THE
MOTORCARAVAN
MANUAL

John Wickersham

Author: John Wickersham

Editor: Robert Davies

Project Manager: Louise McIntyre

Page build: James Robertson

Photographs: John Wickersham

Illustrations: Geoff Denney

© John Wickersham 2004

First published 1998
Reprinted 1999
Reprinted 2001 (twice)
Reprinted 2002 (twice)
Reprinted 2003
Revised 2nd Edition 2004

Published by: Haynes Publishing, Sparkford, Yeovil, Somerset BA22 7JJ, UK

A catalogue record for this book is available from the British Library

ISBN 1 84425 047 4

Printed in Great Britain by J. H. Haynes & Co. Ltd.

While every effort is taken to ensure the accuracy of the information given in this book, no liability can be accepted by the author or publishers for any loss, damage or injury caused by errors in, or omissions from, the information given.

Gas Regulations

Gas Regulations and the way in which appliance manufacturers interpret them regarding the installation of their products are subject to continuing change. It is *strongly recommended* that anyone contemplating the installation of a gas appliance should consult the appliance manufacturer's customer service department before undertaking any work themselves. This may reveal different recommendation. Moreover, there may be reasons why it is unwise and unsafe to undertake installation work in an carpentry and other work in accordance with a qualified fabricator's. However, it is suggested that anyone concerned with systems and appliances that work on the gas can depend on ... the final ... petent and appropriately qualified for the work as defined on page ...

Although ... above ... the Calor ... (3) from ... Winnats ... Ltd.)

Contents

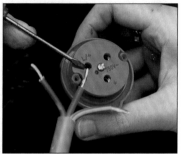

Foreword

The Camping and Caravanning Club understands that the key to enjoyable and safe use of any kind of camping equipment is education, that's why we welcome this major contribution to camping literature which we are sure will be of great use to our 60,000 Camping and Caravanning Club members who use motorcaravans.

Peter Frost
The Camping and Caravanning Club

With nearly 35,000 motorcaravanning members, The Caravan Club warmly welcomes the publication of the Haynes *Motorcaravan Manual*. This readable, yet highly detailed Manual is clearly presented and contains a wealth of useful information, much of it not available from other sources. There are very few such comprehensive guides available to the public, and the information here is presented in an easy-to-follow style with excellent illustrations. The *Motorcaravan Manual* will prove invaluable reading for all motorcaravanners, both for general information and DIY instructions.

Trevor Watson
The Caravan Club

The manual goes into enough depth on the topics it covers to give a clear understanding of the function and workings of the many aspects of the motor caravan without creating a technical minefield that leaves the reader confused and uncertain. As a specialist club for motor caravanners we feel the manual will be an instant hit with our members and will certainly become part of the Club's merchandise for re-sale to its members and also part of the Club's reference library when dealing with the many questions relating to motor caravanning that are directed to the Club Office by both members and non-members. Congratulations on an excellent publication and I hope it generates the success it deserves.

Colin Reay
The Motor Caravanners' Club

Introduction

In a Buyers' Guide published in a recent magazine, there were specifications relating to 263 motorcaravans built in Britain, 405 models imported from mainland Europe and a further 85 "recreational vehicles" (RVs) imported from the United States of America. This adds up to a total of 753 brand new different models currently available in this country.

If you then include all the pre-owned motorcaravans standing on dealer forecourts and all the private sales in classified advertisements, a potential purchaser is presented with a stunning array of vehicles. However, this extraordinary situation also raises a problem.

Noting that there are some many types of motorcaravan available, I found it extremely difficult deciding what ought to be included in this manual. Moreover, the problem didn't end there.

Notwithstanding the remarkable range of models currently on sale, some indefatigable enthusiasts still want to design and build their own motorcaravan. And many do - often with pleasing results! So this approach to ownership deserved recognition, too.

I certainly feel that in a world of ever-increasing restrictions, it would be a sad day if regulations, insurance constraints, and legislation stifled such entrepreneurial endeavour. After all, the origins of many prominent manufacturers can be traced back to the efforts of a lone enthusiast. Siddle Cook and his Elddis caravan, Colin Chapman and his self-build Lotus sports cars, and John Haynes who decided to compile an Austin 7 repair manual - here are three of the many pioneers whose tentative steps subsequently brought pleasure to millions.

Accordingly, the final chapter considers the self-build route to motorcaravan ownership. If that appeals to you, I offer a warning: never underestimate the challenge. Having built several boats and three cars, I presumed that building a motorcaravan would be fairly straightforward. Wrong! It took longer to complete a "campervan" and to iron out its faults than it had taken to complete a substantial self-build house. Nevertheless I learnt a lot in the process and have recently completed a considerably better motorhome - but that took even longer to complete!

With this caveat, I sincerely hope that the content of The Motorcaravan Manual meets the needs of a wide readership. The Second Edition is considerably more detailed than its predecessor and it calls on fresh knowledge gained from testing new models and the invaluable lessons learned from "first hand" experiences.

Needless-to-say, it couldn't have been written without the help of suppliers, designers, manufacturers and the many motorcaravanners I've had the pleasure of meeting at exhibitions and shows. In addition, several technical specialists have painstakingly checked my manuscript for accuracy, the Clubs have been most supportive, and staff at Haynes Publishing have produced a very attractive book. I hope you find it informative.

John Wickersham
April, 2004

Motorcaravan designs

Although we use the word 'motorcaravan', the term encompasses a wide range of different leisure vehicles. In this opening chapter, we compare contrasting designs and draw attention to strengths and weaknesses of different models – both on the road and on-site.

Terminology

A growing number of manufacturers refer to their products as 'motorhomes' whereas others continue to call them 'motorcaravans'. Most people consider the terms to be synonymous and this book could easily have used either word in its title.

Campervans, coachbuilts, recreational vehicles and van conversions are particular types of motorcaravan. Then there are dismountables, high-tops, low-lines, A-Class and more besides! It can all be a bit confusing so the aim of this introductory chapter is to explain what all these terms mean. Distinguishing features are highlighted and critical comments offered because the different vehicles all have their own strengths and weaknesses.

Driving characteristics

The 'perfect' motorcaravan would offer the driving characteristics of a car at the same time as providing spacious comfort in the living area. In reality, there's always a situation of compromise; whereas a few motorcaravans, such as the Starcraft, have been based on cars, the majority use a commercial vehicle as their base unit. Modern commercial products are undoubtedly very comfortable, although none are completely 'car-like'.

This has prompted some manufacturers, such as Wheelhome, to modify 'people carrier' multi-purpose vehicles. The conversion means replacing some of the seats with a kitchen unit and creating a fold-down bed. On the road, acceleration, economy and cornering characteristics are retained, although the living area is inevitably cramped. Setting up a bed can also be awkward because it occupies a significant part of the interior.

In contrast, larger motorcaravans offer spacious accommodation. Their generous living area has been grafted on to a commercial vehicle and life is unquestionably fine on-site. However, when on the road some coachbuilt motorcaravans are slow off the mark and corner with disconcerting body roll. A few models even struggle to reach speeds in excess of 60mph, and owners of large coachbuilt motorhomes recognise that country lanes are often too narrow for this type of vehicle.

Engine options

A key element for any buyer or builder to consider is the engine. As already noted, some models can be slow, and although speed isn't everything, an inability to keep up with the flow of traffic on motorways is disconcerting, if not a little dangerous.

Another key issue is whether to opt for a vehicle with a petrol engine, a diesel engine, or a turbodiesel engine. Fuel prices should help to shape your decision, remembering that in France diesel is far cheaper than petrol. In the UK, however, the pump price for diesel is much the same as the price of petrol. Furthermore, savings on diesel fuel may disappear when the higher costs of servicing a diesel engine are taken into account, and in spite of recent refinements, engine noise can be intrusive.

Many motoring writers and motorcaravan testers have traditionally preferred petrol engines for performance reasons. However, views are changing and if you like the low-rev pulling power of a diesel engine, a turbo undoubtedly adds a little more sparkle. At the same time, it is sometimes claimed that this component can shorten the life of a diesel engine.

Choosing the most suitable engine is important and much depends on your driving style. This is why it would be unwise to buy an expensive motorcaravan without first arranging a test drive on a variety of roads. 'Hire before you buy' schemes are discussed in Chapter 2, as a useful way of ensuring that your choice of engine is the right one.

Chassis type

Another important element is the chassis, which is discussed under *Motorcaravan Types*, and also in Chapter Four

Many potential purchasers overlook this

element, but when buying a coachbuilt motorcaravan, it is a critical design feature. The type of chassis used on a "coachbuilt" has implications for driving characteristics, the suspension, access to the living area, use in winter and interior headroom.

Daily use

Another factor to consider is whether a motorcaravan has to be used for routine transport such as driving to work. Van conversions can fulfil this role quite well whereas coachbuilt models are far less versatile. Height is often a handicap and some public car parks have a barrier at the point of entry which restricts access.

Where funds permit, it is undoubtedly better to run a second vehicle for routine transport. At the same time, a motorcaravan needs to be used regularly, so putting it into store for prolonged periods is best avoided. It is not just a battery that suffers when a vehicle is parked for a long spell; mechanical components can seize up, tyre sidewalls deteriorate and so on.

Motorcaravan types

Although there are many types of motorcaravan, they fall into one of two broad categories. These are:

- models which use the original metal shell of a panel van or multi-purpose vehicle (MPV)
- coachbuilt models where a shell is purpose-built and mounted on a suitable chassis.

This is a broad simplification but it distinguishes the two main routes in design and construction that characterise motorcaravans. Within these groups are a number of variations – including a few vehicles which defy classification.

Articulated units are a case in point. In the United States, 'fifth-wheel' recreational vehicles are relatively common and while their overall size is usually too large for Britain's smaller roads, the flexibility they offer is attractive. Smaller versions have been built in Britain but are seldom seen.

Apart from these special cases, motorcaravans are usually classified into one of the six categories which follow. Three of these are variations on the van conversion product: three are types of coachbuilt models.

FIXED ROOF

Using a panel van as a base is a logical way to create a motorcaravan. The process is often described as a 'conversion', although some manufacturers dislike this term. For the DIY builder, a van conversion is more straightforward than self-building a coachbuilt motorcaravan from scratch.

One problem with most fixed roof base vehicles is that many are too low to permit full standing room. The Murvi Morello is an exception since the base vehicle offers more headroom than most commercial vans. Width is another limiting factor which affects design possibilities in the living area layout.

Motorcaravans based on MPVs are growing in popularity and represent a special example of a fixed roof conversion. This build strategy assures 'car-like' driving characteristics, but the relatively high price of the base vehicle inevitably leads to an expensive end-product.

Plus points
- Good driving characteristics.
- Many models are easy to park – in terms of height as well as width.
- Some models can be garaged.
- Wide access to the interior, by a sliding side door or double rear doors, can be useful.
- Some models can be used as temporary load carriers, for instance to shift furniture.
- Good access makes this type of motorcaravan especially appropriate for wheelchair users.

Minus points
- Greater heat loss from single-glazed windows.
- Lack of standing room imposes a disciplined lifestyle – cooking may have to be done from a seated position.
- Storage space is usually restricted.

Recent examples
There are several fixed-roof van-based motorcaravans, including models from Reimo, Bilbo's, and Murvi. Motorcaravans based on MPVs are available from Wheelhome.

A fixed roof motorcaravan like this Murvi Meteor doesn't provide standing room inside. That's not the case in a Murvi Morello.

Plus points

- As with fixed roof
  conversions, good
  driving, parking
  and garaging are
  key features.
- Good access
  to the interior
  enables the
  vehicle to be used
  as a temporary
  load carrier
  and provides
  wheelchair access.

Minus points

- Heat loss occurs
  from single-glazed
  windows and the
  fabric sides of
  an elevating roof
  structure.
- Interior storage
  space is limited.

Recent examples

There are several
examples based
on light commercial
panel vans including
models from
Auto-Sleepers,
Bilbo's, Design
Developments,
Devon, Drivelodge,
IH Motor Campers,
JC Leisure, Murvi,
Reimo and Young
Conversions.
Motorcaravans
with elevating roofs
based on MPVs
are available from
Wheelhome.

ELEVATING (RISING) ROOF

This type of motorcaravan is an improved version
of the fixed roof type because there's more
headroom inside. However, the installation of
elevating roofs is not a new idea. For instance,
Type 2 Volkswagen Campervans, which enjoyed
great popularity in the 1970s, were often fitted
with this facility. Today, these 'Vee Dubs' have cult
status and many young people run them, renovate
them and revere them. Beautifully restored models
abound and reference is made to a VW renovation
project in Chapter 11.

Today the elevating roof motorcaravan retains its
popularity and numerous models are available on a
variety of base vehicles. Normally the elevating roof

section deploys an attached fabric panel as it rises;
other models have hinged solid sides – for example,
the Holdsworth Villa 3 (1987) and the Auto-Sleeper
Trooper which is still in production.

Some conversions have been carried out using an
ultra-compact vehicle like the Daihatsu Hijetta or the
Citroën Berlingo. The resulting 'micro motorcaravans',
as these products are sometimes called, are suitable
for a single person – or two at a pinch.

While the chief function of an elevating system
is to improve headroom, many rising roof systems
incorporate a high level bed. This may be little
more than a stretcher-style structure to sleep a
young child. On the other hand, some designers
have cleverly incorporated an adult-sized double
bed within a rising roof structure.

HIGH-TOPS

Some panel vans offer good headroom and reference has already been made to the Murvi Morello and la strada motorcaravans under the heading *Fixed roof* on page 7. However, another way to achieve headroom is to fit a 'high-top' roof.

Replacing the original roof on a panel van using a moulded extension unit is a popular ploy. High-top motorcaravans are justifiably popular and the use of glass reinforced plastic (GRP) prevents the structure from being top heavy. Road-holding characteristics when cornering are scarcely affected.

When you step inside this type of motorcaravan, the generous headroom has the effect of making the interior seem surprisingly spacious. Roof-level double-glazed windows or glass panels play a prominent part in creating this impression and the overall effect helps to hide the vehicle's panel van parentage.

Many specialists include high-tops in their product range, but ownership opportunities don't stop there. Advertisements in motorcaravan magazines include independent roof section manufacturers who will install a GRP roof moulding

Plus points

- Driving characteristics are usually good.
- A sliding side door and double rear doors afford good access and load-carrying potential.
- Some models incorporate a separate washroom.
- There's height and a spacious feeling inside.

Minus points

- Heat loss is more acute from single-glazed windows – though many models have double-glazed units.
- Some models are surprisingly expensive.
- High-tops lack the interior space of coachbuilt models.

Recent examples

This is a competitive market with products from Autocruise, Auto-Sleepers, Bilbo's, Reimo and Romahome, as well as many small volume converters like Devon, Drivelodge and Young Conversions. Take note that:
1) The Tardis by Manhattan is unique in that it features a push-out wall section to increase the space in the lounge section.
2) The Design Developments Mediterranee is now built as the Romahome New Dimension.
3) After several years building Mondial models, the Swift Group ceased manufacturing van conversions in 2002.

on a van supplied by the customer. Young Conversions, for example, go one step further and offers a complete roof installation service in which headlining and ventilation facilities are constructed. With this modification complete, many aspiring self-build enthusiasts are then able to fit out the interior to meet their personal needs.

Good headroom is achieved in the la strada Regent which is built on a Mercedes Sprinter panel van.

Setting up beds

When comparing high-top motorcaravans, look closely at the method of erecting the bed (or beds). In some instances the base is created using a multitude of cushion sections; the resulting 'mattress' may lack the integrity you need for a good night's sleep. The Murvi Meteor and Morello are fitted with 'rock and roll' fold-back bench seating which produces a more successful bed base.

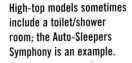

High-top models sometimes include a toilet/shower room; the Auto-Sleepers Symphony is an example.

With regard to the cost of a high-top, professionally-built motorcaravans are often surprisingly expensive. In fact a much larger coachbuilt model might be on sale at a substantially lower price. This is because fitting out a panel van, with all its composite angles, is a labour-intensive exercise. In comparison, a flat-sided coachbuilt constructed from pre-fabricated insulated panels presents a far easier base on which to work. More staff are employed simultaneously and the walls are usually added after all the floor-mounted furniture and appliances are in place. This speed in construction is certainly not possible when converting a panel van – hence the higher price levels.

Variations in layout are also dependent on the base vehicle. Motor manufacturers offer short, medium and long wheelbase vehicles and the choice of model ultimately determines interior size. Some professional conversions, like the Auto-Sleepers Symphony and the Romahome New Dimension, even include a generous-sized washroom and toilet.

Smaller models lack this provision and toilet facilities are rather rudimentary. In some instances a portable toilet has to be retrieved from a locker, located in the living space and then discreetly shielded using a makeshift curtain. This 'back to basics' approach isn't everyone's cup of tea.

DISMOUNTABLES

Sometimes called a 'demountable', this design is particularly popular in the United States where pick-up trucks are comparatively common. Crew cab pick-ups, which have a double line of seats, are especially suitable as base vehicles.

The concept is simple: a purpose-made living compartment is carried 'piggy-back' style on the pick-up and can be detached when necessary. This enables a site pitch to be secured, after which the vehicle can be driven independently.

The same advantage is offered on arriving home; detached 'living capsules' are a common sight in many American back yards, leaving the truck to be used as a day-to-day load carrier.

Plus points

- Being able to detach and park the living accommodation releases the base vehicle for independent use.
- The living accommodation can be surprisingly well-organised, with the benefit of a fixed overcab bed.

Minus points

- A suitable pick-up truck is needed.
- Cab space is not utilised as part of the living accommodation.
- On the road, some dismountables roll badly when cornering; the overall rig is unavoidably top-heavy.

Recent examples

Dismountables are manufactured by Apollo. American products, including folding-roof models, are imported by Niche Marketing.

Dismountable motorcaravans made in Britain by Apollo are often exhibited at outdoor shows.

The versatility of dismountable units is attractive and they're currently imported on a small scale from America. In Britain, the Apollo range has also been popular for a number of years and is often exhibited at outdoor shows.

In theory the idea is sound but in practice there are a few shortcomings. Even supposing you own a suitable pick-up truck, the mounted compartment often produces a top-heavy configuration – though folding-roof models help to resolve this. Driving a dismountable motorcaravan on twisty roads can certainly be disconcerting. Also, the degree of projection beyond the sides of a base vehicle is strictly regulated within European legislation.

Coachbuilt

When a base vehicle 'chassis cab' is used, a coachbuilt construction can offer spacious accommodation. Sometimes the vehicle manufacturer's original chassis is retained (such as on the 2003 Avondale range and on all but a few Auto-Sleepers' models); alternatively a replacement AL-KO Kober lightweight single chassis platform is grafted on to the cab (as on many Bessacarr models). More recently, AL-KO Kober has been manufacturing a double chassis

Once detached from its pick-up truck, this dismountable unit offers generous living space and a canvas-sided 'extension' bedroom.

platform which permits water tanks and services to be mounted in a protected void below the floor panel (recent Hymer and Knauss coachbuilts are examples of this). The merits of these different chassis are evaluated in Chapter 4.

This type of construction also features an over-cab compartment – often referred to as a 'Luton' – and this is either used for storage or sleeping accommodation. In some cases, however, over-cab compartments are a clumsy feature affecting the aerodynamic design of the vehicle – with implications for fuel economy.

This 2001 model Auto-Trail Mohican low profile coachbuilt is based on a rear wheel drive Mercedes-Benz chassis cab with a six-speed Sprintshift automated gearbox.

Plus points

• Many occupants can be accommodated in a large coachbuilt motorcaravan.
• With the benefit of an over-cab bed, the remaining space offers much scope for layout design.
• Several smaller coachbuilts offer a generous amount of living space - especially when compared with van conversions costing a similar amount of money.

Minus points

• Parking a large coachbuilt model may be difficult.
• Versatility in road handling falls short of smaller van conversions.
• Most models are unlikely to be suitable for day-to-day utility transport.
• In some models, the ladder to reach an over-cab bunk cannot be erected when a double bed is made-up beneath it.

Recent examples

Over-cab coachbuilt manufacturers include: Ace, Autocruise CH, Auto-Sleepers, Auto-Trail, Avondale, Benimar, Bessacarr, Buccaneer, Compass, Elddis, Granduca, Hymer, Knauss, Laika, Lunar, Machzone, Mobilvetta, Pilote, Rimor, Roller Team and Swift.

Low profile manufacturers include: Autocruise CH, Auto-Sleepers, Benimar, Bessacarr, Compass, Elddis, Elnagh, Hobby, Laika, Lunar, Pilote, Pioneer Classic, Rapido, and Swift. And there are many others.

Recognising that many people never use an over-cab bed, manufacturers also produce low-profile coachbuilts which have a cleaner line, lower overall height and more likelihood of achieving better fuel economy. Models are manufactured by Bessacarr, formerly by Machzone, and by many Continental constructors. The low-line style has been popular for longer abroad than it has in the United Kingdom.

As regards constructional techniques, different materials are used by different manufacturers. An explanation of coach-building methods is given in Chapter 3, and this form of construction has implications for general maintenance and repair work.

Living accommodation can incorporate a variety of facilities, layouts and bed provision depending on the size of vehicle. However, driving performance in a large coachbuilt is compromised and this should be taken into account. Large models would hardly be practicable for day-to-day utility transport.

A-CLASS

The construction of this kind of motorcaravan starts with a commercial chassis, running gear, power unit, seating, instrumentation – but no cab. This configuration is referred to as a 'chassis cowl', and it means that the entire body can be constructed as an integral unit in which the living area completely embraces the driver's section.

Building an entire body from scratch is undoubtedly a major task and this is reflected in the

Plus points

- All the features of a coachbuilt model apply, with the added bonus that cab space is integrated with the living area.
- A drop-down bed over the cab seats is often fitted and this can be a great asset; it means that a pre-made bed can be accessed in seconds.

Minus points

- Parking an A-class motorcaravan is often difficult.
- There's a disappointingly small kitchen in many of the German models.
- Cab doors are seldom fitted, so entry is via the door to the living quarters.
- The price of an A-class model is considerable.

Recent examples

A-class manufacturers include: Bürstner UK, Carthago, Concorde, Dethleffs, Esterel, Frankia, Hymer, Laika, Le Voyageur, Maess, Mirage, Mobilvetta, Niesmann+Bischoff, Pilote UK, Rapido, and Weinsberg.

Available with right-hand drive, this Arto 69GL Lux from Niesmann+Bischoff exemplifies the distinctive appearance of an A-Class motorhome.

price. In fact, a European A-class motorcaravan is often as costly as a larger American motorhome, although few would argue that it's more suitable for use on our smaller roads. Not only are the external looks usually striking, but the internal layout of an A-class is usually impressive as well.

Most A-Class motorcaravans purchased here have been manufactured in France, Germany or Italy. Few models appear from British manufacturers and neither the Swift Bel-Air nor the models from Machzone are currently in production. Even the Auto-Sleepers Luxor, first launched in Autumn 2002, is effectively a modified version of the Italian-built Mirage.

AMERICAN MOTORHOMES

Calculated on price per square metre of living space, the American motorhome represents incredible value for money. For example, £95,000 could secure a huge vehicle fitted with an eight-litre engine. Typical examples offer a large number of robust external lockers, a built-in generator with dashboard control switch, a permanent double bed, a bath, a large screen over-cab TV set, a powerful turbodiesel engine with automatic transmission, and a multitude of extras.

These substantial vehicles have a keen following and are certainly ideal recreational vehicles in their country of origin. Whether they are suited to Britain's roads is left for the reader to decide. And whilst there are hundreds of American camping grounds offering drive-on/drive-off hard

Like many A-class motorcaravans, the Pilote Galaxy has a drop-down double bed located over the driver and passenger seats.

The lowered bed is soon ready for occupation; if preferred it can be put away with the bedding still in place.

standings equipped with purpose-made couplings for fresh water, waste ('grey') water and sewage ('black water'), facilities like these are seldom found on European sites.

American motorhomes are best suited for countries with wide roads and large open spaces.

Plus points

- Remarkable value for money when measured on floor space and fittings.
- Ideal for large groups – some models sleep up to eight people.

Minus points

- Maintenance costs are likely to be high and relatively few specialists are able to carry out servicing work.
- Obtaining spare parts might present problems.
- A number of camping sites are unable to take American motorhomes.
- Fuel and general maintenance costs are high.
- Parking and access problems limit use.
- The furniture in some American motorhomes is poorly built.
- Many non-standard parts are fitted.

Recent examples

Allegro and Damon (imported by Westcroft Motorhome Centre), Dynamax, Thor and Winnebago (imported by Dudley American Motorhomes), Georgie Boy (imported by Midland International RV Center), Holiday Rambler, Monaco and Newmar (imported by Travelworld American Motorhomes), R-Vision (imported by Freedom Motorhomes).

Buying a motorcaravan

Anyone considering the purchase of a new or pre-owned motorcaravan needs to draw together as much information about different models as possible. Here are some sources of useful advice for you to consider.

Manufacturers promote their products with vigour, so it helps to obtain impartial advice. Accordingly, this chapter looks at ways of building up a clearer picture about the models you like.

In addition, there are different ways to buy a motorcaravan and purchasing opportunities are also discussed. Finally, a prospective owner mustn't overlook things like insurance, breakdown schemes and storage; these topics are covered towards the end of the chapter.

Motorcaravan publications

There are currently five monthly consumer magazines specifically devoted to motorcaravanning. In addition, there are three publications distributed to members of the major caravan and motorcaravan clubs, giving the prodigious total of eight magazines.

Publications like these contain helpful articles about accessories, services and places to visit. The advertisements are useful to read as well. A prospective purchaser can obtain a lot of useful information from the following sections of these magazines:

Data listings of models, specifications and prices

Some magazines publish lists of current models which give information on base vehicles, carrying capacity (payload), external dimensions, the number of beds, price and so on. Information lists covering older models are rather harder to find.

However, the magazine *Motorcaravan Motorhome Monthly* (MMM) publishes ongoing six-part guides to second-hand prices. These currently appear in successive issues under the following headings:

Part One: Panel van conversions with fixed and rising roofs
Part Two: Panel van conversions with high-tops
Part Three: Coachbuilts based on the Fiat/Talbot and Fiat/Peugeot chassis
Part Four: Coachbuilts (other chassis), dismountables
Part Five: A-class models
Part Six: American motorhomes.

Test reports

Monthly magazines run illustrated articles compiled by experienced testers, and these reports include helpful photographs showing a new vehicle in use. Especially informative are the comparative reports where two or three models of similar price and specification have been tested alongside each other.

Older motorcaravans are occasionally tested too. Similarly you will find articles which focus on models which have been inspected on dealers' forecourts, and these reports usually include historical notes about the models offered for sale.

Thoroughness is a feature of most test reports although the degree of critical analysis may vary; some journalists are undoubtedly more incisive than others. And it's also true that some constructional flaws, technical shortcomings and design weaknesses may only become apparent during long-term ownership.

These articles are certainly to be recommended but it also has to be recognised that in this industry there are a lot of small-scale manufacturers, many of whom construct very good products. Their small output seldom allows them the luxury of running a fleet of demonstrator vehicles to supply to magazines for testing – so most test reports are on motorcaravans built by the larger manufacturers.

This is especially true when the editorial staff of a magazine are lent a motorcaravan for an extended period so that its performance can be assessed by a number of different journalists and in a wide variety of conditions. A test that embraces both summer and winter weather undoubtedly provides a more accurate insight into the merits of a particular vehicle.

Recognising the usefulness of published tests to potential purchasers, both *Motor Caravan Monthly* (MCM) and *Motorcaravan Motorhome Monthly* (MMM) operate a service that enables readers to obtain copies of past reports. In the case of MMM, the photocopy service covers every test that has been published since the magazine was first launched in 1966 – and that's quite remarkable.

Calendar of exhibitions and shows

Most magazines include information about exhibitions and shows, which provide yet another opportunity to evaluate vehicles and accessories alike. These dates can also be obtained from the Motorhome Information Service (see page 16).

Even though manufacturer brochures and road test reports are very informative, it's also important to see the products for yourself. One way to do this is to attend a major indoor exhibition such as the long-established National Boat, Caravan and Leisure Show held every February at the National Exhibition Centre near Birmingham. Other indoor caravanning shows are held in London, Manchester, and Glasgow. For example, the one held at Earl's Court, London, in late Autumn always has a pleasing number of exhibits from motorcaravan manufacturers and importers.

Further afield there's a huge late summer show held in Düsseldorf which is claimed to be the largest in Europe. This is probably true and many British motorhome owners drive the relatively short distance to this German city, taking advantage of the well-equipped on-site car park camping facilities. The camp grounds are supported by free bus services to the main entrances of the exhibition centre by day, and the lively old town area of Düsseldorf in the evenings.

Then there are outdoor shows held around the UK, most of which are staged during the warmer months of the year. These events are usually held at a major racecourse or an agricultural showground. Not only are local dealers in attendance displaying new and pre-owned models, but there's also an opportunity to gain advice from existing motorhome owners who bring their vehicles to the event. At outdoor shows you will also find many accessory manufacturers who find it too costly to take stand space at the more elaborate indoor exhibitions.

Address lists of owners' clubs

Some clubs for motorcaravanners are devoted to particular marques; other clubs focus on areas of special interest relating to motorcaravanning. The list currently published in *Motorcaravan Motorhome Monthly* (MMM) gives information on over 90 clubs, four of which cater for owners of American motorhomes; there's even an organisation for DIY enthusiasts called The

Selfbuild Motorcaravanners' Club. The addresses of club secretaries are published in many motorcaravan magazines and these organisations hold regular social events.

Once you've established a shortlist of models that meet your requirements, talking to owners is a good way to find out what a product is really like. Admittedly, some members show great manufacturer loyalty and defend their choice of motorcaravan with eager enthusiasm. Others are more impartial and willingly divulge the problems they've encountered during ownership. So these clubs are undoubtedly an important source of information – particularly if you're interested in a pre-owned model that isn't in production any more.

National caravan and motorcaravan clubs

More than half a million owners are members of the two national clubs concerned with caravanning and motorcaravanning. Both have a significant number of motorcaravanners in membership and the historical development of these two clubs has given them distinctive and individual characteristics. The Camping and Caravanning Club welcomes users of all kinds of units including tents, and there are specialist hobby groups for canoeists, climbers, photographers and so on. The Caravan Club, however, is principally run for caravan and motorcaravan owners although tents are accepted on some of the Club-owned sites.

Differences aside, both organisations provide members with holiday booking services, insurance schemes, instructional courses in driving skills, advisory services, technical leaflets and introductory video programmes.

A third club, The Motor Caravanners' Club, is more specific in purpose, as its title indicates. Its membership is smaller than the two major caravanning clubs, but again there's a members' magazine, advice on technical issues, guidance on choosing a motorcaravan and so on.

A summary of the Clubs' chief publications offering advice on choosing and using a motorcaravan is given in the box overleaf.

Outdoor shows provide an opportunity to gain advice from existing motorcaravan owners.

Website information

The internet has grown in importance as a source of information on motorcaravans in the last few years. Most major manufacturers offer illustrated web sites, and even small scale motorcaravan manufactures are taking advantage of the benefits of this medium. Accessories, appliances, base vehicles, caravan clubs, magazines, the National Caravan Council, and site listings also appear on the web, some with particularly comprehensive coverage.

Then there are specialists such as www.oakwood-village.co.uk, whose periodic road-test reports and technical reviews are also relevant to motorcaravanners.

Murvi Van conversions have achieved consistently high scores in The Caravan Club's Design and Drive contests.

Technical literature

The Motor Caravanners' Club publishes a 36-page booklet entitled *Motor Caravans – Choosing and Using* which is available to members.

The Camping and Caravanning Club publishes technical leaflets for members; one of its special interest groups – The Motor Caravan Section – has members with experience of owning a wide range of models.

The Caravan Club publishes a pamphlet, *Tips for Motorcaravanners*, which is available to members and non-members alike. In addition, members can request a free leaflet titled *Choice of Motor Caravan* together with a number of related technical leaflets on topics such as TV reception and water systems. The free booklet *Getting Started – A Beginner's Guide to Motor Caravanning* is also especially helpful.

Annual design awards

Examples of good practice in design and construction are the focus of attention in two award schemes. One of these is conducted during the annual Caravan and Outdoor Leisure Show at Earl's Court and the competition has been organised for a number of years under the auspices of *Caravan Industry*, a trade journal. Awards are given for various elements with categories such as 'The Best Washroom' and 'The Best Kitchen'.

In addition, The Caravan Club introduced the Motor Caravan Design Awards in 1996. In the first few years of the scheme, the judging was carried out at The National Boat, Caravan & Leisure Show held at the National Exhibition Centre, Birmingham. It entailed a painstaking analysis conducted over five days by a judging panel supported by a team of technical experts who scrutinised matters like payloads, adherence to codes of practice and conformity with dimensional requirements.

The evaluations were conducted with notable thoroughness, but one thing was not included:

the driving experience. Bearing in mind that performance on the road is an important aspect of ownership, the format and title of the award was amended and from 2000 onwards, driving qualities have been incorporated in the judging schedule. The Design & Drive event was thus moved to a venue with access to varying types of public roads and judging is even more searching. Not surprisingly, the results are taken seriously by manufacturers and members of the public alike.

Winners in classes and types (which are subject to change each year) from the Design & Drive event:

2000: Van conversions up to £28,000 Bessacarr E330; **Van conversions over £28,001** Murvi Morello; **Coachbuilts up to £25,000** Swift Sundance 500; **Coachbuilts £25,001-£35,000** Auto-Trail Tracker; **Coachbuilts £35,001 and over** Auto-Sleepers Sherbourne.

2001: Van conversions up to £28,000 Murvi Mallard; **Van conversions over £28,001** Murvi Morello; **Coachbuilts up to £26,000** Swift Sundance 520; **Coachbuilts £26,001-£35,000** Swift Gazelle F61; **Coachbuilts £35,001 and over** Auto-Sleepers Palermo.

2002: All models up to £25,000 Romahome Duo Outlook; **£25,001-£30,000** Auto-Sleepers Nuevo; **£30,001-£40,000** Murvi Mirage; **£40,001 and over** Murvi Morello.

2003: Van conversions up to £28,000 Murvi Mallard; **Van conversions over £28,001** Murvi Morello; **Coachbuilts up to £35,000** Benimar Anthus 6000ST; **Coachbuilts £35,001 and over** Benimar Aereo 6000CC.

Notwithstanding the value of this event, it should be acknowledged that many small-scale manufacturers have such a limited output that they're unable to supply a vehicle. The fact that Murvi, a small van conversion specialist from Devon, has won so many of The Caravan Club's annual awards is evidence indeed that products from small builders are sometimes better than their mass-produced rivals.

Finally, The Caravan Club also commissioned Sewell Information and Research to conduct the first ever survey of motorcaravan quality and reliability. Over 2000 owners of motorcaravans up to six years old were asked a wide range of questions on topics including delivery condition, long term quality and reliability, experience of dealers, servicing, repair and warranties. The results were published in 2002 in a 159-page document and a summary of the findings appeared in the August 2002 Members' Magazine. Research of this kind helps to ensure that the motorcaravans on offer are being built with ever more care.

Cabs in modern light commercial vehicles offer a standard of comfort and quality that rivals many cars.

The base vehicle

In the opening chapter, reference was made to different engine options and the importance of choosing a vehicle whose power and economy meet your requirements. In addition to the engine, the ride quality, transmission, and availability of options like ABS brakes are also important to consider. So, too, is the cab. In truth, most Light Commercial Vehicles (LCVs) now offer car-like comfort. On the other hand, heavier vehicles like the IVEKO commercial products tend to retain the more rugged character of a lorry cab.

Regarding driving details, most British-built motorcaravans are fitted with a manual gearbox since automatic transmission is seldom needed on what is essentially a commercial van. But there are exceptions. For example, it is an option on the Volkswagen T5 (Tiptronic automatic six-speed gearbox with torque converter on five and six-cylinder vehicles). Some Ford Transits can be specified with the Durashift system which links a conventional manual gearbox with an automatic clutch and electronic gear change – which means there's neither a gear stick nor a clutch pedal. On the Mercedes Sprinter there's the optional Sprintshift system which is also an automated gearbox as opposed to a torque converter

An automatic transmission conversion can be fitted to some vehicles by specialists such as Somar Transtec.

Towing a trailer can be a useful asset, but a number of motorcaravans cannot be fitted with a towbar.

automatic transmission. An automatic transmission is now available on the Fiat Ducato, but at the time of writing this was on left-hand drive models only.

Another issue to check concerns the suitability of a motorcaravan for towing. On some models it isn't possible to fit a tow bar – a subject covered in Chapter 4.

If you decide at a later date that a particular feature is required, several specialists are able to help with a retrospective installation. To give some examples:

• A normally-aspirated diesel engine can be fitted with a turbocharger and intercooler by a specialist such as TB Turbo.
• The installation of different central processor units (CPUs) to get more power from an engine is a new area of attention. Specialists like van Aken Developments are offering this service.
• Power-assisted steering can be fitted to some vehicles by a specialist such as TB Turbo.
• Improved radiator cooling and automatic transmission oil cooling units are available from Kenlowe.
• Cruise control can be fitted using an Ultimate Design kit or a system from Adroit Services.
• Automatic transmission can be fitted to some vehicles. Somar Transtec has fitted automatic

The Strikeback alarm system from Van Bitz is specifically designed to protect motorcaravans from theft.

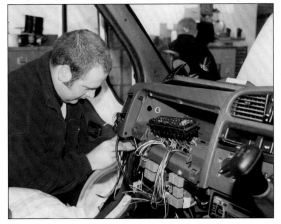

Driving licence

A driving licence valid for cars (Category B or the old Group A) permits the holder to drive a motorcaravan up to 3500kg (3.5 tonnes).

For motorcaravans from 3500 to 7500kg a licence valid for category C is needed. Drivers who passed their car driving test prior to 1997 are entitled to drive a category C vehicle. However, if you passed your test after 1 January 1997, you will need to take a separate category C driving test.

MOT test

Whilst motorcaravans are subject to a Class IV MOT test (the same as cars), coachbuilt and A-Class models are often too large to fit on the ramps at Class IV test stations. In consequence, the test usually has to be undertaken at a Class V or Heavy Goods Vehicle (HGV) test station.

Note: Vehicles with a weight greater than 3500kg are subject to a higher rate of vehicle excise duty (VED).

A few motorcaravans are built on a platform cab which is like a van without its side panels and roof.

Base vehicle engine options on the more popular base vehicles

NOTE: *The information here is accurate at the time of writing. However, manufacturers make frequent changes and you should check the current options with a franchise dealer. There may also be engine variations, such as diesel versions featuring inter-cooling systems.*

FIAT DUCATO/ PEUGEOT BOXER/ CITROEN RELAY	2.0 litre petrol, 2.0 litre turbodiesel, 2.3 litre turbodiesel, 2.8 litre turbodiesel.
FORD TRANSIT	2.0 litre turbodiesel, 2.4 litre turbodiesel.
MERCEDES-BENZ SPRINTER	2.2 litre turbodiesel, 2.7 litre turbodiesel.
VW TRANSPORTER T4 & T5	2.0 litre petrol, 1.9 litre turbodiesel, 2.5 litre petrol.

transmissions to models such as the Citroën Dispatch (alternatively badged the Fiat Scudo).
• The purpose-designed and highly sophisticated Strikeback motorcaravan alarm can be fitted by Van Bitz.

When considering the base vehicles normally used for modern motorcaravans, five different models are prominent. These are the Fiat Ducato, Ford Transit, Mercedes-Benz Sprinter, Peugeot Boxer, VW Transporter T4 and its replacement, the T5.

The Fiat Ducato and Peugeot Boxer were collaboratively developed and are virtually identical; sales, however, are conducted independently and competitively. The Citroën Relay is also a 'badge-engineered' Ducato.

Others appear in lesser numbers, like the Citroën Berlingo, Dispatch (re-badged Fiat Scudo) and Synergie; Daihatsu Hijet; Fiat Scudo; IVEKO Daily and Eurocargo; LDV Convoy, Pilot and Cub (re-badged Nissan Vanette); MAN 4.6TD; Mazda SGL5; Mercedes-Benz Vito; Nissan Vanette; Renault Master, Kangoo and Trafic; Suzuki Carry; Toyota HiAce; and VW LT.

Up-to-date lists of base vehicles are frequently

published in motorcaravan magazines and often form the subject of special supplements. Volkswagen UK also publishes a colourful leaflet listing the British-built motorcaravans which are constructed on the Company's base vehicles.

If you're looking at second-hand motorcaravans, older base vehicles include the Talbot Express/Fiat Ducato (forerunner of the Fiat Ducato/Peugeot Boxer launched in 1994), earlier models of Ford Transit, Renault Trafic, Volkswagen Transporter (T2, T3, and T4), Bedford CF and Leyland Sherpa.

Recognising the options available and acknowledging the differences from one model to another, it is again strongly recommended that a prospective purchaser arranges a test drive. It is only when you take to the road that more subtle aspects of performance become evident. For instance, suspension is important, especially when riding in the back of a motorcaravan. This topic is looked at in greater detail in Chapter 4.

Conversion elements

When comparing motorcaravans, reference is often made to the chassis. However, van conversions are not built on a traditional chassis of heavy steel members. Instead there are strengthened box sections of steel welded to the floor base – often referred to as the 'floor pan'. A few motorcaravans built using a GRP shell such as the CI Carioca 15 and Romahome Duo Outlook are built on what is known as a 'platform cab'. This is rather like a van without its steel side panels and roof. Platform cabs are also used in the construction of French-built Chausson and Challenger low-line coachbuilts. However, most coachbuilt motorcaravans are constructed on what is known as a 'chassis cab'.

The chassis and its fitted running gear, like the suspension and brakes are considered in more detail in Chapter 4. For the moment, bear in mind that some types of chassis are quite high above the ground and this leaves you with a

Manufacturer approval

Some base vehicle manufacturers operate schemes whereby the expertise of certain motorcaravan manufacturers is given an official endorsement. For instance, Volkswagen publishes an annual booklet showing motorcaravans built by 'approved Volkswagen Specialist Converters' – namely Auto-Sleepers, Bilbo's Design, Compass and Reimo (in 2003). In the past there have been *Recognised Converters* (usually larger manufacturers) and *Design Compatible Converters* (many of whom were small volume builders). In 1999, Volkswagen implemented the concept of *Accredited Converters,* a formal confirmation that the motorcaravan manufacturer's additions were not in conflict with the design and construction of the base vehicle.

considerable step-up when climbing aboard. Others are lower and correspondingly easier to enter and their lower centre of gravity is advantageous when cornering. This is the reason why some manufacturers dispense with a manufacturer's chassis and fit a purpose-designed AL-KO AMC unit before constructing the living quarters – but this is normally only done on front-wheel-drive vehicles. The conversion is shown in Chapter 4. Curiously, chassis details are seldom mentioned in motorcaravan magazine data listings – in spite of their importance.

When comparing more general features in a conversion, look at the following:

Layout and sleeping arrangements

This is largely a matter of personal taste but check that bed-making is straightforward. If there's a high-level bed, check access and whether there's provision for bedside items and storage for your clothing. If a bed has to be made using seating cushions, look to see if it's a complicated jigsaw. Fixed beds avoid this but waste a lot of day-time living space. Finally, check if awkwardly shaped seat sections have somewhere to be stowed at night.

Travel safety

Check how many rear seats have a safety belt and relate this to the number of berths. Several models have more berths than belted travel seats and there's a growing feeling that this is most unsatisfactory.

Kitchen

Look at the usable worktop space. Is there adequate food storage? Is there an oven fitted? Some imported models do not have a grill, and many British motorcaravanners regard this as a

Many coachbuilt models are built using the cab, chassis and original suspension designed for commercial vehicles.

serious omission. Is there provision for rubbish? Most British motorcaravan kitchen designers overlook this whereas imported models are usually better equipped.

Storage

Look at storage potential, including inside and outside lockers. A tall locker for skis or fishing rods is useful; so are lockers in the side skirts but check loading weight limits. Consider roof racks and rear ladders, noting that some racks have side rails but no cross bars to support luggage. Tie points are often lacking too.

Spare wheel

Check how easy it is to remove the spare wheel. Some locations are easy to reach; others are quite the reverse. If fitted, rear corner steadies need checking as these items are easily damaged.

Kitchen appliances are usually good, but the amount of worktop space varies from model to model.

Surprisingly few British motorcaravans offer a waste bin; recent models from Auto-Sleepers are an exception.

Provision of external lockers varies, but they are a great asset for outdoor enthusiasts.

The rear stowage facility on this 2001 Swift Gazelle F63 High is extremely useful for storing all sorts of gear.

Habitation codes

Two organisations representing motorcaravan manufacturers in the UK, The Society of Motor Manufacturers & Traders (SMMT) and The National Caravan Council (NCC), worked together to produce the NCC/SMMT Habitation Code 201 concerning health and safety requirements in motorcaravans. Since this was produced, BS EN 1646-2 now sets out the health and safety standards. In consequence, all manufacturers which are members of the SMMT and NCC have to submit prototype and new models for inspection by NCC engineers in order to verify compliance. The NCC test exceeds the minimum requirements specified by British/European standards and involves around 600 or more checks.

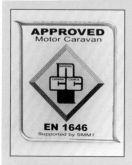

National Caravan Council member manufacturers are required to build to British and European standards.

It includes elements like emergency escape, electricity supply systems, fire precautions, gas, handbook, heating, insulation security, ventilation, payloads, and safety notices. When full compliance is established, subsequent vehicles of the type inspected will display the NCC Approval badge.

Of course, a number of manufacturers – principally the smaller ones – are not members of the NCC/SMMT, so their products are not submitted for testing and do not display the approval badge. It would be wrong to presume, however, that non-badged products would necessarily fail to meet the relevant standards. On the contrary, a non-member such as Murvi manufactures motorhomes to very high standards – as the Company's notable achievements in The Caravan Club's Design Awards have confirmed.

Loading capacity

Establish the maximum user payload and relate this to the number of people you intend to take on holiday. A rough rule of thumb is to allow 75kg for each passenger's personal weight, 100kg for the personal effects of two people (which takes into account cutlery, crockery and cooking utensils) and then 25kg for the personal effects of each subsequent passenger.

Handbooks

Ask to see the handbooks – there should be one for the base vehicle and one for the living facilities. Many handbooks for the latter are surprisingly poor and some converters include no documentation material at all, other than a few leaflets from the manufacturers of individual appliances.

When purchasing a pre-owned coachbuilt motorcaravan, always check the operation of corner steadies, if fitted.

A special platform built at the rear of this Auto-Trail Tracker makes accessing the spare wheel comparatively easy.

Loading terms

Current practice is to express weights in kilograms (1kg = 2.2lbs)

Actual Laden Weight: The total weight of a motorcaravan including all personal contents being carried. This should be measured on a weighbridge to confirm it doesn't exceed the MTPLM.

Maximum Technically Permissible Laden Mass (MTPLM): This refers to a vehicle's gross weight, as defined by the base vehicle manufacturer. Note: It has previously been called 'Maximum Laden Weight' (MLW). Also used are 'Maximum Authorised Mass' (MAM), Gross Vehicle Weight (GVW) and Maximum Authorised Weight (MAW).

Information plates: data relating to weights is usually displayed on a metal plate mounted in the engine bay.

Mass in running order: This is the unladen weight of a vehicle taking into account the maximum fuel weight and a weight allowance for the driver (taken as 75kg).

Maximum user payload: The payload is a vehicle's maximum carrying capacity and is calculated by deducting the vehicle's mass in running order from its maximum technically permissible laden mass.

Maximum axle weights: Both front and rear axles have maximum weights too, and these figures must not be exceeded by the load. On vehicles with front and rear axles, their loading can be checked on a weighbridge by driving one axle at a time on to the weighing plate.

The load carried by this rear axle is measured by parking the vehicle with just its rear wheels on the weighing plate.

Gross Train Weight: This is normally given in the Owner's Manual and refers to the maximum weight permitted for the vehicle plus a trailer and the load being carried on the trailer. This is most important to note when towing heavy items like a support car. It is sometimes referred to as the 'Combined Weight'.

Information plates: Data related to weights is usually displayed on a metal plate. Typically this is fixed in the engine bay (see left).

Weighbridge: To confirm a vehicle doesn't exceed its MTPLM, it is necessary to put the vehicle fully laden with a full petrol tank and its full complement of passengers on a weighbridge.

NOTE: *Sometimes there are minor discrepancies in the way a motorcaravan manufacturer expresses the data. A payload figure, for example, will vary according to the base vehicle option. To give an example, Auto-Sleepers currently expresses the unladen mass weight with the addition of coolants (oil and water), maximum fuel capacity, washer fluid, driver (75kg), spare wheel, crockery, fire extinguisher and tools. So it is important to check details carefully prior to making a purchase to ensure the actual loading potential meets your particular needs. (Since 1999, new motorcaravans are covered within BS EN 1646-2 which sets out how weights and payloads should be expressed.)*

The way to establish that a fully-loaded vehicle doesn't exceed its MTPLM is to have it checked on a weighbridge.

Some recent motorcaravans are constructed with a double layer floor which means that tanks and services are not exposed to the elements.

The la strada Nova is fitted with both inboard and external waste tanks. Normally they're connected, but during cold weather, a red tap shuts off the outside tank as a frost precaution.

Price and hidden costs

Check the total price, ensuring that delivery charges and all 'hidden costs' are included. Most new models are supplied without any user accessories. On the other hand, a model like the Murvi Morello is sold with a complete on-the-road package including gas, cutlery, crockery and leisure battery – but this is unusual.

Health and safety compliance

Check the accompanying panel on page 20 giving information on Habitation Codes.

Nature of use

Some owners use a motorcaravan for day-to-day driving, some for warm weather holidays, others for year-round use irrespective of temperatures. Your particular needs will mean that some models are more suitable than others.

Winter use

If a motorcaravan is going to be used in cold conditions, its design and specification needs to take this into account. For instance, if water tanks are mounted externally, sub-zero temperatures may cause both fresh and waste water to freeze. Since many water tanks are fitted under the floor, purpose-designed immersion heaters are available from specialist CAK. There's also a recent system whereby tanks and services are built within a special under-floor enclosure which keeps them away from the elements. Moreover some Knauss models have a control to direct warm air from the heater into this enclosure. Alternatively models like the la strada Nova have two small waste tanks – one mounted inside and its linked partner under the floor. In winter an isolation lever is used to shut off the underfloor tank so that it remains empty.

Wrapping an underfloor tank with an insulating material will certainly delay its contents from freezing in sub-zero conditions but, conversely, when the water does eventually freeze it correspondingly delays the speed at which it thaws when temperatures rise.

But water isn't the only winterising issue. Some motorcaravans intended for use in cold conditions feature blown-air heating systems whose outlets are directed under bed mattresses (such as in the 1988 Laika Ecovip range) or around a bed (as in the 2000 Mobilvetta Top Driver 52).

Motorhomes for disabled users

Adaptations are possible on a number of models and motorcaravan magazines often publish supplements which describe special products for elderly and disabled users.

With regard to disabled use, HM Customs and Excise has operated a scheme for several years whereby some registered disabled people

Specialists are able to adapt motorcaravans to suit disabled users.

CLEARVIEW
WHEELCHAIR RAMP

FULL WIDTH PLATFORM RAMP

STOWS BELOW WINDOW LEVEL

6FT & 7FT 6INS VERSIONS

AVAILABLE

Interbility

purchasing a new motorcaravan are able to re-claim the VAT. However, this has been revised, and from 1 April 2001 Notice 701/59 Motor Vehicles for Disabled People 701/7 introduced more demanding requirements. In consequence, some disabled owners may not be eligible for VAT reimbursement. Copies of VAT Notice 701/59 may be obtained by telephoning the national VAT Enquiry Line, 0845 010 9000; information is also given on the website www.hmce.gov.uk and by the Motorhome Information Service.

Purchasing considerations

Recognising the considerable cost of a new motorcaravan, a first-time purchaser might be advised to start with a pre-owned model in order to confirm that motorcaravanning comes up to expectation. Sometimes a pre-owned model will be sold with a full complement of items like a fitted roller awning, cutlery, crockery, levelling devices and so on. If you buy a new motorcaravan, many of these items will not be included in the sale.

Pre-owned purchases

Classified advertisements in motorcaravan magazines show that there are plenty of vehicles available for purchase. Vehicles with modest recorded mileages in immaculate condition are often in evidence. It is certainly true that most motorcaravanners look after their vehicles very carefully.

Dealers will also have stocks of pre-owned vehicles and a warranty should be included. Moreover, a full forecourt provides an opportunity to compare models.

Lastly there are auctions. Some are held at local level, often using a storage depot as the venue. On a national scale there's a caravan and motorcaravan division of British Car Auctions (BCA). Periodic sales are programmed around the country; centres at Brighouse and Measham usually offer a good range of stock. Information on a motorcaravan's history is fixed to the screen of each lot in the sale and the process of buying is not the gamble that many people imagine. To assist a prospective bidder, there is a guidebook on buying and selling procedures available from BCA's head office.

Obviously anyone making a purchase of a pre-owned vehicle will accept the meaning of 'caveat emptor' ('buyer beware'). A 'sold as seen' disclaimer emphasises the importance of checking the product. This involves the two elements already discussed – base vehicle and habitation provision. Regarding the base vehicle:

- Check there is an MOT and service vouchers – both of which help to verify the recorded mileage.
- Look at the tyres – irregular wear on the front may indicate steering misalignment.

- Look for worn foot pedals in the cab – a sure sign of a high mileage.
- Check for dirty oil on the dipstick.
- Look for damp under the cab carpets – which suggests there's a faulty screen seal or a leaking heater radiator matrix.
- Insist the owner takes you on a test drive; better still, if all documents are in order, drive the vehicle yourself.

The list could go on and anyone with limited mechanical knowledge is advised to enlist the services of a motoring organisation or better still, a specialist company like Auto Van Services, for an engineer's inspection and report.

Regarding the living area, there are further checks to carry out. These include:

- Turn on the hob and other cooking appliances.
- Confirm the heating system is working.
- Try the fridge (but remember it takes time for cooling to commence).

British Car Auctions hold caravan and motorcaravan sales at a number of their venues.

Auctions for caravans and motorcaravans are sometimes held locally.

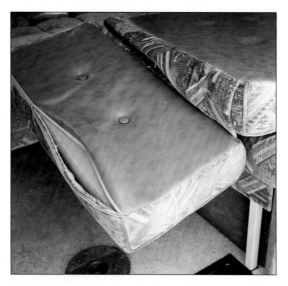

In a pre-owned model, check the upholstery – replacements can be costly.

- Look at cushions, seat backs and bases.
- Check carefully for signs of damp on the walls or inside internal lockers.
- Check documentation regarding habitation servicing.

The next chapter discusses these habitation considerations and a pre-owned motorcaravan being sold with the following documentation is likely to be a reliable purchase:
- Dated habitation servicing certificates.
- Refrigerator servicing confirmation.
- Dated certificates from gas and electrical engineers confirming these supply systems are in safe working order.
- A recent damp test report.

In reality, these important documents are often missing and you would be unwise to put systems into commission until qualified engineers have carried out inspections and service work as described in Chapter 3. Unfortunately, some motorcaravans have never had habitation work servicing carried out since the day they left the factory.

Servicing work is extremely important and dated documents help to support a vehicle when it is subsequently sold.

Buying new

Buying a new motorcaravan doesn't involve the uncertainty that surrounds the purchase of a used model. However, check the scope of any warranties and establish the procedure in the event of an early problem. For instance, if you accept an attractive sales offer from a dealer situated a long way from your home, ask what procedure has to be followed if there are problems in the living area provision. You'll probably have to drive all the way back to the dealer. Similarly, enquire what procedure has to be followed if there's a problem with the base vehicle; mechanical faults can usually be carried out under warranty at any base vehicle franchise dealership.

You can buy a motorcaravan in a number of ways:

- An order can usually be placed at a major exhibition. For instance, a manufacturer's stand is usually staffed by sales representatives from approved dealers around the country as well as by personnel from the factory (or importing agency).
- Alternatively you can make the purchase at the premises of a dealer; there are a number of long-established specialists.
- Buying direct from a manufacturer is normally only possible in the case of low-volume specialists.

Note: Some potential owners contemplate buying direct from abroad. This isn't always a straightforward matter, especially if you want a right-hand drive vehicle. Letters published in magazines show that the exercise can be anything from plain sailing to a frustrating experience fraught with delays and difficulties. Getting warranty work done on habitation elements may be a problem, too, and a lower-than-normal trade-in price is another issue to consider. Nevertheless, as methods of construction, codes of practice and choice of components become more and more standardised, this purchasing strategy will probably become easier.

Whichever route you take, insist on a road test. Sometimes there is diffidence on the part of seller to sanction this. However, parting with a large sum of money without confirming a vehicle's driving characteristics and ride quality is ill-advised.

Bespoke models

A rather different route to ownership is to buy a 'made-to-order' motorcaravan. Small-scale manufacturers like Young Conversions pride themselves on the fact that no two motorcaravans leave their factory the same. Even though the company lists named fixed roof, rising roof and high-top models, in practice most customers make amendments to the standard specification. Some customers even arrange to supply a new or second-hand base vehicle themselves; others get Mike Young, the proprietor, to locate a suitable pre-owned van on their behalf. A number of clients submit drawings of what they require; one client supplied a balsa wood model showing the layout he wanted. Finally there are customers who only want part of the fitting-out work completed because they plan to finish off other elements themselves.

Other manufacturers working along similar lines include Nu Venture Campers in Wigan and Rainbow Conversions in March, Cambridgeshire. The flexibility they offer cannot be matched by large-scale manufacturers, but make an appointment before travelling to their factories to discuss requirements and to see examples of the work.

Self-building and renovating

Other strategies adopted by motorcaravan enthusiasts are:

• Renovating a second-hand vehicle.
• Converting a van themselves.
• Building a motorcaravan from scratch.

It should be appreciated that notable vehicles are sometimes constructed by DIY enthusiasts. Some self-builders have even gone into business (Elddis was originally set up after the late Siddle Cook built himself a DIY caravan).

Much can be learnt from the self-build approach and even an 'armchair builder' who ultimately buys a new motorcaravan can be helpfully informed by seeing what is involved. Accordingly, Chapter 11 is devoted to self-build case studies, all of which are radically different.

Hiring prior to buying

Hiring as a prelude to buying has much to commend it. Around 40 companies nationwide run hiring schemes and the Motor Caravan Information Service supplies a contact list. There are also advertisements placed by hirers in motorcaravan magazines.

Some hirers are small specialists, often run on a private basis. Other operations form part of a dealership and vehicles are often sold second-hand after a year of hiring. In some cases there are offers linked with purchasing. For instance Marquis Motorhomes, which operates Vivanti Motorhome Holiday and Rental, runs a scheme whereby anyone hiring a vehicle can re-claim one week's fee (excluding insurance and VAT) if they purchase a motorcaravan from Marquis within 12 months of the hire.

The majority of hire fleet vehicles are coachbuilt models but you will also find van conversions – and even traditional VW 'campervans' offered for hire.

Hiring before buying makes good sense and most vehicles are equipped with most of the items that a user is going to need. However, bear in mind that fees are considerably higher in the peak summer period compared with prices during the winter months.

Realities of ownership

Choosing and buying is one thing: owning is another. There are certain matters to bear in mind, such as safe driving, insurance, and breakdown assistance.

Driving courses are run by the caravan clubs using venues like old airfields. These are well-run and very popular – so early bookings are needed.

Insurance schemes are often the subject of magazine reviews and there are more than 15 specialists involved. In general, motorcaravan owners represent a good risk and premiums are not normally high.

Breakdown assistance is a service worth considering, but check the extent of cover. For instance, the AA's Relay Service only covers vehicles up to a MTPLM of 3500kg. A large motorcaravan can get damaged when being pulled on to a low-loading transporter, and a commercial collection rescue vehicle might be needed.

Parking at home is sometimes difficult and covenants might restrict the type of vehicle which can be parked by your house. So a prospective purchaser needs to decide if a motorcaravan vehicle would be better kept at a storage specialist. Some centres even provide indoor accommodation.

Servicing is another point to keep in mind and this must include a periodic inspection of appliances and supply systems in the living area. Further guidance on this is given in Chapter 3.

Unlike the larger manufacturers, a specialist such as Young Conversions can build a motorcaravan to suit an individual's requirements.

General maintenance and repair

Looking after a motorcaravan amounts to more than keeping the engine tuned – appliances in the living area also need to be cleaned, serviced and kept in a good state of repair. The exterior bodywork needs regular attention too.

Like any vehicle, a motorcaravan needs regular mechanical servicing and most owners arrange for this to be carried out by a specialist. However, servicing work is also needed in the living area, together with regular tests to confirm that the body structure is free of damp. This second area of attention is referred to as 'habitation servicing' and a surprising number of motorcaravanners ignore this aspect of ownership.

Then there are external features and the chapter includes guidance on different types of body construction. Having an understanding of a motorcaravan's construction is helpful because it has implications for repair work and routine cleaning procedures.

Body construction

Since there are many types of motorcaravan, it's hardly surprising that construction methods are widely dissimilar. On a van conversion, for example, the steel panels can be cleaned using car products. Similarly, repair procedures and re-painting work can be carried out by car body specialists.

However, coachbuilt motorcaravans are different from van conversions and a greater variety of materials are used in their body construction. This again has implications for repair and maintenance work.

The traditional approach to coachbuilding is to build the living quarters on a vehicle's steel chassis, starting with a skeleton framework assembled using wooden struts. A decorative-faced plywood sheeting would then be fixed to this framework to form the interior wall surfaces, with a synthetic fibre quilt placed between the struts to provide thermal insulation. Finally, a cladding material such as pre-painted sheet aluminium would be added on the outside. This technique has its merits and was still used in the 1990s by a few manufacturers such as Buccaneer (before the Company became part of The Explorer Group).

Today, most manufacturers of coachbuilt motorcaravans construct the habitation area using pre-fabricated wall panels. This is sometimes referred to as 'sandwich construction' and the components in the three-layer sandwich are:

• A 3mm-thick decorative-faced plywood.
• Block foam insulation such as Styrafoam.
• Pre-painted aluminium sheet.

Individually, none of these components is particularly strong, but when coated with a high specification adhesive and bonded together in an industrial press, the resulting composite panel assumes noteworthy strength and is also remarkably light. Apertures for the door and windows are prepared before the panel goes into the press and each opening has to be reinforced using a timber framework to provide rigidity. This wooden surround also provides a sound fixing point for the hinges and catches which are added much later.

Bonded sandwich construction is popular and

Prefabricated panels used in many coachbuilt motorcaravans comprise a bonded sandwich of cladding material, insulant and internal decorative ply.

Most coachbuilt motorcaravans are constructed using pre-fabricated wall panels.

At the Explorer Group, roof, sides and floor are assembled using panels pre-fabricated in the factory.

coachbuilding specialists like Auto-Trail, Compass, Elddis and Swift have employed this technique for ten years or more. However, a variation on the theme – which is growing in popularity – is to clad the exterior with a thin layer of pre-coloured glass fibre sheet instead of aluminium. You will see this product on some coachbuilt motorcaravans from the Swift Group, such as the Bessacarr range, together with recent Swift Royale and Kon-Tiki models. Other manufacturers using GRP (glass fibre) sheet for the exterior wall cladding include Auto-Sleepers (on models such as the Ravenna, Pescara and Pollensa) and Avondale (on the Seascape and Seaspirit models). As a rule, this alternative cladding doesn't achieve the high-gloss finish that you see on painted aluminium, but in the event of minor accident damage it is much easier to repair than aluminium sheet because polyester resin-based fillers can be used.

Yet another approach is to commence the conversion using a rigid glass-reinforced plastic (GRP) moulding which is fixed directly to the vehicle chassis. The term 'monocoque construction' is used when this comprises a one-

piece moulded shell. A moulding like this is usually very strong – but it can also be quite heavy. Moreover, the shell needs thermal insulation and this has to be installed on the inside before internal decorative wall panels can be added. Overall it's a labour-intensive way to build a coachbuilt motorcaravan, but it allows a designer to create a living area whose external contours are much more attractive than a 'slab-sided' box. This approach has been used for a number of years by Auto-Sleepers, Design Developments, Island Plastics and, more recently, by la strada in the Nova. In addition, the Starcraft and Rancher self-build motorcaravans both had a moulded GRP shell.

These various approaches to construction emphasise the point that the bodywork on motorcaravans can differ a great deal. Models might have painted steel panels, moulded GRP sections, ABS plastic mouldings, pre-painted smooth-faced aluminium sheet, texture-faced aluminium sheet or a pigmented (pre-coloured) layer of thin GRP sheet. When plastic ventilators, moulded bumpers, acrylic windows, and cab screens of safety glass are taken into account,

Thermal insulation

Anyone planning to purchase a motorcaravan for use in the winter months or in unusually hot places should seek manufacturers' advice concerning the use of insulating materials. Don't forget that a well-insulated living space not only retains the warmth generated by a heating appliance in cold weather: it also helps to prevent the interior becoming an oven when parked in direct sunshine.

Needless-to-say, the level of insulation varies from model to model and some coachbuilt motorcaravans only incorporate a 25mm layer of block foam in the side walls. The insulant is significantly thicker, however, in recent Auto-Trail coachbuilt models as you can see from the stepped portion in the wall around the entrance door.

Sandwich construction sides start with the internal ply; a timber framework is constructed around the perimeter and large apertures such as windows and doors.

A number of recent Bessacarr and Swift coachbuilt models are clad with a thin glass-reinforced plastic (GRP) outer skin instead of aluminium sheeting.

The roughened rear face of this body skirt indicates it is made from GRP, which is easy to repair.

A smooth finish on both surfaces of this moulding shows that it is made from ABS plastic.

Identifying ABS and GRP

GRP stands for 'glass-reinforced plastic' – often called 'glass fibre'. Some GRP is self-coloured because it contains a pigment: other GRP mouldings are painted

ABS stands for acrylonitrile-butadiene-styrene – and is almost always referred to as ABS!

Acrylic-capped ABS has a surface coating of acrylic in order to give it a high gloss finish.

These distinctive types of plastic used for moulded body panels are easy to identify. The rear face of a GRP moulding is normally rough and you will often be able to see the strands of glass used as the reinforcing binder in its laminated construction. In contrast, the rear face of an ABS moulding is smooth and this is often used for vehicle bumpers, albeit with a textured outer face. Acrylic-capped ABS is shiny on both faces and this is often used for fairings on race replica motorbikes, car bumpers made with a body-matching colour, or body panels such as the wings on several recent models of cars (the Ford Focus is an example).

When cracked or split, both GRP and ABS can be repaired but the chemicals required are very different. This is why you need to be quite clear which material has been used for the damaged component. Otherwise, the repair procedures have much in common, but there's a warning. Whereas many body specialists are familiar with GRP repairs, a lot are less willing to repair a damaged ABS panel and prefer to replace the entire section. This can be very costly.

Toilet cleaner

A special cleaning product, previously called Thetford Bathroom Cleaner, was re-launched in 2004 as Thetford Plastic Cleaner. It is specially formulated for cleaning bathroom and toilet components, including the rubber seal and opening blade on a cassette unit.

the sheer diversity of products becomes apparent. This explains why a number of different cleaning agents may be needed to deal with the dissimilar materials. For instance, if you put body polish on dark plastic bumpers, they start to carry white deposits. Put the wrong treatment on an acrylic window and the plastic can develop hairline 'craze' cracks.

Cleaning

Most owners like to keep their motorcaravan clean. This certainly helps when it is offered for sale and the following procedures adopted by valeting specialists are worthy of note.

Cleaning products

Many proprietary car cleaning products can be used for motorcaravans, although some components need a specially-formulated treatment. The acrylic material used for the windows normally fitted in the habitation area is an example.

Recognising the specific characteristics of certain materials, several specialists have responded to the needs of motorcaravanners. For instance, Farécla, a well-established supplier to boat owners, is now marketing Caravan Pride, which is a compound formulated for removing scratches from the acrylic windows fitted in motorcaravans. The Company also sells a GRP surface renovator to revive dulled body panels.

Similarly, Auto Glym cleaning products have

been used by car owners for a long time and this manufacturer has recently formulated Caravan Cleaner, a general-purpose product for caravans and motorhomes. In addition, its more specific products like Bumper Care, Fast Glass, Intensive Tar Remover and Tyre Conditioner are useful for cleaning individual components on cars and motorcaravans alike.

The range of treatments from Mer is also notable. In particular, Mer Car Polish, manufactured in Germany, is easy to apply and versatile in use. It can be used neat as a polish or diluted in water to produce a 'wash 'n' shine' effect. It also removes algae and moss from motorcaravans with ease. Other products in the Mer range include Wheel Cleaning Gel and PVC & Vinyl Cleaner.

The range of colour-specific bumper and trim restoration kits from CarPlan products – manufacturer of the well-known brand T-Cut – is particularly useful because the bumpers on light commercial vehicles are large items which are especially conspicuous when discoloured.

And of course there are many other good cleaning products to consider. But how can a motorcaravanner find out what to use? Unfortunately it's not easy to carry out exacting tests on cleaning compounds and in many instances the owner only finds out through experience what produces the results required. Ease of application is another issue which undoubtedly influences choice. Price plays a part, too. However, never be tempted to experiment using non-proprietary products. For example, some owners found that methylated spirits puts a good shine on acrylic windows. But several weeks later, the plastic developed tiny craze marks, almost certainly caused by a reaction between the acrylic and the meths. So be careful: replacement windows are surprisingly expensive.

Cleaning techniques

The following guidance, based on techniques employed by valet specialists, covers a full cleaning regime.

Tools

A strong bristled brush – for agitating cleaning products when removing resistant brake deposits on wheels. Purpose-made wheel brushes are available, although a traditional stiff brush sold in hardware stores for cleaning large saucepans achieves this function just as well.

A cranked radiator paint brush – the long-handled brushes designed for painting the back of domestic radiators are excellent tools for applying cleaning compounds in difficult-to-reach areas.

Soft nylon floor brush – useful for agitating dust when an upholstery cleaner has been applied to a fabric cover.

Hard compound sponge – upholstery cleaner is often good on interior surfaces such as decorative-faced ply. However, a car cleaning sponge is too soft and a hard sponge used by interior decorators is often better for shifting resistant marks.

Kitchen roll paper – this is used in conjunction with some acrylic window cleaners instead of a conventional rag.

Cotton polishing cloth – a cleaning cloth should not contain lint. Avoid using old T-shirts and other garments which include lint and other mildly abrasive synthetic components. Much to be preferred is open weave cloth which is 100% cotton stock. When polishing with this, any minute abrasive specks get absorbed into the weave of the cloth rather than being held on the surface where they can cause more damage.

Products from CarPlan include treatments for re-vitalising dark plastic bumpers on motorcaravan base vehicles

Cleaning procedure

In a complete valet operation, the strategy is to start with really dirty jobs and then move to more refined tasks and finishing operations. The procedure here describes a full schedule – though you're unlikely to complete the full schedule on every cleaning operation.

The recommended order is:

1) Engine
2) Wheels and tyres
3) Door shuts
4) Body clean or shampoo
5) Interior cleaning
6) Tar spots
7) Body polishing
8) Glass/acrylic windows
9) Finishing jobs including tyre dressing.

ENGINE If you like to keep the engine and its compartment clean, tackle this first. Note the instructions accompanying engine cleaners and remember to tie plastic bags over key electrical items including an electronic alarm. With most

Stain removal

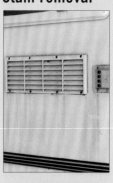

The black carbon trickles that stain bodywork directly under ventilators, door stays and similar attachments can be effectively removed using Auto Glym Engine Cleaner. This is a versatile product which, in addition to engine cleaning, is good for removing grease from tyres, cleaning plastic covers, discoloured vents, fuel stains (especially diesel), exhaust marks, door shuts, ovens and even saucepans that are stained on the outside.

Wheels are hard to get clean, so a wheel-cleaning brush like this one from Auto Glym comes in handy.

A long-handled cranked radiator brush is ideal for cleaning round awkward body fittings.

After a tyre cleaner and grease remover has been applied, the compound should be hosed off.

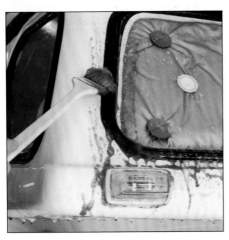

Auto-Glym engine cleaner is equally effective for removing stubborn stains from body panels.

Some upholstery cleaners should be stippled cautiously before removal with a clean cloth.

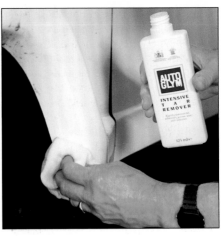

Removing tar spots with a proprietary cleaner should precede any polishing work.

products, the engine should be cold and switched off. The procedure involves: applying the cleaner, agitating with a brush, and then gentle and judicious flooding with fresh water. Experts use pressure hoses but an inexperienced owner is advised not to because a powerful jet can inflict damage.

WHEELS/TYRES Make sure they are cold – hot brake discs can create reactions in some chemicals. Most cleaners should be removed promptly and not allowed to dry, so it is best to complete one wheel at a time. After cleaning the wheel rims or cover, attend to the tyres. Grease should be removed and some engine cleaners are suitable for this. Agitate the cleaner with a brush and hose off. However, leave the final application of a tyre renovation treatment until the end of a valet operation.

DOOR SHUTS A grease remover should be used on door shuts and wheel arches – engine cleaners are often effective here.

BODY CLEAN OR SHAMPOO Either use a purpose-designed product like Auto Glym Caravan Cleaner or use a shampoo conditioner. For really stubborn stains, streaks, algae marks or bird lime, use a product like Auto Glym Engine Cleaner. Agitate this with a radiator brush, then rinse it off with water. On the other hand, if you decide to use a shampoo, remember to rinse it off, but don't use a high pressure hose. This can 'bounce off' the conditioning film that shampoos usually leave after application. Gentle flooding on a metal panel enables some conditioners to electrostatically bond to the surface, thus affording the best protection.

INTERIOR Now work inside. For the upholstery, several manufacturers sell treatments which are suitable on cushion fabrics as well as vehicle seats. Of course, it is always wise to try a product on a small test area first. As a rule, never use a scrubbing action, especially on fabrics like velour. It's better to employ a stippling action using a nylon brush with medium-strength bristles. When the surface is subsequently wiped with a clean, damp, white cotton cloth, the amount of dirt pulled away can be surprising. Where possible, it's best

to carry out upholstery cleaning in warm weather so that cushions can be dried outside. You might also need to open a lot of windows when applying treatments; working in a confined space can lead to discomfort.

TAR REMOVAL Moving outside again, any remaining tar spots should be removed from the body before starting the polishing work. Several proprietary products are specifically made to tackle tar deposits.

BODY POLISH The choice of body treatments is determined by the materials. If your motorcaravan is clad with patterned aluminium, such as a stucco or pimple surface finish, it's wise to leave this alone. Some of the paints used on aluminium sheet can be lifted by polishes so it is better to be content with the sheen left by a shampoo.

However, on painted steel, acrylic-capped ABS and GRP, a good coat of polish will provide a protective finish which may last for six months or more. Take note of the product instructions and when applying a polish, be careful to keep it from black plastic components like motorcaravan door handles and bumpers. These should be coated later with a purpose-made treatment.

WINDOWS Remember that acrylic windows are easily scratched and in some instances a product formulated for use on a windscreen or cab side window might not be suitable for use on a plastic unit. And whereas there are plenty of products available for cleaning safety glass, products intended for a motorcaravan's acrylic windows are harder to find. However, Seitz markets Acrylic Glass Cleaner which is guaranteed not to cause tension cracks and is supplied to motorcaravan accessory shops by Dometic. Another product which can be used on a clean and dust-free window is Auto Glym Fast Glass. This has to be sprayed on to the window from its special container and promptly spread across the surface with a kitchen paper. With equal haste it should be removed using another piece of clean paper from a kitchen roll.

FINISHING JOBS Now the finishing jobs are tackled such as the application of plastic treatments. Several products are available for black fittings – bumper treatments, for example, can just as effectively revive a sheen on a motorcaravan door handle or an external mirror housing.

Finally an application of a tyre dressing treatment completes the valet in style. Note that rubber-based tyre paints are less popular nowadays. Products like Auto Glym Instant Tyre Dressing are much better – as long as you follow the application instructions. When this tyre conditioner is sprayed on to the rubber it forms white streaks which initially look unpleasant – but don't touch the tyre. Leave the dressing to dry for 10 to 15 minutes, after which the effect is most surprising. The milky streaks will have disappeared and the tyres look as if they are new again.

Bodywork sealing

It would be wrong to question the wisdom of adopting traditional cleaning techniques, but anyone confronted with a jumbo jet, a line of railway carriages or a large motor launch would want to find an alternative cleaning strategy. This was one reason why panel sealing products were developed and A-Glaze is one which is being sold in the UK.

Paint-sealing products like this have been used on a number of airliners including Concorde and the British Airways fleet. These treatments are also offered as an extra to anyone buying a high-quality car such as a Porsche or a Ferrari. So these products have provenance and now a kit is being sold by A-Glaze to owners of motorhomes.

The point to appreciate is that this product is neither a polish nor a cleaning compound as such. It is better described as a paint protection system, although its function is equally effective on pigmented GRP which is self-coloured rather than painted. Essentially A-Glaze is a type of surface sealant which protects bodywork from environmental hazards such as weather-induced fading, acid rain, bird lime, oxidation and loss of surface gloss.

The initial application of the product may take a day on a large motorcaravan, but once the surface has been cleaned and coated it lasts for up to two years. All that is needed is the occasional wash, and even a shower of rain has a self cleansing effect. In spite of initial scepticism, the author has found that this product does achieve its claimed objectives. And whereas the treatment kit is expensive when compared with traditional polishes, the long-term benefits are very pleasing, especially if you park a vehicle near trees during the winter months. Green deposits and black streaks don't take a firm hold.

The application procedure is shown alongside and it doesn't matter if the motorhome is clad in dimpled aluminium panels, plain aluminium, GRP sheet or mouldings in GRP or ABS.

The first task is to wash the vehicle thoroughly. Then you treat all metal surfaces and smooth

Ordinary polish can discolour black plastic fittings so a bumper treatment should be used.

plastic mouldings with A-Prep Surface Cleaner. However, textured finishes like plastic bumpers and door handles must NOT be treated. Applying the cleaner is the hard graft stage because it's important to remove smears, black streaks and remnants of cleaning wax. The motorcaravan will then look impressive, but the all-important coating of A-Glaze sealant is needed next.

This sealant is supplied in a surprisingly small container and that's because it has to be applied extremely sparingly with a clean, soft cloth, used in tight circular motions. However, on large areas like the roof, A-Glaze is normally applied using a Squeegee mop fitted with a long handle.

Once the vehicle has been coated with the sealant, you wipe all surfaces using a damp, clean, soft cloth. On larger panels, an atomiser (sold at garden centres) is helpful for applying a fine mist of water which enables the uncured sealant to flow over the surfaces. Finally, you go over everything using a soft, dry polishing cloth to create a pleasing shine.

In the months which follow, a quick wash is all that's needed to re-create the gloss and it's not unusual for the product to maintain its effectiveness for 18 months or more. When the

Areas difficult to reach can be treated using A-Glaze with the help of a telescopic-handled flat mop.

A mist of water sprayed from an atomizer helps A-Glaze sealant to spread during its application.

bodywork eventually loses its glossy surface, it's an indication that air-born deposits have settled on the surface. However, the film can be removed with the Wash and Shine Shampoo included in the A-Glaze kit. The job involves a) a hose down, b) application of the non-foaming shampoo, c) rinse off, and d) leather off. It shouldn't take long and if it helps, a motorcaravan can be cleaned in two halves.

Suffice it to say that using a sealing product like this is a very different way to keep a motorhome looking smart. On the other hand it doesn't help items like texture-finish black plastic door handles and bumpers. To retain a dark satin finish on these components, you still need to use a conventional plastic treatment product.

Reviving acrylic windows

Even the most careful driver will occasionally have to pull close to a hedgerow to avoid an oncoming vehicle when using a narrow lane. That's when brambles are likely to leave a deep scratch on an acrylic window.

The window manufacturer's instructions make it clear that abrasive compounds should NOT be used when cleaning an acrylic pane. However, we are beyond the cleaning situation and to remove a deep scratch, you will certainly need abrasive papers together with a special cutting compound. Products for removing deep scratches are available from both Seitz and Farécla.

As an example, Caravan Pride scratch remover from Farécla is a fine-grade rubbing compound which can be applied either with a slow-rotating

Removing scratches in acrylic windows

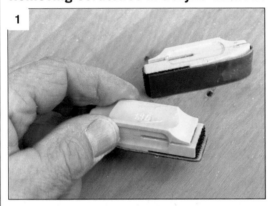

1 Deep scratches are normally removed by starting with 1200 grade wet-and-dry paper mounted on a small block. The water acts as a lubricant.

2 Use an open-weave cloth made from 100% cotton stock and ensure it is wet. A garden spray bottle is useful for delivering a fine mist to the rag.

3 Apply scratch remover over the entire surface and be meticulous about regularly re-applying a fresh mist of water to the surface from a spray bottle.

4 A machine is quicker, but make sure you use only a purpose-made polisher. This revolves much more slowly than a drill fitted with a mop attachment.

- When using wet-and-dry paper on an acrylic window, don't use a circular action until the final polish. Rub in straight lines instead; six to eight in one direction, followed by the same number at right angles. If you see a fresh scratch, this technique allows you to identify which piece of abrasive paper caused the fresh mark. There's no need to work solely across the original scratch mark.

- If the 1200 grade wet-and-dry paper starts to remove the scratches, continue with 1500 grade which is even finer. If it proves too fine, try a 1000 or even 800 grade.

- Remember to change the paper frequently or you will inflict new damage on the surface.

- If a machine is used with a foam mop, water is critical and serves four functions:
  1) It keeps the cleaning compound out of the deep pores of the mop.
  2) It keeps the acrylic surface cooler.
  3) It acts as a lubricant.
  4) It prolongs the life of the mop.

- Whether the scratch is removed manually or by machine, the work should be completed using a clean rag, buffing up the surface using circular motions.

buffing machine or by hand. To carry out the renovation work it isn't necessary to remove a window, although the accompanying sequence is shown using a unit which has been detached and transferred to a bench. Suffice it to say, the product, originally just packaged as 'Boat Pride', has been used successfully for many years on boat windows; its results on motorcaravans are equally impressive.

Leaks and damp problems

When it's driven on a bumpy road, a motorcaravan has to cope with flexing, tension and relentless impact. Thankfully a good design can sustain this kind of treatment, but over a long period, adjacent panels can develop weak spots.

Hardening sealant is another problem. The flexible mastic which waterproofs the junctions between adjacent panels eventually loses its resilience. Moreover, the effects of direct sunshine and the extremes of seasonal temperatures help to hasten its demise. The threat of damage is even more acute if there's a different rate of expansion between two adjacent materials.

Puncture points constitute a further weakness. For instance, screws that hold a length of decorative aluminium strip in place puncture the body cladding material in a number of places. Even components like lamp clusters are notorious weak spots, especially if a rubber mounting gasket loses its resilience. One well-known coachbuilt motorcaravan even had problems when rainwater started to penetrate through the mitred joints on the corners of its rectangular window frames.

Any type of motorcaravan can develop a leak but it is coachbuilt models which are especially prone to problems. Logically it might seem that walls constructed from prefabricated bonded panels wouldn't suffer from seepage as much as traditionally-built non-bonded sections. But this isn't necessarily the case. Rainwater penetrates some types of insulating foam used in the core, whether or not the material is bonded, and a

problem may be developing long before there are visible signs of damp on the interior wall ply.

As always, prevention is better than cure and owners should get a dealer to carry out a damp test every year. A checking instrument normally uses an electric current which can track along zones of moisture to get a reading. Inexpensive damp testers are available from DIY stores but are unlikely to be as accurate as professional damp meters. Moreover, skill and experience are needed to ensure they are used correctly. For instance a professional meter usually expresses the level of damp as a percentage, and an inexperienced owner might reasonably presume that a reading showing 18% damp would show that there's a problem. But that's not the case, because many constructional materials have a

An annual damp check ensures that serious damage can be avoided.

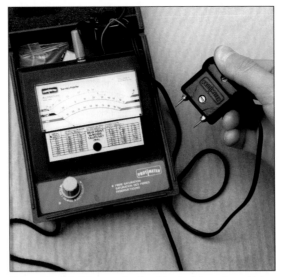

This professional damp meter has two electric probes which reveal developing problems in a motorcaravan's structure.

Readings are typically taken in about 40 places; zones around windows are especially important to check.

natural moisture content and a reading of 18% falls within normally acceptable limits. In fact, body repair specialists only presume that a water ingress problem is developing when there's a reading of 22% or more.

Working to this guideline, a service specialist will take readings by positioning the meter's probes at various points around the perimeter of windows, doors and roof lights, and at the junction points between wall and ceiling panels. If an area of damp is identified, the next task is to ascertain where the moisture's coming from – which isn't always easy.

In a bad case of damp, major re-construction work may be necessary immediately and most owners would entrust this to specialists. Companies like Crossley, with branches in Darlington and Leyland, and Autovan Services at Wimborne, Dorset, are examples of experienced body repairers who undertake major re-building work.

A less demanding remedial measure that some owners tackle themselves involves the removal and reinstatement of decorative aluminium

This screw is badly rusted along its length, which means that rain water could be seeping into the structure here.

strips, wall ventilators, and components like roof windows. Weather-resistance is greatly improved by re-fixing fittings like this on a fresh bed of flexible sealant.

Where decorative aluminium strips are concerned, the job necessitates removal of a plastic cover strip to reveal the screw heads. When the screws which hold the aluminium extrusion in place are removed, check to see if any of them are rusty. If the thread is in bad shape, this is a certain sign that water has crept behind the trim strip and has started to seep into the sub-structure via this particular screw. Replacement screws, together with new flexible sealant, are urgently needed and a zealous repairer will seal up all the original holes and drill new ones.

But there's another approach to consider. It is also possible to attach a trim strip using a high bonding adhesive sealant – described in the next section – instead of using screws. A product like Sikaflex 221 is a good example. A couple of screws are usually needed to hold the strip in place while the adhesive is setting. This may take up to 24 hours, although you can usually expect the adhesion to be good in half that time. However, a motorcaravan manufacturer can't afford to spend time on a job like this, which is why screws are normally used instead. The accompanying illustrations show the procedure being carried out on a caravan, but the job is just the same when re-affixing a trim strip on a motorhome.

Sealants

The ability to retain plasticity is a key requirement of most motorcaravan sealants. However, there are different types of product and these can be classified as follows:
- Butyl rubber-based sealants sold in a cartridge and injected from a dispenser gun.
- Butyl rubber sealant in tape form, supplied with a backing strip for easier handling.

Re-bedding an awning rail

Once the screws are removed, the rail is removed as a unit.

The mastic shown here is still in reasonably good condition, but there are places with poor coverage.

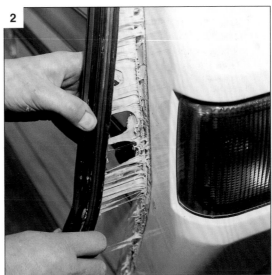

Remains of the old mastic are removed with a cleaner; white spirit is often effective for this.

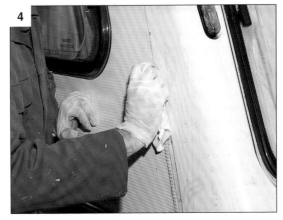

The aluminium seam is meticulously cleaned before starting to apply the sealant.

A bead of Sikaflex 221 sealant is carefully applied all the way around the perimeter of the wall.

Photographs courtesy of Sika

Alternatively Sikaflex 221 can be applied to the awning rail. Two or three self tapping screws may be needed to prevent the rail slipping while the sealant is setting, but a strong bond will ultimately be achieved with no need for mechanical fixings.

Many of the mastic sealants and adhesives used in motorcaravan construction are only available to manufacturers in large batches. However, Carafax can supply small quantities of cartridge sealants by mail order. Sika, another prominent company in the industry, sells its adhesive sealants in car repair shops and in 2004 it will be introducing a product specifically for motorcaravans which will be sold in dealer's accessory shops. Ribbon sealant from W4 Accessories is similarly available from motorcaravan accessory shops.

- Silicone-based sealant sold in a cartridge. This is applied by dispenser gun and many DIY enthusiasts will have applied versions of this product to seal around a bath at home.
- Adhesive sealants which achieve great bonding strength but retain a measure of flexibility.

Note: *As a rough rule of thumb, the higher the strength of a product in terms of its bonding characteristics, the lower its degree of flexibility. Conversely a high level of flexibility is usually off-set by a low level of bonding strength.*

With regard to the last example on the above list, an adhesive sealant is able to bond completely dissimilar materials including metal to glass, wood to metal, GRP to metal and many other combinations. Products in the Sikaflex range, for example, achieve phenomenal bonding strength and this is why they are often used to bond the cab of light commercial vehicles to the coachbuilt living quarters of motorhomes. Furthermore, adhesive sealants like Sikaflex are used to bond modern windscreens directly to a steel frame instead of having to use a rubber moulding strip. Once it has cured – which may take up to 24 hours – an adhesive sealant is dry to the touch. In contrast a butyl rubber-based sealant retains its tackiness for several years and different materials will retain a degree of contact even if their rates of expansion and contraction are dissimilar.

Needless to say, performance characteristics are complex. As far as the DIY enthusiast is concerned, a key issue is to decide which product to use. Whilst butyl sealants sold in cartridge form are used with enviable skill by motorcaravan builders, butyl ribbon sealant is often easier for the amateur repairer to apply.

Ribbon sealant is manufactured in different widths and its working characteristics differ from product to product. The sealant from W4 Accessories – regularly stocked in accessory shops – is particularly easy to use and can be cut to size with a woodworking knife; but its 'pull effect' is modest. In contrast, Caraseal 303 butyl strip from Carafax is very sticky to the touch and achieves

a notable bond as soon as the surfaces make contact. The trouble is, if you position the strip inaccurately, it can be a tricky job to remove it.

If you decide to re-mount a length of aluminium trim, a wall vent, or a component like a roof window, ribbon sealant is recommended. However, if screws are needed to hold a component in place, make puncture points in the strip with a bradawl otherwise the turning screws will wind the sealant round their shaft when you tighten them.

Once excess sealant has been removed, the task is complete – though some owners go one step further and apply a bead of silicone sealant or even Sikaflex around the perimeter of a fitted product. There's nothing wrong with this 'belt and braces' approach, but applying a bead of silicone neatly demands patience. The best strategy is to apply masking tape on either side of the junction.

To achieve a tidy finish, a silicone sealant should be wiped with a finger dipped in methylated spirits, thus producing a bevel along the surface. Then remove the masking tape straight away, bearing in mind that it may be coated with as much sealant as you've left along the junction. This is wasteful admittedly but the resulting line of sealant will look neat.

When applying Sikaflex, many builders smooth over the applied beading using a finger generously coated in spittle. It should be noted that white Sikaflex sealant is much less likely to leave stains on fingers than its black counterpart which seems to get all over the place. Wearing thin gauge surgical gloves is advisable, especially for anyone with sensitive skin.

Body repairs

Before accident damage can be tackled, it's necessary to establish the type of material which needs attention; for instance, steel panels that form part of the base vehicle are tackled in the same way as a similar damaged section on a car.

Guidance on body repairs and painting procedures are given in *The Car Bodywork Repair Manual* by Lindsay Porter, published by Haynes.

When fitting this Remi roof window, a ribbon sealant was applied around the base.

Once installed, the perimeter of the Remi roof window was sealed using Sikaflex 252 for maximum weather protection.

This manual also has a chapter dealing specifically with GRP repair techniques.

On the other hand, many motorcaravans are clad in aluminium or embellished with acrylic-capped ABS mouldings. Repair work here is rather different, so you would need to confirm what the damaged material is before proceeding with remedial work.

Repairing ABS and GRP panels

The tip box printed in the margin on page 28 describes how to establish whether a moulded panel is made from GRP, ABS or acrylic-capped ABS. It also makes a brief reference to repair work.

A notable feature of GRP is the fact that it is relatively easy to repair. Surface damage to the outer layer – called the 'gel coat' – can be remedied by applying fresh self-coloured gel coat or even by using car repair body filler (although this would need painting afterwards). Structural damage, on the other hand, necessitates a repair of cracked or missing sections using chopped strand glass fibre mat; this has to be impregnated with polyester resin, stippled with a brush and pressed down with a laminating roller. Further guidance on GRP products and their use is available from Trylon, a specialist supplier.

Panels in GRP can also be repainted even if the original product was moulded with a polyester resin which contained a colouring pigment. Specialist automotive paint suppliers will mix paint to the exact tint required and can supply the prepared product in an aerosol spray can. However, you would also need an etching primer to ensure the paint adheres to a GRP panel.

Body sections made from acrylic-capped ABS are also repairable and repair kits have been developed by firms such as Gramos and Bradleys.

It is therefore rather disappointing to learn that many dealer workshop staff are unfamiliar with repair procedures and are all-too-eager to completely replace a panel which may have only sustained superficial damage.

The situation is much the same with plastic bumpers and costly replacements are often fitted when a repair could have easily been carried out at a fraction of the price. This is even more inexcusable when specialists like Bradleys supply a specially formulated paint for use on plastic bumpers which dries with a textured finish. Suffice it to say, the illustrations on page 38 show ABS repair procedures being carried out together with an illustration of a white GRP replica bumper for Fiat Ducato or Peugeot Boxer models, which merely slips over the top of one that's damaged or looking old.

As a further tip, it is sometimes found that replacement GRP or ABS moulded panels for older motorcaravans are no longer available – which is a problem when a panel gets damaged beyond

A surface blemish on GRP can be repaired by adding pre-colourised matching gel coat; when dry, this is rubbed down and then polished.

Matching paint

Specialist automotive paint suppliers will mix paint to the exact tint you require, and supply it in an aerosol spray can.

This white GRP bumper from Independence 2000 slips tightly over a damaged one; its fixing screws are discreetly located.

Repairing a split in an acrylic-capped ABS panel

1

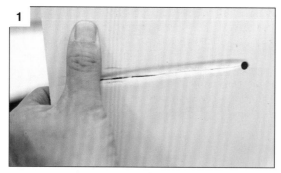

Holes are drilled at the ends of the split to prevent further stress damage; the damaged area is also deepened in order to accommodate the repair compound and roughened with P80 grit paper to achieve a key.

2

Surface cleaner is applied to the damaged area, wiped over with a lint-free cloth, and left to dry. Primer adhesion promoter is then sprayed on and left to dry for 30 minutes.

3

Self-adhesive fibre reinforcing tape is cut to size and stuck to the rear of the damaged panel.

4

A two-part bonding filler is dispensed from a standard sealant gun through the spiral nozzle supplied so that the components are blended. This is applied to fill the split just below the surface.

5

When the bonding filler has fully cured, the area is rubbed down so that no filler appears above the surface.

6

Primer adhesion promoter is applied to the surface once again in readiness for the addition of a final top filler.

7

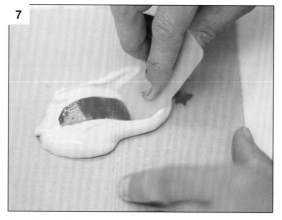

The filler paste is dispensed on to a board and a measured amount of catalyst mixed in thoroughly with a plastic applicator.

8

The filler is applied over the damaged area using the applicator and feathered off at the sides. This will be smoothed when dry using abrasive paper; a matched etching paint suitable for this material will be applied and finally a colour-matched top coat added.

repair. However, V&G is a servicing specialist near Peterborough whose experienced staff can create a one-off mould for a damaged panel irrespective of whether the original was made in ABS or GRP. Having fabricated a mould they then create the new panel in GRP. This is an unusual service which helps to keep older motorcaravans on the road, even if an accident has damaged parts no longer supplied through normal channels.

Finally, there is the matter of repairing aluminium skinned walls. The trouble is that aluminium stretches and dents cannot be beaten out. So the usual way to repair a damaged wall is to fill the depression with a repair filler and then bond a replacement aluminium panel on top. Trim strips help to hide the junctions where old and new panels meet and the human eye doesn't register that one skinned section sticks slightly proud of adjacent panels.

However, on a large wall section, this can be a costly job and in the last few years the HBC repair process – developed in Denmark – has been introduced into the UK. The operation has to be carried out by a trained repairer and it entails making a flexible mould which replicates any type of textured aluminium pattern. A patch slightly larger than the area of damage is then created from the mould and bonded into place. Fairing-in the patching piece and spray-painting it to match the surrounding panel is a skilled operation and the results are usually very good. It's true that

the HBC system isn't a cheap option, but it can cost considerably less than a major re-skinning operation, quite apart from the fact that getting hold of replacement aluminium often takes several weeks.

Delamination

Notwithstanding the merits of pre-fabricated floor and wall panels, it is a serious matter if the insulation foam loses its bond with either of the materials forming the outer part of the sandwich. The condition is referred to as 'delamination' and a panel's strength is seriously affected when it happens. In practice, wall panels are seldom affected by delamination, whereas floors are more likely to give problems.

In a composite floor, the outer parts of the sandwich are formed using plywood which is bonded to both sides of the insulation material. As a point of interest, the overall thickness of the three-part sandwich is usually greater than the thickness of bonded wall panels and there will also be more timber ribs in the core to add torsional strength. In spite of this, the weight of people together with heavy appliances such as a full-size cooker impose a considerable loading. That's why the upper layer of plywood sometimes breaks away from the foam insulation, especially in areas where a motorcaravan's occupants are frequently passing. Places prone to failure are just inside

Repairing a delaminated floor

1

With the floor covering removed, sponginess in the floor panel adjacent to the kitchen units confirmed that delamination had taken place.

2

The straight edge of a spirit level sometimes reveals that there's a slight rise in the delaminating plywood.

3

A repair kit comprises a two-pack bonding agent from Apollo Chemicals, plastic syringes, and beech dowel pegs.

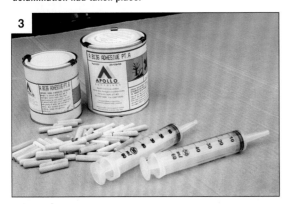

4

You mustn't drill through the ply on the underside of the floor panel, so tape is used as a depth indicator on the twist drill.

5 On this repair, 42 holes were drilled in a measured block that completely covered the delaminating portion of the floor.

6 By temporarily inserting a dowel and pushing it down you establish how much the pegs need to be trimmed before injecting the chemical.

7 Mix in small batches at a time; the two chemicals are measured, mixed in the stated proportions, and then drawn into a syringe.

8 Inject the bonding agent. Hardly any is taken in by the sound areas, but where there's a zone of delamination, a large quantity disperses into the void.

9 When the agent leaks out of a hole, tap in a dowel peg. Wipe away any excess on the floor at once – it's hard to remove when it's dry.

10 Lay a sheet of brown paper over the area, followed by a sheet of thick boarding, then place something heavy such as bricks on top.

the main entrance door and the area around the kitchen sink.

Delamination is easy to detect and a creaking floor is a common sign of a developing problem. Sometimes there's a 'soggy' feeling to the floor, too, and occasionally the plywood section which has delaminated will bubble-up, creating a small rise around the problem zone. Needless to say, a delaminating floor needs urgent attention although a repair is usually fairly easy to carry out.

To begin with a repair kit has to be purchased, containing plastic syringes, wooden dowel pegs and a two-pack bonding agent in liquid form. The manufacturer of these kits is Apollo Chemicals Ltd but the product has to be ordered through a caravan or motorcaravan accessory shop. Aspects of the repair work are shown alongside. The task involves removal of the floor carpet or vinyl, drilling a matrix of holes, mixing the two-part chemicals in measured, workable batches, injecting the catalysed bonding agent, plugging the holes with a dowel peg cut to length to prevent adhesive oozing out of the holes, and finally holding the ply down around the treated area using bricks or a heavy object like a paving slab.

As a rule, it's not a difficult job but some dealers are unwilling to sell repair kits to members of the public. This seems unhelpful, although it's true that if a DIY enthusiast were to make a mistake when injecting the bonding chemical into the core of the board, the process is irreversible. You also

have to mix up small quantities at a time because the reaction of the two chemicals happens fairly quickly. If there's a rush, it then becomes all too easy to forget to add the hardening compound in one of the mixes. So you need to work methodically, and let's face it – the floor is one component that you wouldn't want to fail.

Servicing the living area

Although motorcaravan owners recognise the importance of servicing their vehicle, the living area sometimes gets overlooked. However, this is a serious omission as personal safety could be at stake.

Carrying out a routine pressure check of the gas supply system, for example, is an important task. If leaks are detected, faulty couplings will be repaired by the service engineer since a fault could be fatal. Cases of carbon monoxide poisoning through faulty gas appliances have also occurred, and such accidents could have been avoided if routine servicing work had been carried out.

Handbook advice

Handbooks might advise on items that have to be checked and serviced, but the information is variable – both in quality and detail. In some instances, motorcaravans from smaller volume converters are supplied without a handbook.

It is for this reason that the SMMT and NCC looked particularly closely at the subject.

The SMMT/NCC Annual Habitation Check

Several years ago, The Society of Motor Manufacturers and Traders (SMMT), working in conjunction with The National Caravan Council (NCC), published a booklet entitled the *Recommended Annual Habitation Service Check*. Its objective was to identify areas of attention in a habitation check and provide motorcaravan workshops with useful guidelines. Achieving a consistent level of service is important for a motorcaravan owner.

The SMMT/NCC guide made reference to 11 areas of attention which included:

- The integrity of the body mounting points
- Windows
- Doors
- Attachments to chassis
- Attachments to body exterior
- Internal components
- Rising roof mechanisms
- Gas system
- Water system
- Electrical system
- Ventilation.

Within these eleven areas of attention were further subdivisions which drew attention to specific important tasks. For example, the need to have an annual damp test was highlighted . However, some areas of attention were relevant only for certain types of motorcaravan; one example was the need to check and verify the safe operation of a rising roof mechanism. However, the importance of having appliances serviced regularly applies to any make or model.

Appliance servicing

Carrying out checks on appliances is a safety-critical matter – especially those that operate on gas. When left unused for an extended period, these appliances can start to perform poorly. The accumulation of dust is one contributor to inefficient operation but spiders and insects also create problems. Even a spider's web can upset the shape of a flame, and it can prevent a pilot flame from igniting the main burner on a space heater. This is why a gas specialist needs to clean an appliance together with other tasks recommended by a manufacturer.

But it's not only the shape of a gas flame which needs to be checked by a servicing specialist: the colour of the flame is also a performance indicator. Tips of yellow on the hob burners, for example, might indicate that there's an incorrect gas/air mixture. This leads to sooty deposits being left on pots and pans. More serious is the fact that an incorrect air mixture might signify that there's a carbon monoxide problem. So expert attention is crucial; altering a gas/air mixture should never be attempted by the owner.

Removing dust from gas burners is an important task to be carried out when appliances are serviced.

An absorption refrigerator is another gas-operated appliance that needs periodic attention. For instance, Dometic – formerly trading as Electrolux – has stated that a refrigerator should be serviced annually. This often necessitates removing the appliance from the motorcaravan so that work can be carried out on a bench. A further description of the servicing procedure is given in Chapter 9.

The trouble is that a normal habitation service usually only checks whether a refrigerator achieves cooling. A full service as recommended by the manufacturer is generally regarded by dealers as an additional job. So don't be misled into thinking that the 'service check' is the same as a full fridge service.

Approved Workshop Scheme

Recognising the importance of establishing consistency and quality in the servicing and maintenance of motorcaravans, rigorous standards were set out by The Camping and Caravanning Club, The Caravan Club and The National Caravan Council. This led to the launch of The Approved Caravan Workshop Scheme and the identification of servicing specialists who provide high standards in workshop operation and related customer service. It is managed by the three associations mentioned, but any workshop wishing to join the scheme has to meet exacting standards and be formally approved by an independent inspection agency, Jones Vening Ltd. Thereafter, an accredited workshop has to keep to the strict Codes of Practice and pass the regular re-inspections undertaken by Jones Vening.

Since its inauguration in 1996, the scheme has been extended to embrace motorcaravan habitation servicing and the word 'caravan' has been dropped from the logo. There have also been constant improvements and refinements in the work schedules, as well as a growing list of accredited workshops.

At present there are well over 100 Approved Workshops nationwide and a few accredited specialists who operate a mobile service. Any member of the public can access the latest list of member workshops. You can either contact one of the three management members or check the NCC Web Site: www.the caravan.net.

Toilet servicing

Care of a toilet is regarded as a task for the owner and little maintenance work is included in a workshop service operation. If the toilet has flush water drawn from its own tank, this should be drained down when a vehicle is parked for extended periods in frosty weather. In addition, dry the rubber seal on the cassette, lubricate it with olive oil, and leave the blade OPEN throughout the storage period. Alternatively you can use Thetford "Seal lubricant".

What really needs to be done?

The facing page sets out a typical Service Schedule. It was drawn up using recommendations given in the SMMT/NCC booklet and recommendations from appliance manufacturers. It also takes note of advice and practical guidance received by the author at service engineers' training courses. Finally, it was used as a consultancy/discussion document by the NCC and the Jones Vening Inspection Agency just before this book went to press. The need for an owner to see what a habitation service entails is certainly most important.

Regrettably, some 'non-approved' repair workshops fail to provide customers with documentation showing what work they carry out when conducting a habitation service. This is most unsatisfactory. So check the position very carefully if arranging a service with a dealer whose workshop is not listed in the Approved Workshop Scheme. Written documentation should always be provided afterwards with comments recorded about elements such as structural integrity and the gas and electricity systems. There should also be a diagram showing where the readings were taken when conducting the damp test.

When making a booking, enquire what the dealer will do if something is found to be faulty during the course of the inspection. In some service centres, minor faults like an inoperative interior light will be repaired within the time allotted for the service. Spare parts, of course, will be charged separately. It is the matter of repairing more significant faults that needs prior discussion. Whilst it often makes sense for a repair to be carried out there and then, it is normal for a dealer to seek instruction to proceed from the owner, particularly when an expensive replacement part is needed.

As a rough guide, a standard habitation service – excluding work on a fridge – is likely to involve three or four hours work. The cost varies from dealer to dealer depending on the hourly rate for labour. Parts will be charged separately, of course.

DIY servicing

When a motorcaravan is within its warranty period, it is normal to find that habitation servicing has got to be carried out at an authorised workshop. Once the motorcaravan is outside this period, some owners like to do some of the servicing work themselves.

There's no doubt that owners with practical experience, technical knowledge and the appropriate level of competency would be able to carry out SOME of the tasks listed in the accompanying service schedule. Checking window catches, lubricating door hinges and tightening the spring mechanism on a roller blind are scarcely taxing.

At the same time there are several service operations – like pressure testing a gas system – which must only be undertaken by a qualified gas specialist. Similarly the tests needed on a 230V mains supply system are best carried out by a qualified electrician. In both instances it is worth enquiring if a separate confirmation sheet can be issued with a date and signature verifying that both the gas and electrical systems have been tested and found to be in order. Occasionally there is an extra charge for supplying these certificates, particularly if qualified engineers have to be brought in to do the work. Nevertheless, being able to pass on service records and dated certificates is especially helpful when selling a motorcaravan.

ANNUAL SERVICE SCHEDULE
Motorcaravans

Make:.............................Model:...........Year:..............

Type:
- a) Fixed roof van
- b) Elevating roof
- c) High-top
- d) Dismountable
- e) Coachbuilt
- f) A-Class
- g) American
- h) Other

Circle the type above.

Chassis: i) Original chassis   ii) AL-KO conversion
Circle the type above.

Registration number:...

Vehicle Identification Number.....................................

THE SCHEDULE
Note: ☐ Under Comments, write n/a alongside any element which is not applicable to the model undergoing the service.

Note: ☐ Report under Comments any defect, signs of wear, etc. Report depth of tread on the tyres, including the spare.

Section 1: Undergear
Comments

1. Visually inspect body-mounting fixings ☐ ....
2. Visually inspect cab-to-body junction ☐ ....
3. Check mounting of underfloor tanks ☐ ....
4. Check spare wheel cradle operation and tyre ☐ ....
5. Examine wheel boxes for corrosion/damage ☐ ....
6. Check and lubricate corner steadies (if fitted) ☐ ....
7. Check step operation (if fitted) and lubricate ☐ ....
8. Lubricate axle tube on AL-KO chassis ☐ ....
9. Inspect non-original suspension additions ☐ ....

General comments on undergear.................................

Section 2:
External Bodywork & General Condition
Comments

1. Inspect sealant; check potential leak points. ☐ ....
2. Check/oil door locks; oil hinges. ☐ ....
3. Check body attachments, vents, roof lights, racks ☐ ....
4. Confirm window operation, lubricate hinges/stays ☐ ....
5. Inspect rising roof mechanism (where fitted) ☐ ....

Comments on bodywork/general condition: ....

Section 3: Internal elements
Comments

1. Carry out a damp test; mark on diagram ☐ ....
2. Verify cab seat operation ☐ ....
3. Check furniture; lubricate catches & hinges ☐ ....
4. Confirm blind and curtain operation ☐ ....
5. Check vents (high and low) & drop-out holes ☐ ....
6. Check floor and wall for delamination ☐ ....

Other comments:...

Section 4: Fire warning systems
Comments

1. Smoke alarm – check operation and battery ☐ ....
2. Check expiry date on extinguisher and notices ☐ ....
3. Check operation and safety of DIY additions ☐ ....

Other comments:...

Section 5: Gas/gas appliances
Comments

1. Carry out pressure test on system ☐ ....
2. Replace washer on butane regulator ☐ ....
3. Replace flexible hose; use new hoseclips ☐ ....
4. Fridge: light and test for cooling ☐ ....
5. Light and verify operation of cooking appliances ☐ ....
6. Check space heater operation, clean burners ☐ ....
7. Check water heater operation, clean burners ☐ ....

General comments on gas appliances: ....

Section 6: Electrical
Comments

1. Check RCD and MCBs on central unit ☐ ....
2. Test 13 amp mains sockets ☐ ....
3. Test 12V sockets ☐ ....
4. Check integrity of all wiring and fuses ☐ ....
5. Check operation of all interior lights ☐ ....
6. Check awning lamp/outside pump socket ☐ ....
7. Check auxiliary battery ☐ ....

Other comments:...

Section 7: Water systems
Comments

1. Check operation of water pump, clean grit filter ☐ ....
2. Check waste & fresh water system for leaks ☐ ....
3. Flush through with purifying cleaner ☐ ....
4. Inspect tanks/emptying system ☐ ....
5. Change charcoal water filter, if fitted ☐ ....
6. Check toilet flush and blade operation ☐ ....

Other comments:...

Work completed on: ....

Work completed by:..

These elements relate to a standard service, and further items might be added. These could include:

■ Service refrigerator in accordance with Dometic/Electrolux/Thetford instructions.

■ Check operation/mounting of all seat belts (acknowledging that some are fitted retrospectively by the motorhome manufacturer rather than the base vehicle manufacturer).

■ Check built-in generator for safety.

Chassis, suspension, towing and tyres

Driving characteristics, the comfort of passengers and the amount of equipment you can carry in your motorcaravan are determined by the chassis, suspension and tyres. In addition, features under the floor determine whether it is possible to tow a trailer.

Hardly anyone who is preparing to buy a motorcaravan looks underneath the models that interest them. The layout inside, the smart appliances and the attractive upholstery are much more interesting than the equipment that lies below the floor. But it can be a bad mistake to ignore what is often called the undergear.

When you've purchased a motorcaravan, the importance of its "undergear" soon becomes apparent. In fact a number of new owners change their motorcaravan after just a year or so because of features they failed to check.

To begin with, there are many owners who presume that their vehicle could be used for towing at some time in the future. If, for example, you own a motorhome built on a Fiat Ducato base vehicle and read in a towbar manufacturer's catalogue that there's a bracket to suit a Fiat van and chassis you might conclude that all is well. Sadly that isn't always the case because underfloor obstructions may have subsequently been added when your motorhome was built. For instance water tanks often hide the important fixing points which hold a bracket in place.

Then again there are owners who note with satisfaction that their vehicle's AL-KO Kober chassis – on which many coachbuilt motorhomes are constructed – can be matched with an AL-KO towing bracket, or even a purpose-designed scooter rack. Then they find to great dismay that neither of these items can be fitted after all; that's because British motorhome manufacturers usually construct the body so that it overhangs a small distance rear-wards of AL-KO's all-important chassis cross rail. That's the part, of course, on which the accessories have to be bolted.

The news comes as a shock. But even worse is the realisation that the model you've bought is frequently exceeding its maximum loading limit and that you are breaking the law. In practice, a quoted payload often gives much less scope for carrying personal possessions than was originally expected. That becomes even more apparent after a few accessories have been added like a bike rack, a roof box and a couple of large gas cylinders. It stands to reason that the weight of every accessory you fit represents a corresponding reduction in the personal items that you can carry within your permitted payload. In consequence, it's generally believed that many motorcaravan owners are inadvertently breaking the law by exceeding their vehicle's MTPLM limit as explained in Chapter 2. Without doubt, very few owners have ever checked their laden vehicle on a weighbridge and now that police road-side checks are starting to focus on motorhomes, the realities are all too clear.

In recognition of this, some manufacturers offer payload upgrades which might take the Maximum Technically Permissible Laden Mass (MTPLM – see page 21) from 3400kg to 3850kg. Different MTPLM options have been offered by manufacturers, such as Swift on recent Kon Tiki models. Equally, Auto-Trail has built some of its models on the Fiat Maxi chassis instead of the standard Fiat 14 which means that the MTPLM is raised from 3400kg to

This purpose-made towing bracket can only be fitted to some of the motorcaravans built on an AL-KO chassis.

A chassis cowl is supplied without a cab for A-Class motorcaravan manufacturers.

3850kg, thereby adding considerably more loading potential. This option costs a little over £1000 and a Maxi-base vehicle has bigger wheels, bigger brakes and a stronger suspension – and you can't always add these upgraded items after a motorhome has been completed.

Unfortunately this upgrade option tends to appear in the catalogue small print but it's really very important.

Chassis variations

It was pointed out in Chapter 2 that a panel van doesn't have a chassis in the traditional sense. Like a car, its structure has strong box sections which form part of the steel floor or 'floor pan'. In consequence, the following passage describing types of chassis does not include van conversions. However, the later sections on suspension systems and towing matters are relevant for all types of motorcaravan.

Having an understanding about types of traditional chassis is certainly useful for anyone intending to purchase a coachbuilt or A-Class model. The former is constructed using both the base vehicle's cab and an attached chassis (see illustration on page 19); the latter uses just a chassis and an abbreviated cab referred to as a chassis cowl. On a chassis cowl, illustrated above, the fascia and its instruments are supplied but there are no doors, no windscreen and no roof. After all, the A-Class builder will be creating these elements as part of the integrated construction.

There are three different types of chassis used by motorcaravan manufacturers: a) light commercial vehicle (LCV) chassis; b) heavy goods vehicle (HGV) chassis; and c) the AL-KO Kober AMC conversion.

The original commercial chassis

In practice, the majority of motorcaravans are built on a base vehicle whose chassis was principally designed for commercial applications rather than for leisure use. In consequence its design and accompanying suspension system is specified

more for the carriage of goods than people.

Most types of chassis cab and chassis cowl are classified as light commercial vehicles (LCVs). Only very large (and expensive) European motorhomes are constructed using the heavy goods vehicle (HGV)

The Niesmann+Bischoff Flair 8000i is constructed on an Iveco Daily chassis.

Heavy goods vehicle chassis from Iveco are used by several manufacturers of large A-Class motorcaravans.

This floor panel extends outwards beyond the main chassis rails, but it has no outrigger supports.

Galvanised extension members are mounted on a Fiat chassis to support the rear overhang on a Swift Sundance.

chassis used for large lorries. Models from IVEKO and MAN are examples. Many American motorhomes are built on similar heavy structures.

The original LCV and HGV chassis are robustly built and have both advantages and disadvantages in respect of motorcaravan construction:

Advantages

- The structure is rigid.
- The chassis has been developed in conjunction with the cab and running gear as a whole.

Disadvantages

- Chassis sections are thoroughly painted but a galvanised construction might afford better protection.
- Outriggers which project outside the main longitudinal members are seldom provided and a motorcaravan builder has to find a way to provide good support for the floor panel which serves the living area.
- The structure is usually quite high above the ground so steps have to be provided on the finished motorcaravan.
- The higher the finished vehicle, the greater the likelihood of body roll when cornering.

Irrespective of these features, many motorcaravans are built on a standard commercial base which essentially has two longitudinal main members, but no side members to support a wider structure. If you look underneath a coachbuilt motorcaravan, some floors have little or no side support whereas others have added outriggers that help to spread the load. If the support is poor, it's hardly surprising that the composite floor panels used on most motorcaravans are able to flex, and this may hasten the delamination problems described in the previous chapter.

However, that's a matter for the motorcaravan designer to resolve; the base vehicle manufacturer doesn't normally get involved. On the other hand, Ford has been an exception.

Ford-modified chassis design

Before the arrival of the latest generation of Ford Transit models, the Company announced its interest in motorcaravans at the Earl's Court Caravan and Leisure Show in Autumn 1994. This led to the announcement of chassis modifications for rear-wheel drive Transits which would afford better support to the living area structure.

The modified chassis cab product was immediately used by Herald Motorcaravans which were always built on a Ford base vehicle in the 1990s (this independent manufacturer later became part of the Explorer Group). In addition, Auto-Sleepers used the modified chassis on the company's Ford-based coachbuilt models.

Designers at Ford's special vehicle engineering division lowered the height of the main longitudinal chassis members by 75mm (3in). This reduction was made on both the medium and long wheelbase vehicles. In addition, the main members incorporated a facility for the attachment of outriggers and side assemblies which would provide good support for the wide floor panel needed on a motorcaravan.

To assist the motorcaravan manufacturer further, the rear closing member of the chassis was also removable, thereby allowing the builder to extend the construction rearwards. With extension units bolted to the main chassis, the rear section of the living quarters was thus fully supported. However, since a rear-ward extension meant that the standard exhaust system then wouldn't be long enough, an altered design took the pipe to one side. The Ford rear suspension also had an anti-roll bar fitted.

Other differences included a cab with a higher specification and Ford's modifications certainly made the Transit a very appealing base vehicle in the later part of the 1990s. Since then the Transit range has been radically changed and now there are a number of models, including front-wheel drive vehicles. Moreover, a motorcaravan package like the one launched in 1994 is no longer offered.

Rear overhang and chassis extensions

When a coachbuilt motorcaravan is built on an original chassis, a common practice is to extend the rearmost part of the structure using additional rails or a complete bolt-on framework. The body subsequently mounted on the elongated platform is thus extended ever further behind the rear axle. This creates what is described as a rear overhang. Type Approval Regulations together with Construction and Use guidelines state that this must not extend rear-wards of the back axle by more than 60 per cent of the wheelbase dimension.

When you take a wheelbase dimension (the distance between the centre of the front and the centre of the rear wheels) and then calculate the maximum permitted overhang, you soon see that some models are built to the limit. Whilst this might create a large living space on a relatively short chassis, there are a number of implications to bear in mind.

Basic geometry, a rudimentary knowledge of the principles of leverage and simple common sense indicate that loading a heavy item at the very back of a motorhome is going to compound the loading on the rear axle to a considerable degree. What's more, there are strict loading limits on all rear axles and it is an offence – and obviously potentially dangerous – to exceed the limit stated on a vehicle's plate details. The longer the overhang, the greater the effect of a given weight. But it is not just the rear axle loading which would suffer.

Where there's a single rear axle, this can act as the pivot point on what is effectively a kind of see-saw. The heavier the load bearing down at the back, the more the front end of the vehicle wants to lift upwards. In extreme cases, this can be dangerous because the front tyres then have less positive contact with the road. This can affect the steering, braking, and in the case of front-wheel driven vehicles, the traction.

Bearing this in mind, you can appreciate the problems that might arise if you want to transport a motorcycle or an electric mobility scooter on a rear-mounted carrier – especially if the overhang on your motorcaravan is near the 60 per cent limit.

A similar situation can arise if you want to tow a trailer. For example, when there's a substantial noseweight bearing down on a towball, the load also affects rear axle loading limits and tends to lighten the front of the vehicle. Some owners wrongly believe that upgrading the rear springs will solve this – it doesn't. The load carried by the rear axle, and related issues like braking effectiveness are not changed simply by firming-up the suspension. Suffice it to say, anyone planning to carry scooters or similar heavy items on a rack at the back would be strongly advised to purchase a vehicle with as short a rear overhang as possible. In addition, carrying substantial loads is better managed on a base vehicle which has an upgraded rear axle, larger wheels, brakes and so on. The advantages of having a full air suspension system installed with reactive height-adjusting facilities are also very clear,

Carrying a heavy mobility scooter on a rear-mounted rack adds a considerable extra load to the back axle and suspension.

but the designers of British motorcaravans seem slow to recognise the merits of these products.

A further way in which a motorcaravan manufacturer can overcome the problems magnified by a large overhang is to have the base vehicle's chassis extended between the axles. One manufacturer which has adopted this is Lunar Motorcaravans, with work being carried out by

The chassis for this Lunar motorcaravan is being extended at Drinkwater Engineering works.

Extending a chassis 'amidships' shifts the back axle rearwards, thus avoiding a large rear overhang.

Fiat back-to-back cabs are now supplied when an AL-KO chassis is going to be fitted.

motorcaravan described in Chapter 11.

There is certainly scope with a light commercial chassis to accomplish modifications which meet owners' particular carrying requirements. On the other hand, some manufacturers decide not to build on a commercial structure at all and prefer to use a purpose-built motorcaravan chassis supplied and installed by AL-KO Kober.

The AL-KO Kober AMC conversion

A chassis designed specifically for motorcaravans is manufactured by AL-KO Kober and this can be fitted as a replacement on a number of front-wheel drive vehicles before the body-build process commences. Replacements can also be fitted on rear-wheel drive Mercedes Sprinter base vehicles, but this is currently requested only by German motorcaravan manufacturers.

The AL-KO AMC conversion involves a radical alteration to the base vehicle but these conversions are approved by the manufacturers. There's also unsatisfactory wastage because the unused original chassis has to be scrapped; in response to this, Fiat now supplies back-to-back 'chassis-less' units as shown alongside.

Without question, the AL-KO product has proved successful on a large number of vehicles, including small buses, mobile libraries and motorcaravans. In fact over 20,000 conversions have been completed since 1985.

Drinkwater Engineering – now merged with TVAC engineering specialists. A modification carried out at Drinkwater Engineering, and shown on page 48, is approved by base vehicle manufacturers. Moreover, in this strategy where the chassis length is increased amidships there is an accompanying shift of the back axle towards the rear of the motorhome. In order to be able to carry heavy loads while avoiding a large rear overhang, the author had this modification carried out on the self-build

Installation of an AL-KO Kober AMC conversion to a Fiat Ducato chassis cab

With the vehicle supported and a guiding jig in place, the original chassis is sawn away from the cab.

The original chassis is severed; some of its parts will be reclaimed and remounted.

The junction point to the rear of the cab is cleaned and prepared for welding.

Using a jig to achieve accuracy, connecting flanges are welded to the stub chassis behind the cab.

Several components from the original chassis will be re-used including the wheels and the brake assemblies.

An AL-KO Kober chassis is constructed using hot dip galvanised sections that are bolted together.

The cab flanges, coated with protective brown wax, are coupled to the new chassis; eight bolts are inserted.

A new extended hand-brake mechanism is fitted to the AL-KO Kober chassis.

Using a rolling road, the brakes are checked and adjusted with concrete blocks simulating a typical load.

The replacement chassis is galvanised, lighter than the original and it provides good support for the floor panel.

However, the alteration involves more than just the installation of a purpose-built chassis; it also includes the installation of a replacement rear axle tube fitted with a different suspension system as described in the later section. Only the brake drums, bearing assemblies and wheels are retained from the original chassis cab.

The photographs here show a brief synopsis of the conversion operation process being carried out at AL-KO's factory in 1999. A number of minor features are not illustrated, such as rearranging the road light system and altering brake hydraulics, but the main procedures are recorded pictorially. If you purchase an AL-KO-based vehicle of this period,

The connecting system on the latest Fiat cabs has been modified to couple with an AL-KO chassis.

this is what the foundation will look like.

More recently, further developments have taken place to coincide with the replacement Fiat vehicles which appeared in January 2002. As the photograph on page 49 illustrates, the connecting assembly which links the replacement chassis to the cab has been altered. Also there has been another conversion option in which a double floor is fitted.

Recognising that many more people are using their motorcaravans in winter, and acknowledging the need to prevent water freezing in the fresh and waste tanks, models with a double-layer floor have become popular. By using a particular type of AL-KO chassis, the motorhome manufacturer is able to install tanks, warm-air central heating ducting, cables and gas pipes in an enclosed void under the floor of the living area. This places them away from road dirt, snow and driven rain. In some vehicles, such as the Knauss Traveller range, one of the heating outlets can be redirected into this void as a precautionary measure when temperatures drop below freezing.

Many motorhomes built with a double floor, such as the 1992 Swift Gazelle F63 High, also incorporate large lockers for outdoor equipment in the underfloor space. This places weight where it's best when driving: low down. So the system has several advantages, although it inevitably means that the floor of the living area is higher than on a stepped down AL-KO chassis and therefore good access steps are essential. Its success also depends on the manufacturer making sure that all pipe runs, couplings and other accessories have access points for repairs and maintenance. One or two manufacturers provide rather limited access and even simple repairs such as the replacement of a faulty pipe coupling then become a major operation.

However, that's not the fault of the AL-KO chassis specialists and a critical appraisal of the Company's AMC products includes the following points:

Advantages

- Computer-designed chassis members contribute to a very light construction without compromising rigidity.
- Installation of hot-dip zinc galvanised sections ensure notable longevity.
- Where requested by the motorcaravan manufacturer, AL-KO Kober can fit a 'stepped-down' chassis that is 225mm (9in) lower than the original one. A lower floor height provides easier access to the living quarters and a lower centre of gravity is likely to reduce body roll when cornering.
- Single or tandem axle units can be fitted irrespective of the original back axle configuration.
- A suspension system offering increased load potential can be installed if requested by the motorcaravan manufacturer.
- Since the chassis sections are bolted together, replacement of a damaged unit may be possible although it would be an involved operation.

The purpose-designed outriggers on an AL-KO chassis provide good support for a floor panel.

Where required, AL-KO can install a 'stepped down' chassis which will provide a lower floor height.

- AL-KO Kober-designed towing brackets and motorcycle racks are available for attachment to the chassis if required (but see the earlier comments on page 44 about this).
- The least-expensive short-wheelbase chassis cab base vehicle can be converted to a long-wheelbase unit, with a minimum wastage of original materials.

Note: *Further advantages in respect of the suspension system are detailed later.*

Disadvantages

- Additional items must not be welded to an AL-KO Kober chassis – this would invalidate the warranty.

Note: *Great reliance is placed on the bolts, flanges and fabrication which connect the new chassis to the donor cab. This is not a method of conversion that should be tackled by a self-builder.*

Clearly there is much to be gained by this constructional approach and it is used for ambulance conversions, buses, mobile libraries and removal vans, as well as motorcaravans. Manufacturers who have used AL-KO Kober chassis on some of the models in their ranges include Autocruise, Auto-Trail, Buccaneer, Compass, Elddis, Lunar, Machzone and Swift.

The choice of chassis clearly has structural implications, but the suspension system is also an important part of the structure, since it is a key contributor to comfort on the move. This is discussed next.

Suspension systems

Ride comfort in a motorcaravan is governed largely by the suspension and this can be a problem where a commercial vehicle has been used as the base vehicle.

Leaf-spring suspension

Often described as 'cart springs', the typical leaf-spring arrangement used on most commercial vehicles is fine for bags of cement or crates of lemonade. But for a discerning motorcaravanner this form of suspension is seldom satisfactory without some degree of modification.

The main drawback is a harsh ride, which is especially evident on poor road surfaces.

Then there's the disconcerting feeling of body roll on sharp bends, twisting roads and small roundabouts. Tall vehicles which have a high centre of gravity receive the worst of this. Poor load distribution doesn't help, and the carriage of heavy items in a roof box also makes things worse. Disconcerting deflections are also exaggerated when a high-sided vehicle overtakes a motorcaravan on a fast road.

To reduce roll, some manufacturers fit anti-roll bars; other improvements include the installation of stiffer shock absorbers on the front.

Making improvements by the addition of support

Load data

Motorcaravans built on an AL-KO Kober chassis and rear axle conversion will have a plate mounted in the engine compartment giving details about weight limits. The one shown here was mounted in a late 1990s coachbuilt. On more recent models, different loading terminology would be used as described in Chapter 2. For instance, Gross Vehicle Weight is now expressed as Maximum Technically Permitted Laden Mass (MTPLM). Irrespective of changes in words, the need to work within these limits is very important.

Gross Vehicle Weight (maximum total vehicle weight).

Gross Train Weight (maximum total weight of vehicle with towed trailer).

Maximum weight Axle 1 (permitted axle loading, front).

Maximum weight Axle 2 (permitted axle loading, axle number two).

Maximum weight Axle 3 (permitted axle loading, axle number three in the case of twin rear axle models).

Further details of the AL-KO Kober conversion are given in the AL-KO AMC Handbook which is included with the documentation accompanying a new motorcaravan. If mislaid, copies are available from AL-KO Kober using the address given in the Appendix.

systems like air-assistance units can also be accomplished at a later date but note the section on spring assistance products and the influences on braking which arise when modifications like this are made. Also make sure you recognise the clear distinction between air suspension and air assistance as described in the safety panel on page 53.

Coil springs

Whilst fitted to the rear suspension of many cars, coil springs have not been widely used on commercial vehicles. However, the T4 Volkswagen Transporter was different because it had an independent suspension system at the rear, using mini coil springs and a semi-trailing arm configuration. The refined ride it offers has been favourably reported in many independent motorcaravan tests.

As regards the springs, these are short coils mounted at a slight angle in order not to intrude into the habitation area. Rear coil springs on a car, for example, typically take up space in the boot – hence Volkswagen's use of 'mini' coil springs. Moreover, the semi-trailing arm is not unlike a wishbone configuration and independent springing undoubtedly provides good ride characteristics.

Manufacturers which have used the Volkswagen Transporter include Compass for the coachbuilt Calypso, Bilbo's with the high-top Nektar, Auto-Sleepers with the high-top Trident, and many more.

If a conversion is based on a people carrier, again there would normally be coil spring suspension. Wheelhome conversions are an example.

Torsion bar

Different yet again is a system which uses torsion bars. In this arrangement, a swinging arm suspension unit provides the mounting point for a wheel hub at one end and a long, fixed bar at the other. As the vehicle rides the bumps, the bar is subjected to a

Servicing

AL-KO Kober torsion bar system

The rear axle of a motorcaravan built on the AL-KO Kober torsion bar system must be lubricated every 20,000km (12,500 miles). The procedure that a workshop engineer has to carry out is as follows:

1) Jack up the vehicle and provide support so that the wheels are clear of the ground.

2) Identify the grease points on the outer ends of the axle tube on either the forward-facing side or the underside. They lie just inside the main longitudinal chassis members.

3) Pump in grease using a pressure gun – about six pumps, ensuring that there is no likelihood of overfilling (a hand gun is not adequate).

4) Use a product such as Shell Retinax LX grease.

5) Record the mileage at the time of greasing in the service record.

Owners often try to cure a sagging rear suspension by having air assistance units fitted.

A new shock absorber is fitted when the AL-KO Kober torsion spring axle is installed.

twisting action which it naturally resists. This is what is meant by a torsion bar and the system has been employed in many popular vehicles – the Renault 5 hatchback of the early 1980s is a good example.

An engineer might point out that what might appear to be a curious action to the lay person is no different from the similar twisting action that a coil spring has to endure. The only difference is that the torsion bar is rather like a coil spring that has been unwound to form a long rod.

When setting up a vehicle, a torsion bar can be tightened by inducing a twist to alter the vehicle ride height and driving characteristics. On the road, a torsion bar system works well – although the bar takes up space. On a Renault 5, for example, the front torsion bars are 1.22m (4ft) long and run behind the sills of the car.

If this appears a rather clumsy arrangement, it is no problem in respect of the rear suspension employed in an AL-KO Kober AMC chassis. In this application, the torsion bars are mounted within the axle tube. The bars couple to the swinging arms that provide the mounting point for the wheel hubs, and replacement telescopic shock absorbers are fitted during the conversion to suit the system.

The AL-KO Kober torsion suspension undoubtedly provides improved road handling, and weight options of 3200, 3400, 3500 and 3850kg can be specified. In other words the payload can be increased to suit a motorcaravan designer's specifications – ultimately providing the user with more, or less, scope when loading up.

In motorcaravan tests, the good ride achieved using an AL-KO Kober torsion bar system is frequently acknowledged during road tests.

Spring assistance and braking

Springs don't retain their resilience for ever and after several years in use it's not unusual to find that the rear end of a motorcaravan has started to sag. When this occurs the best answer would be to have the springs replaced with new ones, but it's a costly exercise. Instead, many owners have a spring assisting device added, such as:

• compressible rubber supports
• auxiliary coil springs
• air-inflatable units.

Note: *A compressible rubber support is often fitted on brand new vehicles as the photograph shows.*

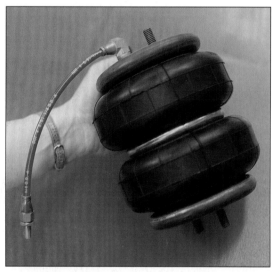

A compressible rubber assister is fitted to this new Swift Royale coachbuilt motorcaravan.

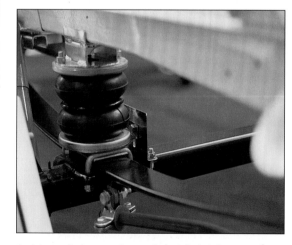

Assistance devices are frequently installed at the central point of a leaf spring.

This brake sensor and control unit on an air suspension system automatically adjusts the proportion of front/rear braking according to the load.

These products are often installed at the central point of a leaf spring, directly above the axle mounting as shown in the accompanying photograph. Their function, of course, is to bear some of the weight hitherto taken entirely by the springs, and this can help to elevate a depressed rear end. However, a retro-fit installation has to take into account the calibration of the vehicle's braking system for the following reason.

Brakes do not normally provide a 50-50 front/rear balance. Usually a greater proportion of the braking effect is applied to the front wheels. However, vehicles may also be fitted with a device which alters the front-rear balance to suit the load being carried at the back. Put simply, the device registers the depression of the rear suspension and reacts by altering the braking to achieve optimum performance under that load condition. This facility isn't just fitted to commercial vehicles; estate cars and even some small hatchbacks and saloons have these brake control units.

In the case of a motorcaravan with a depressed rear, the brake balancing device interprets this as a sign of heavy loading and responds by setting the balance of front/rear braking to suit that situation. However, it stands to reason that if the sagging rear of a heavily-laden motorhome is subsequently elevated by fitting a height-raising product, a brake sensing device which hasn't been appropriately re-adjusted is fooled into interpreting the revised ride height as an indication that a light load is being carried. The balance of braking applied to the front/rear wheels is then automatically set to suit a lightly-laden situation, when in reality, the vehicle might be heavily-laden.

Clearly the installation of retro-fitted spring assisters isn't as straightforward as many people imagine. At the time of installation, the braking load

Technical Tip

Air assistance or air suspension?

Air assistance describes inflatable devices designed to work in conjunction with the original springing system. For instance, if leaf springs have lost their resilience, a motorcaravan might develop a sag at the back. The addition of inflatable units may help to overcome this and give additional support to a deteriorating suspension. However, check the comments in the main text about the detrimental effects that incorrectly installed air assistance products can have on braking operation.

Air suspension is installed on vehicles which need to provide supreme comfort (such as accident and emergency ambulances) or provide an extremely smooth ride (as in lorries transporting sensitive loads such as aero engines). The original spring suspension system on these vehicles will have been completely removed and scrapped. The replacement suspension comprises air chambers, a compressor pump, an air reservoir, a computer-controlled monitoring system and a revised brake compensation system. These systems are fitted on high quality motorcaravans.

Large air chambers have been fitted in the place of leaf springs on this Drinkwater suspension.

An air suspension system is fitted with a compressor.

Pressurised air from the compressor is stored in a steel reservoir mounted on the chassis.

The author had Drinkwater air suspension fitted to a new Fiat Ducato chassis on his self-build motorcaravan.

sensing system must be adjusted in accordance with the base vehicle manufacturer's guidelines. If this all-important feature is ignored, braking performance could be compromised.

For this reason, if you consider having a spring assistance device fitted, it is most important to ascertain what the installer will do to re-calibrate the load sensing system and to confirm that the product and its installation meets with the approval of the base vehicle manufacturer. You may see advertisements with convincing claims about ride improvement, better road holding and the reduction in body roll, whereas the subject of the braking set-up is often not mentioned at all.

In contrast, when reactive, computer-controlled full air suspension is installed, a sophisticated brake sensor and control unit is fitted to suit the new system as described later.

Air suspension

In spite of the extensive use of air suspension in public service vehicles and by lorry operators whose business involves transporting sensitive loads, the product is seldom used

Many motorcaravan owners want to tow, but the weight of a trailer and its load must not exceed the gross train weight listed for the towing vehicle.

in motorcaravans manufactured in Britain. However, it has been an option offered by Lunar Motorcaravans and the author also had a Drinkwater system installed on the Fiat chassis of his self-built motorcaravan in 1999.

In Germany, the situation is different. The merits of this system are more widely recognised and a number of motorcaravans are built using air suspension. Moreover, the AL-KO chassis has been available for some time with controllable air assistance units to supplement the torsion bar suspension. Taking the idea further, a full AL-KO air suspension system was exhibited in Britain in 2003.

A number of manufacturers specialise in this type of suspension and developments are ongoing. In Europe, for example, air suspension units are normally fitted just to the rear axle, and coil springs provide the suspension at the front. However, there is little doubt that a full air suspension system will be available some time in the future.

When air units are mounted on the back axle, this assists fore and aft levelling; when you are on a sloping pitch, the air can be 'dumped' or released, as much or as little as needed. There is even a small degree of lateral levelling possible on a few air conversions, but only when both front and rear air chambers are installed does this facility truly offer levelling in every plane. However, levelling is only one of the benefits of air suspension.

For example, the comfort experienced when 'riding on air' is of particular note. This is an essential requirement for some disabled users, but for any motorcaravanner, comfort on the road is important. Then there is the ability to keep your motorcaravan level, even when a heavy load like a scooter is added on the back – or later removed. This feature is achieved automatically by sensors, an air inflation/release facility, and a controlling computer. In other words, when a heavy load is added, pressure monitoring in the air chambers interprets the extra loading and further air is pumped into the units. Conversely, when items are removed, the reduced loading is recognised and air is automatically released.

This reactive facility which raises or lowers the rear to suit the loading is also accompanied by the all-important brake adjustments highlighted in the earlier section. Further comments on a Drinkwater air suspension installation are given in Chapter 11 and it is very likely that systems like this will become more prominent in the future.

Shock absorbers

When considering a suspension system, many people presume – quite wrongly – that fitting higher specification shock absorbers will stiffen the springs and increase ride height. This reveals a misconception about the function and design of products commonly referred to as 'shockers'.

Driven without shock absorbers, a vehicle

bounces along in wild leaps – as any Banger Racing enthusiast will have seen when a shocker fails on the race track. Irrespective of whether it is a telescopic shock absorber filled with gas or one containing oil, the component's job is to dampen down the movements as a vehicle rides the bumps. Shock absorbers simply do what their name implies and a standard shocker is not a spring device. Incidentally, gas shockers are often considered better than oil-filled versions but can be costly.

Towing

Most motorcaravans are powerful enough to tow a sizeable trailer carrying a reasonable load. The base vehicle's commercial origin usually means the engine has good pulling power at low revs and this characteristic is especially evident with diesel engines. However, the weight of a loaded trailer must be checked on a weighbridge and related to the Actual Laden Weight (ALW) of the towing vehicle.

A Fiat Ducato is reversed on to support ramps.

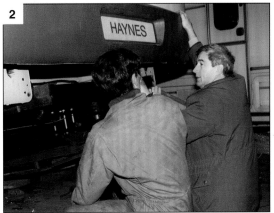

The installation is explained to a fitter by the designer.

Design and fitting of a Watling Engineers 'one-off' towbar

A bracket with detachable ball facility is built in situ.

The rear projection of the tow ball plate is carefully checked.

The completed bracket assembly is removed for painting.

Finally, all the fixing bolts are checked with a torque wrench.

Using an A-frame is a popular way to tow a car, but several points should be borne in mind.

Technical Tip

Towing with an A-frame

All but a very few cars (such as the Fun Tech and the Microcar) weigh more than 750kg – and a trailer adds more to the total trailed weight. When a car is pulled on an A-frame it is deemed to be a trailer, and because it exceeds 750kg it must have independent braking. Several devices, both mechanical and electrical, can be fitted to bring the towed car's brakes into play when needed. However, the question arises whether towing with an A-frame is legal throughout Europe.

■ The Caravan Club contacted all EU motoring organisations and established that a braked car towed behind a motorcaravan on a purpose-designed frame appears to be permitted in the United Kingdom and 'tolerated' in both Germany and the Netherlands. In other European countries the practice is normally reserved for the police or recovery operators.

■ Not withstanding EC arrangements, if a visitor is using a vehicle deemed acceptable in his or her country of residence, the host nation will not take action even if the visitor isn't complying with legislation in the receiving country. Unfortunately, where towing with an A-frame is concerned, police forces in some EC countries appear to ignore this and a number of motorcaravanners report that they have been stopped. To avoid difficulties in these countries, carrying a car on an approved trailer might be the preferred option.

■ Modifying the electrics in a towing vehicle, the wiring allocation of pins in plugs and sockets, and stability devices are discussed in *The Caravan Manual*, published by Haynes.

■ An A-frame coupled with a motorcaravan doesn't articulate like a trailer. Reversing when using an A-frame is virtually impossible.

Touring caravanners work on the basis that to achieve the ideal match, the total weight of the trailer should not exceed 85 per cent of the ALW of the towing vehicle. This ensures that the 'tail doesn't wag the dog', and most motorcaravans are likely to meet this recommended weight ratio, presuming the trailer isn't carrying a heavy load such as a cabin cruiser or a heavy motor vehicle. Only a lightweight micro motorcaravan would find it difficult to adhere to the 85 per cent vehicle/trailer guideline.

In some circumstances, an experienced driver might tow a trailer whose loaded weight is the same as the ALW of the towing vehicle (a 100 per cent match). But both national caravan clubs strongly recommend adherence to the 85 per cent limit wherever possible. Furthermore, a loaded trailer should never be heavier than the actual laden weight of the vehicle towing it.

Another factor to keep in mind is the 'gross train weight' (GTW). Adherence to this limit is a mandatory matter and the GTW, normally given in the base vehicle handbook, relates to the total weight of both the towing vehicle and the trailer. Problems occur if you want to tow something heavy like a support car, and precise data concerning the weights of both the motorcaravan and its fully laden trailer should be obtained.

There are also issues concerning the towbar (or 'tow bracket') to take into account. There is now a legal requirement under Directive 94/20/EC that only an EC type approved towbar can be fitted to light passenger vehicles. For the time being, this directive does not apply to commercial vehicles – as explained in the Appendix. On the other hand, it seems unlikely that motorcaravan base vehicles will always remain exempt from towbar type approval requirements.

Also serious is the matter of fitting a towbar. A major manufacturer like Witter lists brackets designed for many popular base vehicles including the Peugeot Boxer, Fiat Scudo and Mercedes Sprinter. However, these brackets are designed for an unmodified base vehicle. If, in the process of the motorcaravan build, additions such as a chassis extension or under-floor water tanks are fitted, the bracket designer's original fixing points are unlikely to be usable. With this in mind, it is essential to discuss the matter with the motorcaravan manufacturer before purchasing a bracket.

It is much the same in respect of AL-KO Kober towing systems. The brackets are designed to bolt directly on to AL-KO's rear cross member, but British motorcaravan manufacturers usually fit a body which is carried further rear-wards of this structural component. So a purpose-made AL-KO bracket cannot be fitted after all.

Of course, there are always bespoke bracket designers, such as Watling Engineers, and the sequence of photographs on page 55 shows a 'one-off' towbar being designed and fitted.

Finally on this theme, there is the issue of towing a small car for use on site. This practice is popular in the United States and it is also growing in Europe. When towing a trailer which carries the car, the position is clear and to comply with the law, virtually all vehicle trailers are fitted with an over-run braking system as standard. However, trailing a car independently without a trailer, by using what is known as an A-frame, can raise legal questions as described in the panel on the left.

To achieve braking compliance when using an A-frame, there are now several systems which bring the towed vehicle's own brakes into play. This meets the braking requirement, but there's still the need to ensure that the total weight of the car plus the motorcaravan doesn't exceed the listed gross train weight.

Tyres

Just as driving characteristics are dictated by chassis design and the suspension system, tyres play an important part, too.

Tyre pressures – which should be checked regularly – will be given in the base vehicle's handbook. However, the handbook recommendations may apply to commercial situations and be less appropriate for a leisure vehicle. For this reason, the manufacturer of a motorcaravan is the first point of contact for guidance on tyre pressures. Owners' clubs are often helpful as well.

Current practice is not to swap tyres to equalise tread wear. However, it's usually acceptable to switch a front tyre to the rear and vice versa on the same side. This ensures the tyre will rotate in the same direction throughout its life. If you note irregular wear on your tyres, this usually indicates there's a suspension or steering fault. Getting a specialist to readjust tracking on the front

steering assembly often cures irregular wear on front tyres.

When laying-up a vehicle for an extended period, tyre sidewalls soon sustain damage. You should therefore periodically move the vehicle a short distance to ensure that a different section of the sidewall is distended during the lay-up. To lessen the likelihood of sidewall damage during a lay-up, some manufacturers recommend that tyre pressures are temporarily increased by 0.3bar (5lb per sq inch). Bear in mind that vehicles used irregularly usually need new tyres as soon as there are signs of deterioration on the sidewalls, and it's this element rather than tread wear which signals the need for new tyres. In fact products like Michelin's Camping Tyres are made with extra reinforcing in the sidewalls for this reason.

When it is necessary to change a wheel, the jacking points and the tightening order for wheel fixings are specific to each vehicle. Consult your vehicle and motorcaravan handbooks for the appropriate guidelines.

Finally, comply with all legal requirements relating to tyres. Seek advice from a specialist about matters like tyre wall markings and note that free literature from the British Rubber Manufacturers' Association (BRMA) includes tyre wall diagrams and explains several technical issues. The address of the BRMA is given in the Appendix.

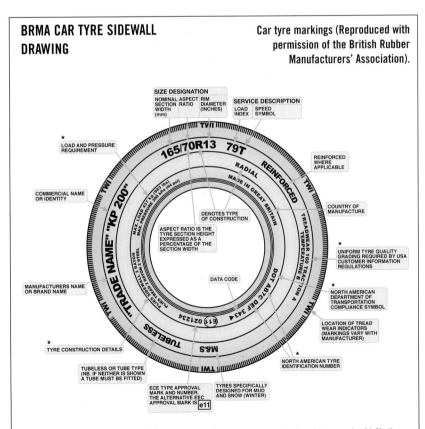

BRMA CAR TYRE SIDEWALL DRAWING

Car tyre markings (Reproduced with permission of the British Rubber Manufacturers' Association).

Some tyres have sidewall markings, e.g. "loads and pressures", which are given in order to comply with North American requirements. They DO NOT apply in the U.K. and Europe; the examples shown here have an asterisk."

5

Electrical systems

The electrical provision in a motorcaravan is more complicated than the electrical system in our homes. Not only is there a mains system, there's also an independent low-voltage supply.

This chapter looks at electricity in the living quarters. It comprises a 230V AC system, known as the **mains supply**; and a 12V DC provision, described here as the **low-voltage system**.

The system which serves the base vehicle is different yet again, and this is covered in textbooks that deal specifically with automotive wiring. For example, the Haynes Manual *Automobile Electrical & Electronic Systems*, by Tony Tranter, includes topics such as wiring procedure, ignition, electrical accessories and engine management systems.

Returning to the provision in the living quarters, the exact rating of the electricity supply needs clarifying. For example the 230V supply on a busy site sometimes drops below 200V, and this can affect the operation of appliances such as a refrigerator which the user has set to operate on mains. Similarly, a 12V provision is another misnomer. If a vehicle or leisure battery gives a meter reading of 12V across the terminals, this indicates that it is in a discharged condition. A battery in a full state of charge will give a reading of 12.7V. This is explained more thoroughly under the heading *Checking charge level and condition* on page 63.

Not surprisingly, the subject of electricity in motorcaravans is wide-ranging so it helps to break it down into seven sections:

1) Low-voltage systems (12V DC)
2) Leisure batteries
3) Charging
4) Mains systems (230V AC)
5) Portable petrol generators
6) Solar and wind generators
7) Inverters.

Low-voltage systems

A safe and efficient 12V system is dependent on a number of elements. A well-designed circuit is one feature; a dependable supply is another.

The circuit

Nearly all motorcaravans use a battery to supply the low-voltage system. On the other hand, transformer/rectifiers *are* available for motorcaravans and the Ranger PA10 Power Pack from Breckland Leisure

is often used on exhibition stands to power the 12V accessories in show models. However, for normal use a 12V battery is the source of power.

To be more accurate, *two* batteries are available. The normal source is a leisure battery (often referred to as the auxiliary battery) which is exclusively designed to run lights and appliances in a living space. If this fails, the vehicle battery can be switched into use as an alternative. However, this should be regarded as only a temporary arrangement – if the charge level drops too low, vehicle starting might be affected.

Recognising the diversity of appliances that run on a low-voltage supply, a circuit designer now follows a practice which is adopted in the mains supply in our homes. This is where the original feed is sub-divided into separate routes which, in turn, branch out to supply distinct groups of appliances.

Each branch is independently protected by a fuse, the rating of which is appropriate for the appliances being served. For instance a radio-cassette player has a low consumption, so it is normally protected by a 5 amp fuse. On the other hand, a water pump has a higher consumption, and a 10 amp fuse is usually fitted.

Quite often the separate branches are also fitted with a switch, so if you need to look at a troublesome water pump on a dark evening, you can switch off its supply without having to interrupt the operation of the interior lights. This is very convenient, though some motorcaravan control units don't incorporate switches. In this instance, to

A 12v distribution unit divides a low-voltage supply into separate fuse-protected feeds.

The rear connections provided on this low-voltage distribution unit are clearly marked.

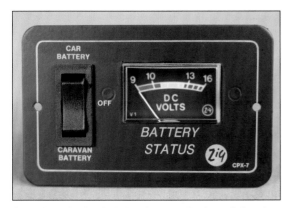

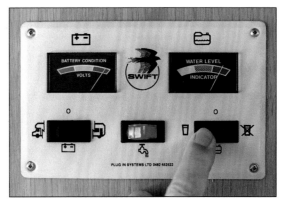

Control panels often include a battery selection switch and a meter shows the state of charge as well.

The panel on this Swift motorcaravan includes a water level indicator for the fresh and waste water tanks.

isolate a particular supply you have to take out the appropriate fuse instead.

The device which divides a supply into individually protected branches is called a fused distribution unit. In Britain, the units fitted in motorcaravans are usually made by BCA Leisure, Plug-in-Systems, Sargent Electrical Services or Zig Electronics. Quite often the fuses are mounted in a switched control panel and these are sometimes conspicuous in location: others are more discreet and may be mounted in a cupboard or behind a hinged cover.

Other features commonly fitted are:

• a battery selection switch,
• a battery condition indicator,
• a gauge showing the water levels in the tanks.

The selection switch enables you to choose whether the supply is drawn from your auxiliary

battery or the vehicle battery. Some switches have three positions, the centre of which isolates the circuit and draws from *neither* supply.

The battery condition indicator provides warning when recharging is needed. A few have a meter fitted to indicate a battery's state of charge and the markings on the scale can provide very precise information. However, most distribution units are fitted with light-emitting diodes. Typically a green light on the panel confirms that a battery is in a good state of charge; a red light warns that recharging is needed. These warning systems are useful for other reasons; for instance if the automatic shut-down on a water heater comes into operation, it's all too easy to presume that the gas cylinder is empty. On the other hand, if the battery warning light is on, it might mean there is insufficient power to operate the water heater's electronic circuits – hence the triggering of its automatic shut-down mechanism.

Anyone who has limited experience of 12V circuits can find all this rather daunting. It also doesn't help that some motorcaravan Owners' Manuals contain no wiring diagrams at all. That is why the wiring display board that Plug-In-Systems

Safety

• The principal supply cable coming from a battery's live (positive) terminal to serve the low-voltage circuits *must* be protected by an in-line fuse fitted close to the source. However, when a leisure battery is installed in a ventilated locker, the fuse should be positioned *outside* this enclosure. This is because a battery sometimes gives off an inflammable gas while being charged. Since a fuse often sparks when it fails, the wisdom of situating it *outside* a battery compartment is clear.

• The rating of a battery supply fuse varies. Plug-In-Systems recommends that for most motorcaravans, a 15 amp fuse is appropriate. However, in a large model full of electrical appliances, if everything were to be operated at once the full complement of 12V appliances would draw a total current of 15–20 amps and blow the fuse. In practice, this operating pattern is most unlikely and circuit designers usually consider 60 per cent of total demand a realistic maximum.

A typical caravan or motorcaravan wiring layout.

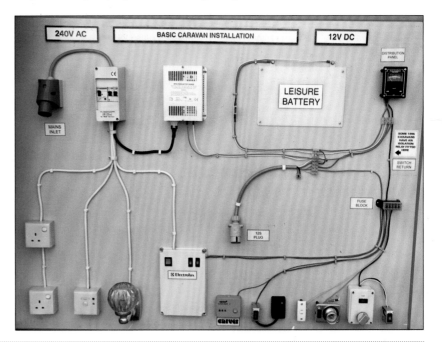

Terminology

Volts, Amps and Watts

A practical illustration often helps a beginner to understand the theory behind electricity. For example:

To be hit by a fast-moving lead shot could be very unpleasant. It might only be small but the pressure it imposes at the time of impact would hurt. However, speed isn't everything. Being hit by a much slower object – like a double-decker bus – could be far worse since the size of the object comes into play. Now combine the two elements and the result is infinitely more potent. These mental pictures help to illustrate the difference between volts (pressure), amps (amount) and watts (the amount and pressure combined).

Volts – This unit of measurement is concerned with *pressure*. However, in a practical situation, a cable offers a resistance that can lead to a loss of pressure – especially if the cable is too thin. Furthermore, the greater the length of a cable, the more you get a drop in the voltage.

Amps – Amperes or 'amps' refer to the *amount* of electricity. In practical terms, a motorcaravan fridge needs a large amount of electricity to work properly (8 amps), and requires a relatively thick connecting cable. In contrast, an interior strip light only needs a small amount of electricity (0.7 amps), and works quite successfully with a much thinner connecting cable.

Watts – This is the *rate* at which electrical energy is used and some appliances are more greedy than others. Watts are a combination of both the pressure of flow (volts) and the amount of current (amps). The formulae to remember are:

$$\text{Watts} = \text{Volts} \times \text{Amps}$$
$$\text{Volts} = \text{Watts} \div \text{Amps}$$
$$\text{Amps} = \text{Watts} \div \text{Volts}$$

No of strands	Cross sectional area in mm^2	Current rating in Amps	Application in motorcaravans
14	1.0	8.75	Interior lights
21	1.5	12.75	Wire to extractor fans, but check the model
28	2.0	17.50	Feed to fridge (minimum) See note on Page 61
36	2.5	21.75	Feed to battery from the charger Feed to a diaphragm water pump

• A cable that is too thin for a high-consumption appliance may start to get warm as a result of the cable's resistance. If the rise in temperature starts to cause the insulation to melt, there's a serious problem ahead. If several supply cables are wrapped together, for example, melting insulation could lead to a short circuit.

• A low-voltage supply doesn't pose a threat of electrocution like a mains supply, but if you've seen the powerful spark that is caused when there's a short circuit, you'll appreciate the acute fire risk that accompanies a 12V system. Melting insulation is sometimes the cause of short circuits. Fuses in a circuit are intended to prevent this risk but they have to be of the correct rating and appropriately located in the supply system.

has taken to outdoor shows is so helpful. It shows how everything is connected up; in addition, accompanying wiring diagrams clarify typical systems even further. The accompanying illustration reproduces Plug-In-Systems' visual aid and readers intending to carry out a self-build conversion or re-fit will find the guidance invaluable. So, too, will a motorcaravan owner whose Owners' Manual only provides brief guidance.

Nevertheless, the wiring diagram on Page 67 conveys only part of the picture. One thing not explained is the fact that cables have different ratings and the correct type must be matched to the appliance it has to serve. The following section explains this further.

Cable rating

Whilst the layman often talks about 'wire', an electrician usually prefers the term 'cable'. Using the correct terminology is important and the panel on the left explains several other key words.

When coupling up appliances, both the thickness of the connecting cable and its length are significant; for instance, thick cable is needed to ensure there's a good flow of current. If the cable is too thin, there's a resistance to current flow – a situation that might cause the plastic insulation around the wire to get warm or overheat.

The length of a cable run also needs consideration; the longer the run, the greater the drop in volts. So if your leisure battery is situated a long way from the vehicle's alternator, a significant voltage loss is inevitable when charging the battery while driving. The shorter the connecting cable, the better the charge rate. Voltage loss is less pronounced, however, if a thicker cable is fitted.

As regards the type of cable needed, a motorcaravan low-voltage system is usually wired using automotive cable. This has good flexibility because it is made from separate strands or 'filaments' and these normally have a standard thickness of 0.33mm. A flexible core made up of separate strands also achieves a more permanent connection when used in screw-fitted terminals.

A low-consumption appliance like a fluorescent light needs connecting up with thin (1.0mm^2) cable.

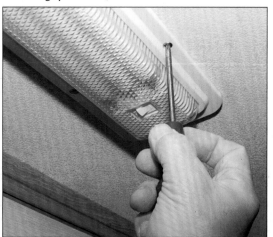

Cable gauge is shown on the label here, but you can also work it out by counting up the strands.

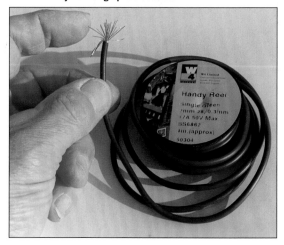

A low-consumption appliance like a fluorescent light only needs a thin cable whereas a high-consumption appliance, like a refrigerator working on 12V, needs a cable whose core is of a much thicker gauge. But this is a simplification and a more precise specification is needed.

Cable rating is indicated on its supply drum and this information is sometimes expressed in respect of its cross sectional area in mm². Alternatively the label might quote an *approximate continuous current rating* in amps. On a practical note, if a label is missing, you can confirm the cable rating by carefully counting the filaments, presuming the strands are of standard size. The table in the panel on page 60 relates the ratings to typical motorcaravan applications.

NOTE: *For a number of years, Electrolux installation manuals stated that if 2.0mm² cable is fitted, the cable run must not exceed 8 metres. Longer cable runs – between 8 and 10.5 metres – need 2.5mm² cable to avoid an unacceptable drop in voltage. However, Dometic (the former Electrolux brand) now recommends that on most models only 2.5mm² cable should be fitted. In the case of Dometic's Automatic Energy Selector (AES) models the 12V supply cable should be 6.0mm². To confirm that an installation is satisfactory, a voltmeter should be used to take a reading at the low-voltage connector block on top of the refrigerator. This would be done when the engine is running and if the reading falls below 12V, a cable of higher rating is needed.*

Making connections

Sometimes additional electrical accessories are needed in a motorcaravan. It's not unusual to find that an extra spotlight or a 12V socket would prove useful. If you're competent in electrical work, the job isn't difficult provided the appropriate cable is chosen and the appliance is coupled into the existing circuit correctly.

For instance, if you wanted to fit a 12V socket for a colour television, large models may have a rating as high as 100 watts. Thus it would be quite wrong to take the feed from a supply cable

An extra reading light is not a difficult component to fit.

that had been installed to serve the lights. A 0.7 amp fluorescent light draws around 8 watts, so the manufacturer would probably have connected this up using 1.0mm² cable (as shown in the table); a colour TV would be more appropriately served by a cable of 2.0mm². **Note**: *The Watt rating of appliances can vary greatly: for example, small portable TV sets are rated at just 50 Watts.*

Where possible, it is best to route the cable for a proposed socket back to the distribution unit since that usually has fuses serving the different supply branches; however, visible cable pinned to the surface looks unattractive and could be obstructive, so time should be spent finding a route that keeps it out of sight.

Coupling up a spotlight is less of a problem because there's likely to be a feed to another light fitting not too far away. Forming the join is the next consideration and sometimes a connecting block is used for this.

Another product often used for making a connection is the 'snap lock', sometimes referred to as a Scotchlock. This connector creates an electrical connection with an existing cable by means of a small metal tag which slices its way through the insulation sleeve on both feeds. Using a snap lock means you don't have to cut the original cable.

Notwithstanding the simplicity of the snap lock system, many electricians dislike it and prefer to use crimp connectors. If you have never used

Fitting a connecting block is a commonly-used way to add extra lights to a motorcaravan.

Snap locks allow a new cable to be coupled into an existing feed wire.

Crimp connectors are easy to fit, and are the connection method favoured by many electricians.

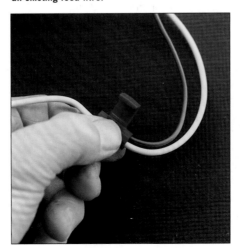

Owners of recent models are puzzled why the lighting in the living area is inoperable when the engine is running. There is a good reason for this, as explained in the section titled *Electromagnetic compatibility*. Overriding this safety system could be very dangerous, as the text points out.

these products, it is a good idea to buy a starter kit. This includes a crimping tool, together with a selection of different crimp couplings. The photograph on page 61 shows how a typical fitting is pressed on to the prepared end of the cable.

The use of soft solder is less common, although some auto electricians favour its use in particular circumstances.

Electromagnetic compatibility

Purchasers of recent motorcaravans have found that electrical appliances in the living quarters, with the exception of the refrigerator, will not operate while the engine is running; for example, the interior lights cannot be used. This can be a hindrance – but there's a good reason for this new wiring practice.

It has been prompted by a phenomenon referred to as 'electromagnetic compatibility' or EMC for short. Installers acknowledge that many forms of transport are reliant on electronic control systems; for instance, when travelling by air, passengers are not permitted to use electronic equipment during a flight. Similarly there's a potential risk in modern vehicles in which electronic circuits control the operation of items like ABS braking and engine management systems.

Regrettably the correct operation of these control devices might be influenced when other electrical equipment is used – which is potentially dangerous. So the less auxiliary electrical equipment being put to use when a motorcaravan is being driven the better – and that's why an automatic isolation switch has been incorporated in recent 12V circuits. In effect, the 'isolation switch' is a component more commonly called a 'relay'; this detects when the engine is running and automatically cuts off the supply of electricity to the living area.

Not surprisingly, the owners of older motorcaravans might not need such a system; sophisticated electronics in motor vehicles are comparatively recent. However, an attempt to by-pass this control on a newer model might lead to a serious accident caused, for instance, by interference with brake operation. This matter has raised questions and the concession to keep a fridge running on a 12V supply has been challenged by manufacturers whose fan-operated heaters are disabled automatically, even though they've

apparently been approved for operation during driving. This is a debate which has only just started.

Leisure batteries

Neither the base vehicle battery, nor an auxiliary leisure battery, should be seen as 'fit and forget' accessories. On the contrary, they need regular attention and special measures have to be taken if the vehicle is likely to remain unused for an extended period.

Construction and use

In both construction and use, vehicle and leisure batteries are different.

A vehicle battery is designed to produce a surge of power to operate a starter motor. This is a demanding task, but once the engine is running, the battery gains an immediate recharge from the vehicle's alternator.

In contrast, a leisure battery has to provide a steady flow of current over an extended period – and time might elapse before recharging is possible. However, a recharge mustn't be delayed too long; battery manufacturers advise strongly against completely discharging a battery because this can cause permanent damage.

The continued pattern of charge/discharge (referred to as deep cycling) is something that a vehicle battery can't endure for long. The lead plates sustain damage quickly and an all-important paste held within them can fall away. In a leisure battery, however, the plates are constructed with separators so that their paste is held *in situ* more effectively. This is reflected in the higher cost of the product – though if looked after well, it's not unusual for a leisure battery to last longer than a vehicle battery.

In Elecsol leisure batteries, carbon fibre is used in the plate construction. This is an unusual

A relay is an electrically operated switch; a magnetic coil and contacts can be seen in this example.

Technical tip

Lead acid and gel batteries
Motorcaravans manufactured and sold in Germany are usually fitted with a gel leisure battery rather than the lead acid product. It would appear that this strategy is principally led by safety requirements. In the event of a serious road accident, it means that there's no acid to spill. That's precisely why gel batteries are fitted in jet skis and quad bikes.

Gel batteries are also noteworthy because they do not emit an explosive gas when being charged. But that is probably as far as the advantages go. When it comes to performance, lead acid batteries are usually regarded as the better product. There is also a very significant price difference and some gel batteries are four times the price of an equivalent lead acid version. Moreover, many makes of charger can be used without causing damage to a lead acid battery. In contrast the right type of charger is critically important when using a gel product – and this is discussed in a later section.

development and early indications suggest that Elecsol batteries will give notably long service. Without doubt, the inclusion of a five-year warranty is proof of the manufacturer's confidence in its product.

Notwithstanding the cautionary advice about avoiding a total discharge, it is worth stating that a leisure battery installed in a motorcaravan is more likely to receive a periodic charge than a battery in a touring caravan. This is because a tourer is often left on a pitch for a long period and if there's no mains hook-up, recharging a leisure battery can pose problems. The fact that most motorcaravans are driven off-site regularly means there's a periodic recharge from the alternator.

Guidance on use

To get the best from a leisure battery, the following recommendations are suggested by manufacturers:

- The terminals should be smeared with grease, like Triflow, or petroleum jelly (Vaseline).
- Check the electrolyte periodically, and if the level falls below the top of the plates, top it up with de-ionised water. This is sold in car accessory shops.
- A battery must not be left in a discharged state; this is often the reason why a battery becomes irreparably damaged.
- If your motorcaravan is parked for an extended period, make provision for keeping the leisure battery in a charged condition. This might involve transferring it to a bench for charging; alternatively some owners use a trickle charger which is left permanently connected. Products from Airflow and Carcoon are used on classic cars, but are equally useful for maintaining the charge in a motorcaravan's batteries.
- Completely sealed non-spill gel electrolyte batteries, such as the Varta Drymobil, are less common and you should seek the manufacturer's advice about care and maintenance. Many chargers designed for lead acid batteries are **not** suitable for use with a gel battery.
- When removing a battery on a 'negative earth' vehicle, disconnect the negative terminal first; when installing a battery, connect the negative terminal last.

If the electrolyte drops low in a cell, add de-ionised water.

Checking charge level and condition

To check a battery's state of charge it is usual to test with a meter, although specific gravity testing is an alternative.

Obviously it's best to take a voltage reading directly from its terminals, but several points need to be borne in mind.

- The use of a digital voltmeter is recommended since these are easy to read and their accuracy is usually good. At one time these were expensive, but prices have dropped considerably.
- Make sure all the motorcaravan's appliances are disconnected – even a permanently connected clock can falsify the reading.
- If a battery has just been disconnected from a charger, or you've recently been driving your motorcaravan, the reading will be high but this isn't a true indication of its state of charge once it has stabilised. So you need to let it settle before carrying out a voltmeter test, which means waiting for at least four hours – longer if possible. The reason for this is that an elderly battery in poor condition has a problem holding its charge; once a charger has been disconnected it's no surprise to see a good reading; but that's misleading because it might drop to a much lower reading a day or two later and that's what counts. In contrast, a battery in good condition which isn't supplying power is able to hold its charge level for two months or more.
- Although this type of battery is described as providing a 12V power supply, that's just a nominal description and many motorcaravanners are surprised to learn that a reading of 12V indicates a poor charge level. In fact, the following table clarifies the situation:

Voltmeter reading	Approx. state of charge
12.7V or over	100%
12.5V	75%
12.4V	50%
12.2V	25%
12V or under	Discharged

A digital multimeter is used to take voltage readings.

Battery condition and charge level

A reference to the 'condition' of a leisure battery normally refers to its state of charge. This is certainly the case if you see a meter installed in a motorcaravan which bears the words 'Battery condition'. Unfortunately, this is rather confusing because an ageing battery whose casing is cracked and whose reliability in electrical terms has clearly diminished could equally be described as being 'in a poor condition'. In attempt to acknowledge these two completely different issues, the title of the accompanying section (see left) intentionally treats the terms: 'charge level' and 'condition', as separate features.

Battery output between charges

The capacity of a battery is expressed in Amp-hours (Ah) and this indicates how long it can provide an output before needing a recharge. As a rule, the external dimensions of a leisure battery are related to its Ah capacity and whilst a 90Ah battery needs a recharge less frequently than a 60Ah version, there isn't always sufficient stowage space for one. The assigned location for a motorcaravan leisure battery is often unable to accommodate the larger 90Ah battery.

In practice, this may not present a problem. Motorcaravanners who are constantly on the move are unlikely to be affected too badly. It is only when you park a vehicle for an extended period – perhaps because you're travelling out of the site by other means of transport – that you realise that a 90Ah battery would be better. Moreover the demand on a battery during dark and cold winter nights is very different from the situation in the summer. But what does the Ah capacity rating mean in practical terms?

To get a rough estimate of how long a battery will provide power between charges, make the following simple calculation:

1) Establish the wattage of appliances. Typical examples are: a single tube strip light – 8 watts; a spotlight – 10 watts; a water pump – 50 watts; a colour TV – 50 watts (*can vary – some TVs like the Roadstar CTV 1020 are as low as 30w*).
2. Work out how many hours (or fractions of an hour) they will be used in a 24-hour period.
3. Calculate watt hours for each appliance by multiplying wattage by hours in use.
4. Add together the total of watt hours.

This is shown in the following table:

Equipment	Rating in watts	Hours in use	Watt hours
Two 8 watt lights	16	5	80
Two 10 watt spot lights	20	1	20
Water pump	50	0.2	10
Colour TV	50	5	250
Total watt hours 360			

Divide watt hours by volts to get ampere hours:

$$360 \div 12 = 30Ah$$

Inspecting the cells in a leisure battery can be difficult when it's fitted under the driver's seat.

Technical tip

Variations in battery output between charges:

· The stated capacity of a battery, expressed in Amp-hours, presumes the ambient temperature is 25°C (77°F).

For approximately every 1°C drop in temperature, there's a one per cent fall in battery capacity, so when a battery which is nominally rated as 60Ah is operating in a temperature of 15°C (60°F) it effectively becomes a 54Ah battery.

Problems are even more acute for winter motorcaravanners. Not only will a battery work harder to provide lighting and fan-assisted heating on long, dark evenings, but the actual capacity of the battery is considerably less than its Ah rating might suggest.

· Performance between charges also deteriorates as a battery ages.

· If a variety of appliances are used at the same time, thereby creating a more rapid discharge rate, battery performance characteristics are affected detrimentally. This is why German batteries often have two Ah ratings marked on the casing. The lower of the two shows a battery's reduced Ah capacity if a lot of items are used simultaneously.

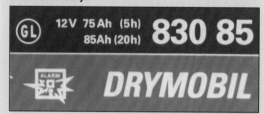

This Varta battery has a 75Ah or 85Ah stated capacity depending on the rate of discharge.

So if your motorcaravan is fitted with a 60Ah battery, at this rate of use (30Ah consumed in 24 hours) it should last for around two days before a recharge is needed. This is only a rough guide, however, and the point was made earlier that running a battery to the point of total discharge is a bad practice. Newcomers to motorcaravanning are often surprised how quickly a leisure battery loses its charge. The above guidance clarifies the position and also confirms the merit of fitting a larger capacity 90Ah battery where there's space.

Leisure battery location

The closer a leisure battery is to the alternator, the better the charge rate when you're driving, and provided there's ventilation and adequate space, the engine compartment undoubtedly meets this requirement. In practice, there isn't always space under the bonnet; an alternative therefore, is under a cab seat – presuming that the base vehicle has its engine at the front. (Older VW base vehicles had rear engines).

The reason for this, as discussed earlier, is that a long run of connecting cable leads to a fall-off in voltage and a poorer charge rate as a

Motorcaravan manufacturers seem reluctant to use the battery boxes fitted in touring caravans.

During charging, a battery sometimes gives off a mixture of hydrogen and oxygen. This is lighter than air, explosive, and has a distinctive odour. Should the gas accidentally ignite – and a cigarette can cause this – the casing of a battery may be blown apart and corrosive acid forcibly ejected. Eye injury and flesh burns are likely.

There are two ways of venting the explosive gas to the outside. If a battery is housed in a purpose-made locker, an outlet vent is needed. This should be installed above the top of the battery because hydrogen rises. The alternative is to couple up a venting tube – most leisure batteries have a connector nozzle that accepts flexible tubing. Provided this joint is perfectly sound, the plastic tubing can be led through a hole in a side wall or floor, dispersing the gas to the outside. If dispersal is done this way as opposed to a wall vent, the outlet can now be at a low level since the emitted gas is contained within the plastic tube and will be forced downwards.

result. Admittedly a thicker gauge of cable helps to reduce voltage loss on long cable runs, but putting a leisure battery in a locker right at the back of a vehicle or in a distant wardrobe is not advantageous from an electrical standpoint.

Other points regarding location are as follows:

- A battery must not share a locker with gas cylinders. (A spark from a battery terminal next to a leaking gas cylinder could cause an explosion.) The ideal location is in a separate locker, sealed from the interior but vented to the outside of the vehicle. It is curious that purpose-made battery compartments are fitted in touring caravans but you seldom find them in a motorcaravan.
- Avoid using crocodile clips on battery terminals. A clip might become dislodged and a spark across a poor connection can be powerful. Traditional bolt-on clamps sold in auto shops are recommended, although clamping clips sold at motorcaravan accessory shops are also good.
- A battery location must have ventilation. The reason for this is given in the Safety panel (above right).

Charging

A leisure battery can be charged using any of the following:

- a portable or fixed mains charger
- the engine alternator
- a petrol generator
- a wind or solar system.

Mains chargers

The following points concerning mains chargers are worth noting:

- The amp output of a charger influences how quickly a battery is revived. Too high an amperage, however, is not good for a battery in the long term.
- A leisure battery needs a different charging regime compared with a vehicle battery. This is why an inexpensive portable car battery charger isn't recommended. On the other hand, some of the better car chargers incorporate a selection

switch; this provides the appropriate regime for either an auto or a leisure battery.

- A battery can be 'over-charged' and when this occurs, the electrolyte (the diluted sulphuric acid in the casing) may start to evaporate. If this happens, top up the battery using de-ionised water.
- Periodic checking of the electrolyte level is important; it should just cover the plates in each cell.
- There are several separate cells in a battery, each of which has its own top-up point. Sometimes a cell can fail and this upsets an automatic charger's sensing system. Instead of switching off automatically when the other cells are recharged, it maintains its full output on account of the failed cell.
- When a motorcaravan is connected to a mains hook-up, most owners keep its built-in charger running constantly – even when it is supplying 12V accessories. However, the fact that a normal motorcaravan charger's output is no more than 13.8V means that the tolerance of 12V accessories allows them to operate *at the same* time without the risk of damage. On the other hand, a charger whose starting output is 14.7 or 14.8V would be much more likely to damage a 12V accessory. The trouble is that battery manufacturers claim that a 14.7 or 14.8V voltage is needed in order to allow a battery to recharge completely – a topic that's explained later. It is also true that a few manufacturers of built-in chargers have recommended that they should be switched off once the battery had become recharged. Information regarding the best practice for a particular charging product should be sought from its manufacturer.
- The initial charge in a stepped regime for a gel-type battery (as opposed to one containing diluted sulphuric acid) should not exceed 14.4V.
- In spite of warnings, some motorcaravanners still attempt to use a 12V supply without a leisure battery in circuit (that is, by drawing directly from a charger as if it were a transformer/rectifier). This is bad practice because its output might

Vehicle battery charging

Although a motorcaravan's built-in charger looks after the leisure battery, it may not be switchable to charge the vehicle battery. To achieve this, some motorcaravanners carry a conventional portable charger. Another solution is to fit the Van Bitz Battery Master which provides a trickle charge to the vehicle battery using the motorcaravan's built-in charger. It is completely automatic in operation. Installation involves coupling the positive terminals of both the vehicle and leisure batteries via the Battery Master control relay product. The device monitors the charge in the leisure battery and whenever it achieves a higher voltage than the vehicle battery, it diverts some of its power. This happens, for example, when the leisure battery is being charged. A red LED indicates when the sharing is taking effect.

The Van Bitz Battery Master is about the size of a matchbox

fluctuate, whereas some appliances need a stable supply. Having a battery in the circuit smoothes out irregularities and prevents damage to appliances. Suffice it to say, this is one reason why manufacturers of fixed chargers installed in motorcaravans limit their output to 13.8V. The trouble is that this introduces a problem with lead acid batteries, as the next point emphasises.

• When initiating charging, particularly when a lead acid battery is heavily discharged, battery manufacturers usually state that the process should begin with a start-up voltage of 14.7 to 14.8V. Some battery manufacturers even go further and point out that a discharged battery might **never** re-achieve its peak condition if a charger doesn't provide a high start-up voltage. Suffice it to say, the duration of this initial boost might only last for 10 to 20 minutes, and when a stepped charger is used the voltage will then drop automatically in stages. In practice, not many chargers offer a stepped regime and the number of stages varies from product to product. However, when the battery regains a good state, the unit then adopts a trickle charge mode designed to maintain the voltage level.

Gassing

When a charger gives an output of 14.4V or more, a lead acid battery starts to 'gas'. This refers to the situation in which the acid electrolyte emits an explosive gas – which is why you should never smoke or have a naked flame in the vicinity of a charging battery. If an explosion occurs, the battery casing is usually blown apart and the highly corrosive acid flies everywhere. Bearing in mind the earlier point that some motorcaravan manufacturers fit batteries in rather silly places within the living space, the risks become clear. For instance if a leisure battery is mounted under a cab seat and the gas relief tube becomes detached (which it often does), anyone smoking nearby might initiate an explosion. It would be so much better if sealed, purpose-made battery compartments with external venting were used – as they are in modern touring caravans. Here is one of the reasons why fixed battery charges are limited to a 13.8V output; this normally only causes gassing if one of the cells

in the battery fails. The other reason mentioned above is that most owners run 12V appliances at the same time as the charger is in use – and 14.7 to 14.8V could damage them.

These comments might make it sound that gassing should be avoided. That's not the case. Over a period of time, the performance of a leisure battery deteriorates quite noticeably and this occurs when there's a build-up of sulphate on the plates. A starting voltage of around 14.8V and the resulting gassing action, helps to overcome this condition. It is even claimed that many leisure batteries are scrapped long before they ought to be – simply because of sulphate build-up which could have been avoided by using a high output charger. Nevertheless, a gassing battery needs good ventilation, an environment free of naked flames, and far more regular top-ups with de-ionised water.

It stands to reason, of course, that if an owner periodically transfers a leisure battery to a bench situated in a ventilated environment, a high output charger with a stepped regime can then be used without risk. For instance RoadPro retails Sterling chargers which are well-known in the marine industry. These chargers create the regime recommended by battery manufacturers; they also offer a setting control for gel batteries whose charge voltage must never exceed 14.4V. However, these sophisticated products are not cheap.

Other stepped chargers include the less-expensive CTEK products from RoadPro which are designed to charge several types of lead acid and gel batteries, including the kind fitted on motorcycles. The CTEK chargers are unusual in that they offer a pulsed output and the Multi XS 7000 model operates with up to six charge level steps. A maximum boost setting of 16V operating for four hours can also be chosen for a battery which has been neglected and needs full reconditioning. CTEK products employ automatic timing and current-controlled charging so that the needs of a battery are identified and met by an appropriate stepped charge regime.

Trickle charging

The situation so far has focused on procedures for dealing with a discharged leisure battery.

The battery charger and power supply units from Sterling are often used in cabin cruisers.

The CTEK Multi XS 7000 pulse charger offers up to six charge level steps and a maximum boost of 16V.

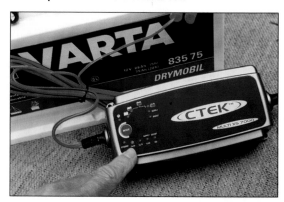

The Carcoon trickle charger includes a short lead with eyelets which can be left permanently on a battery.

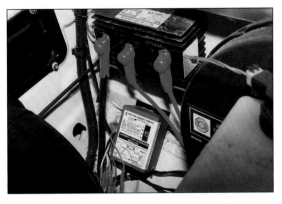

To maximise output from an alternator, some manufacturers are fitting the Sterling 4 Step Alternator Regulator.

However, there's also the matter of maintaining a charged battery – for instance during a period of storage. This is when a trickle charger is useful and products like the Airflow Battery Conditioner and the Carcoon Trickle Charger are often used by owners of classic cars. Now they are being used by motorcaravanners as well. These compact units indicate the battery charge state by light emitting diodes (LEDs) and, when connected to the mains, they provide a charge whenever their electronic circuit detects that a battery needs it. This electronic monitoring and activation element is a special feature and the products are designed to be left wired-up for long storage periods.

The engine alternator

When a motorhome is being driven, the alternator is able to charge a leisure battery. To maximise its output, some owners fit a Sterling Advanced Four Step Alternator Regulator.

To enable a leisure battery to receive a charge from the alternator while an engine is running isn't merely a matter of linking the vehicle batteries together in parallel (parallel is where the terminals are connected positive to positive and negative to negative). If those connections were made, current would be pulled from *both* batteries when starting the vehicle. This can damage a leisure battery and sometimes a fuse is blown in the process.

Wiring for fridge, battery charging and isolating relays in a motorcaravan.

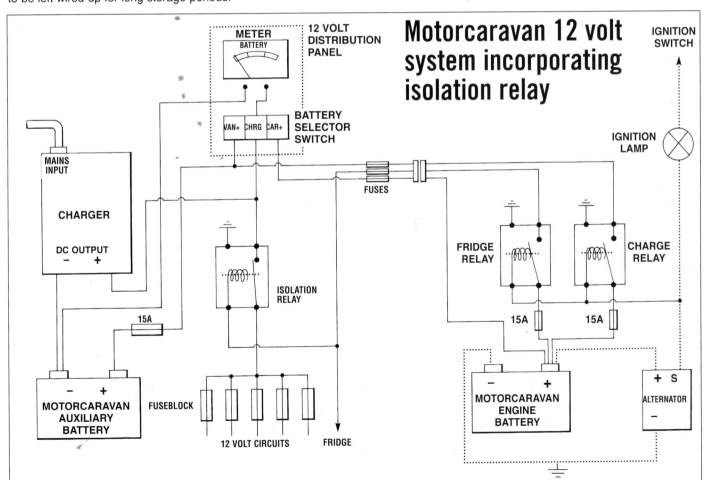

The batteries have to be isolated whenever the engine isn't running, but if a special relay is fitted, a connection can be achieved automatically as soon as the vehicle has been started. A 'relay' is an electrically operated switch and when wired into the system, the two batteries retain their independence until the engine is running. Incidentally, a similar relay is also fitted if you need to run a refrigerator on a 12V supply when you're on the road.

Several manufacturers specialise in these relays, including Hella, Lucas, Ring and Ryder, and installation kits are made for both motor and touring caravans. Wiring instructions are provided and the diagram on the previous page from Plug-In-Systems shows how a fridge relay, a battery charging relay and the isolation relay for the low-voltage supply in the living quarters are all connected up.

The fridge and charging relays are activated by connecting into the ignition light supply from the alternator. In practice, forming this connection isn't easy in some vehicles and an auto electrician at a franchise dealer should be consulted. Taking a supply from an ignition-controlled accessory on the base vehicle may not be a suitable alternative either. Some accessories are activated as soon as the starter is cranked and thus the vehicle battery is inappropriately augmented by power from the leisure battery. That can cause damage to a leisure battery.

Finally, a number of auto electricians suggest it is better to fit two separate relays for charging and

fridge operation. It is true that combination relays *are* available, but if faults occur, it's undoubtedly easier to identify a problem if the functions are kept independent.

Petrol generators for charging

Although a generator is useful for running mains appliances, most types deliver a fluctuating supply and power surges are not unusual – for example, when a low-wattage electric kettle is switched off there's a momentary surge of power. That might cause problems. Not only are there electronic products which need a smooth supply of mains electricity (such as a lap top computer), there's also a widespread use of 'switched-mode' battery chargers in motorcaravans. Switched-mode chargers are conveniently light in weight but a surge in the supply can damage their sensitive electronic circuits. The chargers fitted to motorcaravans in the 1980s were built around a transformer and are less susceptible to damage; but they're heavier than the switched-mode chargers which have superseded them.

To avoid causing damage:
• If you just want a generator to charge your battery and it provides a separate 12V output you can disconnect the battery from the motorcaravan and couple suitable cables (often sold as accessory items) to its terminals and the 12V output point on the generator. This gives a direct charge and completely eliminates the built-in charger from the system.
• The risk of damage occurs if you plug the 230V output from a generator into your motorcaravan mains input socket (as you would a mains hook-up lead), completely forget to switch off the consumer unit and appliances, and then start the generator. That causes damage. To avoid a generator's start-up surge, it is essential that you have all the electrical items switched off in the motorcaravan – although the hook-up lead between generator and the inlet socket can be connected. Then start the generator in accordance with its instructions. Wait until it is running at normal speed. Then – and only then – switch on the RCD and the power to the charger.

This Powerpart battery charger embodies the advantages of switched-mode electronics.

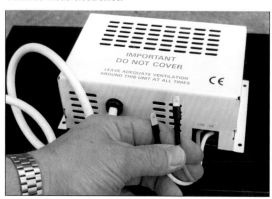

The latest Honda leisure generators use an inverter system to create smooth, surge-free mains electricity.

- Perhaps the smoothest supply from a generator is obtainable from Honda's latest models such as the EU10i and EU20i. These employ a completely different method of creating mains power and their supply is claimed to be surge-free and more stable than a normal mains supply. To achieve this, Honda's products generate 12V DC power which is then passed through an inverter to raise and rectify the supply to 230V AC.
- To be certain that the correct use of a generator is not going to damage a charger, it would be prudent to confirm the position with your motorcaravan's manufacturer. It is also essential to follow the instructions accompanying your petrol generator as well.

Solar and wind generators

The idea of getting 'something for nothing' is very attractive. On the other hand, solar and wind generators only provide a trickle charge for a battery. They do not create mains electricity.

Strictly speaking, the term 'solar' is inaccurate because photovoltaic cells (which produce power from light) also produce electricity in cloudy weather; they don't depend on sunshine. Solar panels are popular products and a number of specialists fit them to the roofs of motorcaravans.

With both wind and solar products, a regulator is needed to ensure that a battery isn't overcharged. For example, an abnormally high output produced by a wind generator during a gale could easily lead to damage. Similarly, the output from a large solar panel on a bright day can exceed the safe limit.

Several types of solar panel are available, complete with installation kits, although large panels cost a lot of money. Equally it mustn't be forgotten that the time when a battery works

Specialists like A B Butt can install photovoltaic solar panels on the roofs of motorcaravans.

hardest is during the long dark evenings in winter. It is therefore unfortunate that a solar panel is most effective during the long daylight hours of summer.

Mains systems

This section describes the components used in a mains supply and provides general safety guidance, including procedures for coupling-up on site.

As regards owner installation, some good kits are available and a competent and careful practitioner should find it easy to install a mains supply if one hasn't already been fitted. Many owners would entrust this work to a qualified electrician, but some DIY enthusiasts undoubtedly have the knowledge and ability to fit a mains kit themselves.

Note: *DIY installations must be tested by a qualified electrician and should have a signed test certificate to verify compliance with the current IEE regulations. Contact the NICEIC or ECA for details of approved inspectors in your area.*

The kit itself should comprise:
- A supply circuit wired to IEE standards. This means 2.5mm^2 flexible cable to connect the Input Socket to the RCD; 1.5mm^2 flexible cable is required for all other circuits served by the MCBs.
- A mains consumer unit manufactured with a Residual Current Device (RCD); this immediately cuts off the supply if anyone touches a live wire accidentally. It also includes Miniature Circuit Breakers (MCBs) to protect individual circuits – there's usually one MCB for the fridge and another for the sockets - although three MCBs are fitted in larger motorcaravans.

DIY mains wiring is possible; the Powerpart Mains wiring kit is supplied with full fitting instructions.

Technical tip

Mains hook-ups

A site hook-up is limited in its supply. Some supplies are as low as 5 amps; others as high as 16 amps. Some sites offer two levels of supply and charge accordingly. On arrival at a site you need to ask the site warden about the amperage rating.

Using the figure given (amps), multiply this by 230 (volts) to establish the total wattage it can supply. For instance if a site offers a 10 amp supply, 10 x 230 = 2300 watts.

Now look closely at your appliances to see their wattage rating. Typically these are:

Light bulb	60w
Small colour TV	50w
Fridge	125w
Battery charger	100w
Microwave cooker	1,200w
Domestic kettle	2,000w

Now add up the wattages of the appliances you expect to have in use at any one time to assess whether you'll overload the site supply.

Note 1. If you overload the system, you'll activate the hook-up pillar's trip switch and will have to ask the warden to reinstate the supply.

Note 2. A site is not able to supply all hook-up pillars simultaneously with a maximum or near-maximum output. Advice posters often encourage users not to operate 230V items unnecessarily. This is especially true in winter when central heating systems are often run on electricity rather than gas and many owners spent long evening hours watching television and using interior lighting.

- An earth wire, covered with green and yellow sheathing, must be connected from the earth bar in the consumer unit and bolted to the chassis. A warning plate should also be attached to the point of fixing.
- 'Three-pin' 13 amp sockets are fitted in a motorcaravan and it is best to have the latest types which feature double-pole switching.
- The input socket must comply with BS EN 60309-2.
- The connecting cable, which should comply with BS EN 60309-2, must not exceed 25 metres. It contains three flexible cores for live (positive), neutral (negative) and earth connections, each of which must have a cross-sectional area of 2.5mm². You are NOT recommended to link up more than one extension lead to reach distant hook-up points.

NOTE:

1. An MCB is a trip switch which provides over-current protection. This is a modern equivalent of the old-fashioned rewirable fuse.

2. An RCD used to be called an 'Earth Leakage Circuit Breaker' or a 'Residual Current Circuit Breaker'. In recent years, these incorporate double-pole switching which means they control current flow on both live and neutral connections. Bear in mind that the RCD affords no protection from a shock received from the site pillar, the hook-up lead and that short length of cable which links a motorcaravan's inlet socket with its consumer unit.

3. Most consumer units deal solely with 230V electricity but some control units, such as the Plug-In-Systems PMS3 (fitted in Bilbo's conversions) embrace mains, charging and 12V systems in a single control box.

The system fitted in a motorcaravan is designed to connect with site 'hook-up' pillars in the UK, fitted with an industrial socket. If you want to connect the supply lead to a 13 amp socket at home – perhaps to pre-cool a fridge prior to departure – you'll need an adaptor. Similarly an adaptor is needed to connect into many hook-up pillars on the Continent.

Bilbo's fits a Plug-in-Systems power unit which combines mains and 12v controls in a single unit.

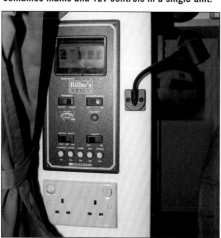

An earth cable bolted to the chassis must be clearly labelled.

An adaptor is needed before a hook-up cable can draw electricity from a 13 amp domestic socket.

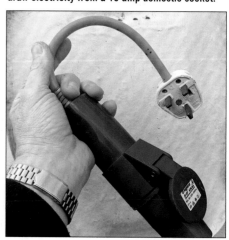

At some caravan sites the electrical hook-up pillars have a red release button, and. . .

. . . an inserted plug has to be turned clockwise to lock it in place and to activate the electricity supply.

On this mains consumer unit, the RCD control is on the right, a yellow test button is above it, and the MCBs are on the left.

Connecting up to a site supply

When you've gained a warden's approval to have a mains supply, always follow this hook-up routine:

1) Switch off the RCD on the consumer unit (photo above), and all mains appliances.
2) Uncoil the hook-up lead. Never leave it coiled on a drum because this can lead to overheating.
3) Insert the hook-up plug with recessed tubes (female) into your motorcaravan input socket.
4) Insert the opposite end with pins (male) into the site supply point. On some sites you have to rotate the connector clockwise until it locks and this action activates the flow of current.
5) Turn on the RCD of the consumer unit to put the system into operation.
6) Press the trip button to confirm that the RCD cuts out as it should.
7) Re-set the RCD switch to reinstate the supply.
8) Check the polarity of the supply. Sometimes there's a reverse polarity warning light on the

A test device to confirm if the supply polarity is correct or reversed can be a useful accessory when heading abroad.

consumer unit. If there isn't, make sure you purchase a socket tester from a dealer or electrical factor.

When disconnecting a supply, switch off all the mains appliances and the RCD control switch. Then withdraw the supply plug from the site's hook-up pillar. In the case of the twist-socket fitted on several sites, you need to depress a red button to release the connector. Similarly the inlet sockets on some motorcaravans are also fitted with a plug release catch. Coil and stow the hook-up lead.

Polarity

In the UK, it is traditional for a switch to create a break in the live feed serving an appliance or lamp fitting. In other words if a light is switched off, no current reaches the bulb or its socket.

However, in many other European countries, a switch operates on both live *and* neutral connections, a system known as double-pole

On some motorcaravan mains inlets, you cannot remove the plug until you've depressed a release button.

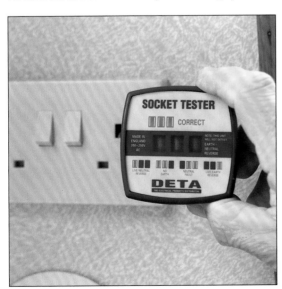

To deal with reversed polarity some owners wire-up a plug with the live and neutral connections reversed.

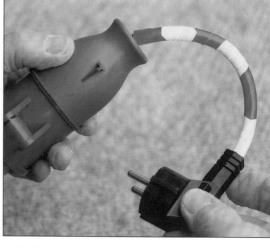

Red and white stripes remind the user that this foreign adapter has been specially wired to deal with reversed polarity.

switching. This is undoubtedly very safe, but it then seems that less care is taken abroad when contractors install campsite hook-ups. Live and neutral feeds are often reversed although the situation, called 'reverse polarity', is not such a safety threat in countries where all electric controls adopt double-pole switching.

On the other hand, reverse polarity is potentially very dangerous for the UK tourist whose motorcaravan is normally fitted with only single-pole switches. When you switch off an appliance with a reversed polarity supply it's true that it ceases to function. But – if we take a light as an example – *the light fitting remains live* because switching is now on the cable leading *out* of the unit.

If you encounter a reversed polarity supply, you are strongly advised not to use a mains hook-up just in case you were to touch a live connection accidentally. However, some owners create a practical solution for dealing with reversed polarity by intentionally wiring up a continental adaptor with its live and neutral connections reversed. Obviously you cannot buy a 'wrongly wired' adaptor but one of these remedies the problem at source – the supply pillar. By carrying

The Concept Range from W4 Accessories features double-pole switching and can be fitted in place of single-pole sockets

both adaptors when touring abroad, together with a polarity tester plug, the situation can be immediately solved.

Motorcaravans manufactured since 1993 now have double-pole switched RCDs so the problem is less acute. But regrettably, single-pole 13 amp sockets are still fitted in motorcaravans – even though double-pole 13 amp switched sockets have been available for some time. The Concept Range sold by W4 Accessories is an example. Without question, it is worth changing the original single-pole switched sockets for double-pole versions. This is an inexpensive modification which follows the practice adopted in a number of continental countries.

Petrol generators

Earlier in this chapter, reference was made to the problem of power surges from petrol generators when used in conjunction with battery chargers. However, when stopping at sites which do not have mains supply points, a generator is an undoubted asset.

They can be noisy, of course, and on a crowded site they're undoubtedly intrusive. But owners who use their motorcaravans in remote areas regard them as important items of equipment.

That said, it needs to be recognised that a generator's output is far lower than the output obtainable from a mains supply hook-up. For example, a site providing 16 amps is able to operate appliances whose combined rate of consumption adds up to roughly 3680 Watts. That's considerably more than the output from a Honda EU10i generator, which has a rated output of 900 Watts. In the event, this isn't a problem if you want a generator to run mains lighting, a TV, a mobile phone charger, a shaver, or even a low-wattage electric kettle. However, many owners expect a mains supply to be able to run a microwave oven and that leads to confusion.

To illustrate the point, let's imagine that someone has a microwave rated at 600 watts (sometimes referred to as 600 watts cooking power). The trouble is that this figure relates to the oven's output as opposed to the input it requires. In order to establish which generators are powerful enough to run microwave ovens, the usual advice is to double the oven's quoted wattage and then deduct ten per cent. Hence a microwave oven rated at 600 watts would need a generator producing at least 1080 watts. That's not a problem for a Honda EU20i which is surprisingly silent, but industrial machines offering a higher output are considerably noisier and less compact than the leisure machines.

Provided this is understood, generators have a useful place and some motorcaravans have a metal-lined locker to transport one – although it's not vented so you cannot operate the machine *in situ*. A ventilated cover is also needed when a generator is running in the rain.

On larger motorcaravans, a special compartment is made to house a permanently mounted generator. Dometic and Onan generators are often fitted in large motorhomes, with a remote control panel usually situated inside the living area. On an American RV, this kind of provision is commonplace.

Inverters

Another way to gain mains power is to take a 12V supply from a leisure battery and to convert it into 230V AC using an inverter. For example, inverters like the Xcell from Driftgate 2000 are well respected, although they are better-known in marine circles.

Where lighting is concerned, an inverter permits operation of mains bulbs, although the Ah rating of the supplying battery determines how long these will run before it's discharged. For example, a

250 watt inverter – even if 100 per cent efficient – would draw more than 20 amps from a battery when working to its limit. In consequence a 60Ah battery would be completely discharged in less than three hours. In reality, the battery discharge rate is even more rapid because no inverter can be 100 per cent efficient.

However, if you want to run a couple of 60 watt bulbs and nothing else, the limitations are less severe, especially if you follow the earlier advice and fit a 90Ah battery. That will produce good lighting for a number of hours. Even longer hours of light are possible if you use the inverter to run 230V 10w 'long-life' lamp units.

Higher wattage items like a travel hair dryer or a shaver can also be run from an inverter. These appliances are used for only a short period and, since a sound battery has a self-recovery element, the loss of charge is not likely to be too serious.

This permanently-fixed 2.5kW Electrolux generator was mounted in a Murvi van conversion as a special project.

Starting and operating a permanently installed generator is sometimes controlled by a remote panel.

The Xcell inverter from Driftgate 2000 converts 12V DC from a battery to 230V AC mains power.

6

Contents

Gas supply systems & heating appliances

The most common fuel for heating and cooking in motorcaravans is liquefied petroleum gas (LPG). This is produced in two different forms and an understanding of its characteristics, storage and supply ensures that the fuel is used efficiently and safely.

Gas is not the only fuel used in a motorcaravan; mains electricity is sometimes used for heating the living space. In the latest motorcaravans there may even be a 230V hot plate on the hob.

Also gaining in popularity are heating systems (for both space and water) which use diesel or petrol drawn from the base vehicle's fuel tank. Notwithstanding these interesting alternatives, gas is still by far the most common fuel used in motorcaravans.

Characteristics of gas

The name for this fuel is Liquefied Petroleum Gas, or LPG for short. For convenience it is usually supplied in portable steel cylinders, although some motorcaravanners choose to have a refillable bulk tank fitted underneath their vehicle. For owners embarking on long continental trips, a refillable tank has its merits because the types of portable cylinders sold abroad have different couplings and there's little standardisation. But what about the product itself?

LPG in its natural state is neither poisonous, nor does it have a smell; so a leak could occur unnoticed. But it is highly flammable, so for consumer safety a 'stenching agent' is added to the gas during processing. The distinctive odour is very unpleasant and it ensures that a leak is detected at once.

In addition, LPG is heavier than air, so 'drop out' holes (sometimes called gas dispersal holes) are built into a motorcaravan's structure to provide escape routes for leaking gas. It is for this reason that vents built into the floor and under gas appliances should never be covered up. Anyone buying a second-hand vehicle should carefully check that a previous owner has kept all the ventilators unobstructed.

For added convenience, some owners have a refillable bulk gas tank fitted under their motorcaravan.

Never cover a gas 'drop-out' hole; if a gas leak were to occur, this is one of the escape points.

There are two types of LPG: butane and propane. Their characteristics are different but the appliances fitted to motorcaravans built in Europe are designed to run on either gas without need for adjustments. The differences between butane and propane are as follows:

Butane:

- has a higher calorific value than propane which means that it is a more efficient heat producer. Accordingly butane is a popular choice – as long as the weather is warm.

- does not change from its liquefied state to a gas vapour when temperatures are lower than 0°C (32°F) at atmospheric pressure. Even a cylinder brim-full with liquefied butane cannot deliver gas into the motorcaravan's supply system when temperatures fall below freezing – so it is seldom used in winter.

- is heavier than propane, so although the smallest Calor Gas cylinders for the two products are the same size, the propane version holds 3.9kg (8.6lb), and an equivalent cylinder filled with butane holds 4.5kg (10lb) of liquefied gas.

Propane:

- changes from a liquefied state into a gas in temperatures as low as –40°C (–44°F) – so it is the preferred winter fuel. However, it is unfortunate that suppliers on the Continent sell mainly butane, though processing companies sometimes add a small quantity of propane to butane cylinders in order to give improved cold weather performance.

- in its liquefied state it is lighter than butane. That's why, in two cylinders of identical size, there is less propane by weight than butane.

- is better for running a system in which several gas appliances are operating simultaneously and where the demand for gas is high. When describing this feature, technical specialists often say that a propane cylinder has a better off-take rate than a similar butane cylinder.

- has a vapour pressure between three and four times that of butane at 15°C and it's for this reason that different regulators are normally required for these two gases. But note the following paragraph.

To ensure that motorcaravanners fit the appropriate regulator when switching from butane to propane, or vice versa, gas suppliers intentionally fit different couplings on the cylinders. However, special dual-use regulators were introduced in 2003 when new gas standards were implemented; this subject is discussed later. All that needs to be said at this point is that dual-use regulators should only be used in conjunction with the purpose-built appliances first fitted in 2004 models.

● Before taking to the road, it is important to turn off the gas supply at source. Even though there are isolation valves in modern motorcaravans for controlling different appliances, the best precaution is to turn off the supply *at the cylinder*. Prior to starting the engine, turning off the supply should always be part of a motorcaravanner's routine. This precautionary measure ensures that no appliances (especially a fridge) can be accidentally left running on gas. When you drive into a filling station for fuel, it is strictly illegal for a motorcaravan to have a naked flame and this would pose a very serious threat to people's safety.

Always turn off your gas supply at the cylinder before embarking on a journey.

● Always transport a cylinder in its *upright* position. If a cylinder is laid on its side, the liquefied gas *might* prevent the pressure relief safety valve from functioning correctly. Gas can also escape from a faulty valve. When it's acknowledged that in the transfer from liquid to vapour there's approximately a *two hundred times increase in volume*, the potential hazard arising from a leak is clearly apparent.

Supply

Portable LPG cylinders are sold in several sizes, some of which are more suited to a motorcaravanner's needs than others. A Calor cylinder is obtained by way of a hire agreement, and the fee is paid when the contract is first signed; this means that a cylinder remains in the ownership of Calor Gas Ltd. If you cease being a Calor customer, the initial hire fee can be reclaimed, provided you are able to present the original agreement form.

The arrangement with Campingaz is different – you *do* purchase your first cylinder and when it's empty, you pay to exchange it for a full one again.

An advantage with Calor Gas is the fact that you can usually change from butane to propane or vice versa. In other words, an empty 3.9kg propane cylinder can be exchanged for a full 4.5kg butane one without paying any more than the cost of the gas. Similarly a 4.5kg butane cylinder can usually be changed for a larger 7kg cylinder. Occasionally there are restrictions when a particular size of cylinder is in short supply.

Calor cylinder sizes

3.9kg (8.6lb) propane
4.5kg (10lb) butane
6kg (13.2lb) propane
7kg (15.4lb) butane
13kg (28.7lb) propane
15kg (33lb) butane
Calor Gas butane cylinders are painted blue
Calor Gas propane cylinders are painted red.

Note: *The 19kg (41.9lb) propane cylinders are too large to transport safely in a motorcaravan. The 13kg propane and 15kg butane cylinders present similar problems although the gas lockers on some coachbuilt models **are** large enough to transport and secure cylinders of this size in an upright position.*

Gas lockers on some coachbuilt models are large enough to accommodate one or even two 13kg Calor propane cylinders.

Campingaz cylinder sizes

0.45kg (1lb) butane
1.81kg (4lb) butane
2.72kg (6lb) butane
Campingaz cylinders are painted blue.

Note: *Only the 2.72kg (Type 907) butane cylinder is a practical proposition for motorcaravanning. The two smaller cylinders might be kept for emergency back-up to operate a cooker burner but they are really intended for use in backpacker tents.*

The design of a motorcaravan gas locker should incorporate an effective means of securing a cylinder and there are distinct disadvantages if there isn't room to accommodate a back-up supply

Only the Campingaz 907 cylinder is large enough for normal use in a motorcaravan.

cylinder. A few small motorcaravans only have single cylinder lockers which is most unsatisfactory.

Storage

With a coachbuilt motorcaravan, it is relatively straightforward to manufacture a purpose-built gas cylinder locker offering external access. It is less easy in a van conversion and some manufacturers construct an internal locker, albeit with a thoroughly sealed access door to isolate it from the living quarters. However, in both cases, the storage locker has to be fitted with a substantial drop-out ventilator at the lowest point of the enclosure.

Gas availability

Calor Gas is widely available in Britain, and is sold in several different sized cylinders. Both butane *and* propane are sold by Calor Gas but the company doesn't operate abroad.

Campingaz is another product available in Britain, although the largest cylinder (the 907) is only a modest size 2.72kg (6lb). Moreover, propane is not available in Campingaz cylinders.

Nevertheless, Campingaz is available in over one hundred countries and prices vary quite a lot. It is notably inexpensive in Spain because butane cylinders are used in many less-affluent households, so it receives a heavy subsidy from the Spanish Government; propane in Spain is normally only supplied for commercial use. Campingaz is not available in Finland or Sweden and is seldom stocked in Norway.

Other products are available abroad and in Germany there are several examples, such as SKG 5kg propane cylinders. However, the gas appliances in older German motorcaravans have been designed to run at higher operating pressures than British appliances. So if you own a British-built motorcaravan built before the 2004 model year, it's not just a matter of buying a German regulator and cylinder when touring in that country. On later motorcaravans, the revised gas standards have helped to resolve this kind of problem.

Various methods are used to anchor a gas cylinder; a collar and webbing straps are provided in this Swift motorcaravan.

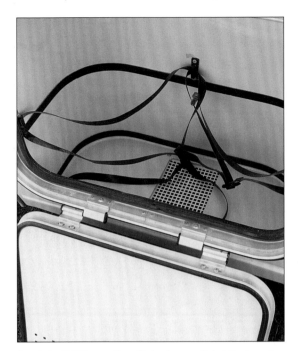

A substantial 'drop-out' ventilator is essential at the lowest point of a gas cylinder locker.

The internal locker in a van conversion must be effectively sealed from the living quarters.

In addition, electrical products such as a leisure battery or a light should never be installed in a gas locker. Leaks *can* occur at a cylinder valve and if a spark is generated when coupling the terminals of a battery, there would be an explosion.

On returning home, many owners remove gas cylinders from the vehicle as a precautionary measure. This is fine, but storage of the cylinders at home presents new problems. Under no circumstances should cylinders be left in a cellar, for example, since leaking gas would have no means of escaping. Moreover, *Gas Safety Regulations (Installation & Use)* state clearly that propane cylinders must not be stored inside any dwellings; nor should they be stored anywhere that lacks low level ventilation outlets. A shed or outhouse might prove suitable; but it is safer to adopt the practice of the suppliers whose cylinders are kept in a roofed storage cage situated well away from any source of flame. And remember. cylinders must always be stored upright!

Pressure regulation

A key component in a motorcaravan's gas supply system is the regulator. This device ensures that gas is delivered from a cylinder at a stable and constant pressure to suit the fitted appliances. this means a new replacement cylinder will not deliver gas at a higher rate than one which is nearly empty.

Regulators are set at the time of manufacture and must not be dismantled. Inside the sealed casing, a diaphragm moves up or down and this operates a lever mechanism which controls the flow of gas. There is *nothing* to adjust and that is why regulators are sealed at the time of manufacture. They also give many years service

although if one gets damaged, replace it. Some specialists advise you to change a regulator as a matter of course every three years.

Gas supply arrangements in motorcaravans built towards the end of 2003 underwent a radical change. The alterations were prompted by an obvious need to standardise practices in all European Community member states. Changes were laid down in:

a) European Norm (EN)12864:2001 which led to the publication in March 2002 of BS EN 12864:2001 which is the official English language version. This particularly focuses on regulators.
b) European Norm (EN)1949:2002 which led to the publication in September 2002 of BS EN 1949:2002 which is the official English language version. This specifies LPG installations, including pressure regulation.

If it took a long time to get these standards agreed and published; it also took time to get new gas products manufactured. But some German motorcaravans sold in the summer of 2003 were fitted with the new systems. In Britain, manufacturers which were members of the National Caravan Council were required to implement the new systems from 1 September 2003 – which effectively means the 2004 model ranges. Many non-member manufacturers also elected to adopt the new standards even though compliance was not obligatory.

Moreover, there is no requirement for pre-2004 models to be altered and this means there are now two very distinct systems in use, which either use a cylinder-mounted regulator or one which is permanently installed in the supply system.

New identity

The product often referred to as Camping Gaz has been available for many years. However, in late 1997 its name was changed to 'Campingaz' and a new identification logo was also introduced. The change of brand name is recognised throughout this manual.

Sealing washers for this type of regulator must be changed periodically and are sold in packs.

• Remember to buy a supply of sealing washers if you use a Calor screw-on butane cylinder-mounted regulator. Contrary to popular belief, the washer that comes in the black screw-on blanking cap that you get with a new cylinder must not be transferred for use in a regulator. It is not made of the correct material.

• A cylinder-mounted butane regulator is rated at 11.2 inch water gauge (28m bar); a propane regulator is rated at 14.8 inch water gauge (37m bar). So if a service engineer connects a glass U-tube holding water to a butane supply, the pressure is sufficient to force the water 11.2 inches up the tube; propane would force the water 14.8 inches up the tube. The device which employs this water-gauge test principle is called a manometer.

• A regulator has a tiny hole in the casing. If this becomes blocked, the diaphragm is unable to move inside. The problem sometimes occurs in windy and dusty conditions. A similar situation arises in winter if moisture gets into the breather hole and then freezes. When this happens, the diaphragm can get stuck in its fully open position. Should you find that the flame on a cooker becomes far higher than normal, this 'over-gassing' situation is nearly always the result of a regulator malfunction.

The sealing cap washer supplied with this type of cylinder is NOT suitable for use on a regulator.

The label on this cylinder-mounted propane regulator confirms its 37mbar output pressure.

A regulator will fail to work properly if the breather hole on its casing gets blocked.

Cylinder-mounted regulators

Until Britain's 2004 models were sold on or after 1 September 2003, anyone purchasing a new motorcaravan had to buy a regulator to suit the fitting on the cylinder that he or she intended to use. These regulators are compact, inexpensive and specific to either butane or propane.

(NOTE: *The term 'cylinder-mounted regulator' is used in this manual to differentiate these products from the 'fixed' regulators whose introduction was prompted by the 2001 and 2002 Standards mentioned on page 77.*)

Cylinder-mounted regulators are made to suit particular appliances. In Britain, for example, a motorcaravan's gas appliances were designed and built to run on gas supplied at a pressure of 28-37mbar. Accordingly a cylinder-mounted butane regulator delivers gas at a pressure of 28mbar and a propane regulator delivers gas at a pressure of 37mbar. However, in Germany, the jets fitted in appliances require gas to be delivered at a higher pressure. For that reason, imported German motorcaravans sold in Britain prior to Summer 2003 had to be fitted with replacement gas appliances which suited the lower pressures adopted in British motorcaravans.

That aside, it has been the practice for a

regulator to be coupled directly to the top of a cylinder. The trouble is that there are so many different types of cylinder fittings.

Standardisation of some kind was clearly needed and that's why the new European Norms (ENs) are now in place. Without doubt, the revised supply system certainly helps anyone travelling abroad because non-British gas cylinders can be easily coupled up to a British motorcaravan. However, owners of pre-2004 models cannot have their motorcaravan fitted with this revised gas system without major alterations.

As it happens, many motorcaravanners wouldn't want to do this anyway and are thoroughly content with the safe, simple, inexpensive cylinder-mounted regulators which have served them well for many years. These are some of their key features:

1) When a regulator fits directly to a cylinder, its design includes a ribbed nozzle to accept a length of LOW PRESSURE flexible hose for coupling to the nozzle on the metal pipes of the gas supply system. The hose should be secured using hose clips.

2) The Calor Butane and Propane cylinders which have threaded couplings are made with a reverse thread. This means that to tighten

The low pressure hose fitted on pre-2004 motorcaravans should be secured with pipe clips.

A spanner for securing regulators fitted with a cap nut is sold at motorcaravan accessory shops.

a coupling, the flanged nut on the regulator has to be turned in an anti-clockwise direction. A spanner is also needed and you can buy one at an accessory shop. Unfortunately it is sometimes too flimsy to undo a really tight connection – especially on a propane cylinder.

3) To connect to a propane cylinder the regulator is manufactured with a carefully machined threaded insert (male) which has to engage tightly in the receiving socket (female) of the cylinder. No washer is used and to achieve a leak-proof connection, there must be a close metal-to-metal register.

4) There are various types of butane coupling, namely:
   • A Calor screw-on butane regulator to suit 4.5kg cylinders – for which an open-ended spanner is needed.
   • A Calor clip-on butane regulator with ON/OFF control to suit 7kg and 15kg cylinders.
   • A Campingaz butane regulator with ON/OFF control to suit threaded couplings.

Disconnecting a 541 regulator from a 7kg Calor Gas butane cylinder

1

When the regulator switch is in the 6 o'clock position, the gas supply is turned ON.

2

To stop the gas flow, turn the switch to the 9 o'clock OFF position; wait for all gas flames to go out.

3

With the switch in the OFF position, the disconnecting lever can be lifted and the regulator removed.

4

The orange safety cap must always be replaced – even if the gas cylinder is empty.

Though not always easy to find, these adaptor connectors for Campingaz cylinders are sold at many motorcaravan accessory shops.

These three makes of fixed universal regulator have been made to comply with the new gas standards published in 2002.

5) Calor propane cylinders and Calor 4.5kg butane cylinders are the only type to have a hand wheel on the top for opening or closing the gas supply valve. The larger butane Calor cylinders just have a clip-on coupling and this means that a control tap has to form part of the regulator.

6) A Campingaz regulator is also made with a control tap. However, many people buy an adaptor from their dealer (which is made with a control tap) to pair up with their Calor 4.5kg butane cylinder-mounted regulator.

7. Check the accompanying photographs and Technical Tips panel for further information.

Permanent 'universal' regulators

The attempt to harmonise the gas systems fitted in motorcaravans throughout Europe was well-intentioned and two important changes were made. Firstly the operating pressures of appliances running on butane and propane had to be brought in line throughout EC countries. Secondly it was considered necessary for all new motorcaravans to be equipped with a permanently-mounted regulator which would a) serve the standardised appliances, and b) accept either butane or propane without need for adjustment.

Meeting the technical requirements was onerous, but 'universal' butane/propane regulators were designed and manufactured by CLESSE (for Comap UK), GOK (for Truma UK), and RECA (for the Cavagna Group). A motorcaravan manufacturer has to couple these directly to the copper or steel supply pipework and mount the regulator in a gas cylinder locker.

In addition to accepting butane and propane, the output from one of these regulators must comply with the standardised European pressure of 30mbar. In addition, gas appliances fitted in motorcaravans equipped with one of these regulators have to be manufactured and fitted with a data plate to confirm that they are built to operate at 30mbar. Retro-fitting a permanently mounted universal regulator to a pre-2004 model of motorcaravan is not approved by specialist gas engineers. The Calor Gas leaflet *New Requirements for LPG in Caravans,* distributed in 2003 states: 'The gas pressures of the new regulator and your existing installation are NOT compatible. You should continue to use the appropriate cylinder-mounted regulator. . .'

Motorcaravans built to the 2002 gas standards must have high pressure coupling hose; this is made in several colours but it's always appropriately stamped on the side.

Under the revised gas systems, the butane/propane regulator is fixed to a wall and a special high pressure connecting hose is needed to couple up with the cylinder.

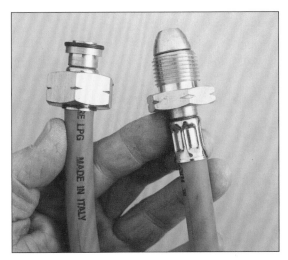

High-pressure hose cannot use standard hose clips; it has to use factory-fitted bonded or crimped couplings.

Under the most recent gas standards, connecting hoses are made to suit cylinders used in many European countries.

Using a mounted universal regulator

To use the latest system, an owner has to purchase a special coupling hose – sometimes called a 'pig-tail' connector – to link the chosen cylinder with the permanently-mounted regulator.

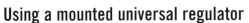

Technical Tips

Flexible hose:

· **This is made from a special composition to comply with BS EN specifications. It is *not* rubber.**
· **There should only be one flexible hose in the entire system – to couple up with the gas cylinder. Elsewhere, metal pipes have to be used and copper is the most common material.**
· **In a pre-2004 system, low pressure hose is pushed on to ribbed unions (nozzles), but the standards recommend that hose clips are used.**
· **Flexible hose deteriorates very little when kept in stock at a suppliers. In use, however, it is affected by LPG and will need changing periodically. It is also affected by ultra violet light when a cylinder is used in sunlight, such as on a gas barbecue.**
· **The hose bears a date to indicate when it left the factory; this may be a year of so *before* you purchase it from a dealer depending on stock turnover.**
· **It is important to note the *precise* date when a new length of hose is installed. The *Calor Gas Dealer Directory 1995* recommends that it is replaced at five-yearly intervals or more frequently if there's evidence of deterioration.**

Flexible gas hose is stamped with a date on the side which indicates when it was manufactured.

This has to convey gas coming from the cylinder at full pressure and is more expensive than the clipped length of low-pressure hose used in the previous system. A pig-tail connector comprises high pressure hose and bonded or crimped purpose-made couplings which are factory-fitted. A hose-clip system would ***not*** be acceptable. In addition, the new standards limit its length to 450mm (about 18in), although if cylinders are stowed on a pull-out tray, a hose up to a maximum length of 750mm (about 30in) is permitted.

These connectors are well-made but are quite costly. Versions are available to suit the cylinders sold in a number of European countries but there's still a need to buy adaptors to suit less popular cylinder fittings.

With this system you can obtain cylinders in countries you want to visit and then purchase the appropriate coupling hose. The only problem might

Unfortunately there are so many different cylinder couplings that adaptors will still occasionally be needed in post-2003 gas installations.

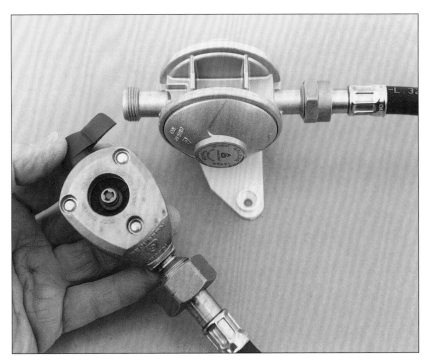

The weight of an empty Calor Gas cylinder is shown on the collar in pounds and ounces, which can be converted to kilograms by dividing by 2.2.

Once you know the weight of an empty cylinder, the amount of remaining gas can be confirmed by weighing it on some bathroom scales.

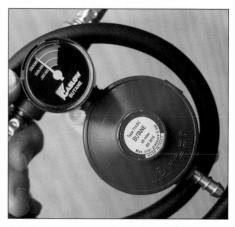

A Gaslow gauge can be used to assess the amount of gas in a cylinder – and it also indicates if there is a leak in the system.

arise if you want to visit a number of countries; you could start collecting a variety of different gas cylinders, together with suitable coupling hoses as you travel from place to place!

Cylinder state

Assessing the amount of gas remaining in a cylinder can be difficult. There are several devices intended to show how much gas is available as well as the following weighing procedure.

If using a Calor cylinder, you need to establish its 'tare' weight, which is its weight when empty; this is indicated on the aluminium collar below the valve. The information is expressed in lbs/ozs – if you prefer to work in kilograms, pounds have to be divided by 2.2. Then a part-used cylinder can be weighed on bathroom scales to establish by how much its weight exceeds the empty weight.

Alternatively, cylinder pressure can be monitored using a Gaslow gauge (this can also be used as a leak detector, as explained later).

To assess the condition of a cylinder using a Gaslow gauge, at least one appliance must be

in use. Taking into account the load imposed by the working appliance(s), a Gaslow gauge then indicates if the supply is in: a) a good state, b) mediocre condition, or c) approaching exhaustion. Earlier gauges used a needle which pointed to 'traffic light' segments on the dial; for example, the red section warned of a nearly empty cylinder. On the latest gauges it is the segment that moves, and to achieve even greater accuracy there are separate read-outs marked on the segments for use on 'cold days', 'cool days' and 'hot days'.

Changeover systems

Running out of gas is always inconvenient. Even if there's a back-up cylinder, the business of disconnecting the empty cylinder and coupling-up its replacement isn't pleasant in the dark, especially if it's raining. It's also a nuisance if a meal is being cooked or it's a severe winter night and you need to keep the heating on. This is why a changeover system is useful – especially one which is completely automatic.

Changeover products are available from Gaslow whose manual and automatic systems have been used in conjunction with transferable regulator systems for many years. Another product is the Truma Triomatic automatic changeover, which has a control panel mounted in the living quarters. This enables you to keep a close watch on the cylinders without having to go outside. There is also a defroster to ensure the Triomatic doesn't freeze.

Pipework and installation

Moving 'downstream' from the cylinder, regulator and flexible coupling hose, a gas system is built using rigid pipes – copper being the most popular material. The following points about a supply system should be noted:

To avoid a serious accident, neither the rigid gas supply system nor the connections to gas appliances should be modified, repaired or coupled-up by a non-qualified person. In the *Calor Caravan Check Scheme* booklet (May 1995

Some motorcaravanners have had an automatic changeover device such as the Truma Trionic fitted.

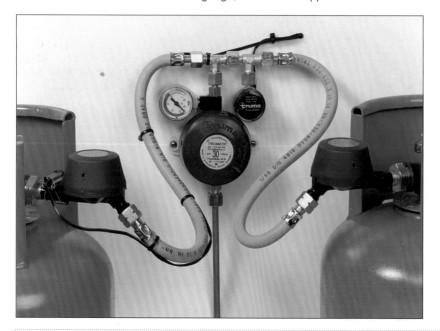

Compression fittings have three principal items: the component itself, a cap nut and an olive.

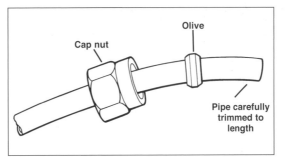

When connections are formed, the cap nut is fitted on the supply pipe first, followed by the olive. The pipe is then inserted into the coupling as far as the stop point and the cap nut tightened.

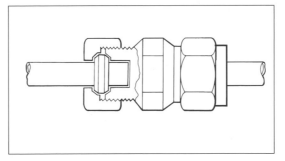

As a cap nut is tightened, the olive bears harder against the shoulder of the fitting and is squeezed inwards, gripping the gas pipe tightly.

Gas engineering qualifications

For some time it has been stated that work on gas connections, flues and supply systems should be undertaken only by a competent gas engineer. More recently, however, this prescription has been deemed too vague and some advisers insist that only a CORGI registered engineer tackles this kind of work. Others assert that the requirement is even more stringent and state that a CORGI qualified person must have successfully completed a course which embraces training in LPG installations in leisure vehicles. This caveat is added because some CORGI registered engineers are only trained to deal with domestic household installations. NOTE: *CORGI stands for Council for Registered Gas Installers. Registration is a requirement for those who install and maintain LPG installations as laid down in the Gas Safety (Installation & Use) Regulations 1994.*

edition) it states: *'Gas installation is an expert's job and by law must only be undertaken by an experienced gas fitter.'* A CORGI registered engineer fulfils this requirement.

This principle is endorsed here and the following technical descriptions are provided for information only. In practice, the task of connecting up copper gas pipe using a proprietary pressure fitting is not difficult – particularly for anyone familiar with similar pressure fittings used in domestic plumbing; but an inexperienced person will not know how much to tighten a coupling to achieve a leak-free joint. Over-tightening can deform the pipe and a leak is inevitable – as it is if the coupling is under-tightened. It's a job to leave to a qualified LPG fitter.

Copper pipe for gas systems is made in the following sizes:

5mm (3/16in) outside diameter (OD) = feed to a gas lamp as used in historic models.
6mm (1/4in) OD = feed to many types of appliance (such as the fridge).
8mm/10mm (5/16in) OD = main trunk feed in a

motorcaravan; feed for space heating appliances.
NOTE: *Some fittings designed for metric pipes will not fit imperial pipes.*

Pressure couplings are made to suit specific pipe diameters and there are reducing fittings because a branch supply normally uses a narrower diameter pipe than the main trunk-way. The accompanying diagram shows the key components such as the 'olive' and the 'cap nut'. *The Dealer Information Booklet*, published by Calor Gas, points out that jointing compound should not be used. Jointing compound is only intended to seal thread-to-thread couplings.

Bending copper gas pipe is often done by hand; but for more precise work, especially when forming a tight bend, a pipe bending tool is used. This supports the walls of the pipe and prevents kinking. It follows the same principle of operation as a pipe bender used for domestic copper water pipes.

As regards the final coupling to appliances, this often employs a thread-to-thread union rather than

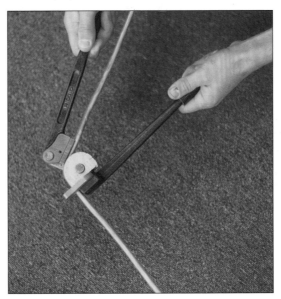

Bending copper gas pipe can be done by hand; but a pipe-bending tool is used for more precise work, especially when forming acute angles.

In a modern installation, isolation valves are fitted so that individual gas appliances can be controlled separately.

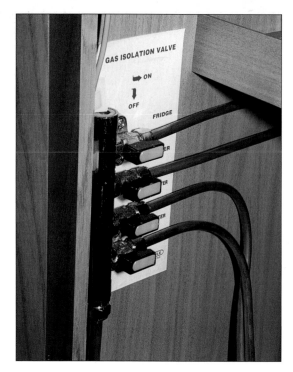

a compression fitting. In this instance, a special LPG jointing paste is required to seal the threads; Calortite is one of the products used.

In modern installations, it is also necessary for individual appliances to be controlled by a separate isolation valve. If an oven were to develop a fault on holiday, for example, the supply to this appliance could be completely shut off while other appliances remain in use.

Leak Detection

Whereas work on a gas supply system should not be undertaken by a DIY owner, exercising vigilance over the system's integrity is important. For example, a leak detection device can be fitted. In addition, if you want reassurance that couplings are sound, there is no reason why you shouldn't check them using a leak detection liquid.

To carry out this procedure, firstly make sure that the system is switched on at the cylinder

and all appliances are off. Cigarettes and naked flames should be extinguished. Then smear all couplings with either a proprietary product or diluted washing-up fluid. Once applied, check for bubbles – which indicate a leak. It is usual to apply the mixture with a small brush and to hold your fingers around the joint to prevent the fluid running away. If you find a leak, switch the system off at once and get the coupling tightened or replaced by a gas fitter.

A more convenient way to monitor a system is to fit a Gaslow gauge at the gas supply cylinder. These products were mentioned earlier because they are also used to show the pressure in a cylinder. The test procedure is as follows:

- Turn off *all* gas appliances.
- Turn *on* the gas supply cylinder; the gauge should show a green segment.
- Turn *off* the gas supply at the cylinder.
- Provided there is no leak, gas will be held in the supply pipes and the gauge will continue to show the green segment.
- Using a standard Gaslow product, if the gauge remains green for at least a minute, the system is considered sound; over a longer period, the gauge will eventually return to the red sector.

Another way to keep a long-term check is to have an Alde leak detector fitted into the supply line by a gas fitter. This incorporates a small glass sighting chamber filled with a glycol liquid. To conduct the test, switch the gas supply on and turn all appliances off. When a red test button on the top of the detector is depressed, a regular flow of bubbles in the sighting chamber gives away the fact that gas is escaping somewhere in the system.

Different again are leak detectors that give an audible warning when a sensor detects gas. This type of device *could* be fitted by a careful DIY owner. For instance, the First Alert electronic alarm warns of a leak using a piercing 85dB siren. The unit has to be connected to a 12V DC supply and should be fixed to a secure base in an appropriate location. Recognising that LPG is *heavier* than air, it needs fitting low down.

An Alde leak detector can be installed in the supply line – bubbles in the sighting glass indicate the passage of gas.

The First Alert gas alarm emits a loud sound when the smell of gas is detected – and it is an easy product to fit.

Cooking appliances

All motorcaravans are fitted with a hob, and larger vehicles often have an oven as well. Overall a kitchen with its accompanying work tops, sink and drainer forms a prominent feature. Only in respect of rubbish disposal are most British manufacturers lacking, being extraordinarily poor in providing a bin for kitchen waste. Continental manufacturers seldom make this mistake.

Not that European motorhomes are perfect. On the contrary, many luxury vehicles – including top-notch German A-Class models – often have a disappointingly small kitchen. Apparently many owners from mainland Europe prefer to eat out instead. Equally, very few motorcaravans imported from the Continent feature a grill, since toast is seldom on the menu. Importers often fit these appliances later in order to make a kitchen more acceptable to the British public.

And it doesn't end there. In this country, the cooker hobs fitted since the early 1990s are usually equipped with an electronic spark igniter on each burner. Curiously, many German-designed hobs have no ignition facility at all. It seems perverse having to use a hand igniter or matches in an expensive motorhome!

On another topic, since 1994 it has been mandatory to have a flame failure device (sometimes called a 'flame supervision device') fitted to all the gas burners. If a burner blows out, the device immediately cuts off its supply. You will see the small bi-metallic probe that projects into the flame of the burner; when this is hot, an electric current is generated. The current then flows to an electromagnetic gas valve that stays open all the time the probe is hot. However, as soon as the flame is extinguished, current is no longer produced; the electromagnet in the gas valve fails and a small spring closes off the supply.

With this system, when you want to light a burner, the spring has to be compressed to open the gas valve. This is done by pushing in the

control knob and holding it down until the newly lit flame has made the probe hot again. When these systems fail, it is often because the general vibration in a motorcaravan has caused a break in the electrical connections between the probe assembly and the electromagnet in the gas control. Re-tightening the connections on both ends of the metal linking conductor often solves this problem.

Also of interest is the fact that modern appliances now have to bear the CE approval mark which confirms that a product has passed requisite safety testing procedures. They also have to operate on both butane and propane at the specified pressures mentioned earlier.

Finally, a few motorcaravans have one burner on the hob which operates on mains electricity. That can provide a useful back-up if the gas runs out. On the other hand, not everyone wants to stay exclusively on sites which offer mains supplies.

Many British motorcaravans are equipped with a full cooker comprising a hob, a grill and an oven.

Since 1994, gas appliance manufacturers have fitted a flame failure device (FFD) to each hob burner.

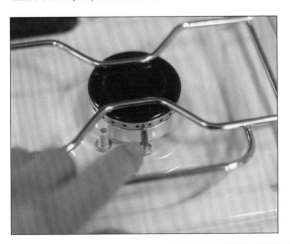

Technical tip

- Apart from cleaning, there are no servicing tasks on cookers that an owner can carry out.

- Like the supply system, cooking appliances must be checked by a qualified gas engineer in accordance with the manufacturer's instructions. This is one of the tasks that should come within an annual habitation service check.

- Ventilation is essential in a kitchen and a professional manufacturer will have provided permanent vents. These are needed to provide oxygen for combustion and also to provide an escape for the products of combustion. Additionally the ventilators help with the removal of steam which leads to condensation.

- A good improvement project is to fit a fan-assisted cooker hood over a hob. The model manufactured by Dometic helps to extract steam by venting it to the outside.

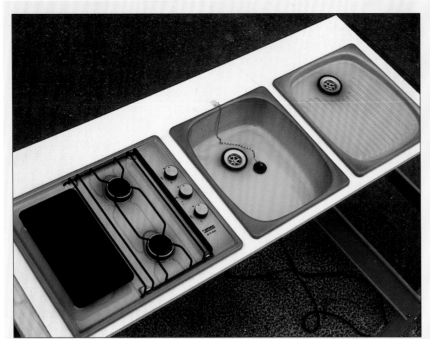

In this DIY project, the kitchen units were first fitted to a plastic laminated board, then installed into the new kitchen as a entire module.

Owner improvement work

Constructing a kitchen and fitting appliances is tackled by many DIY builders. Needless to say, the support structures have to be sound because units take a lot of buffeting when driving on bumpy roads; but meeting this requirement is not a difficult job for a good joiner.

The equipment manufacturers' instructions must be strictly followed. Clearances are one of several important factors. There must be plenty of space between a hob, for example, and combustible surfaces. And don't forget that a frying pan of bacon has a nasty habit of spitting. Even motorcaravan manufacturers sometimes fit curtains which are too close for comfort.

Many self-builders also install heating appliances and the manufacturers' instructions are usually very clear, with templates to help. Some tasks like coupling up heating ducting are really quite straightforward.

But there is one thing that an unqualified person mustn't do, and that is to make the gas connections. This is a job that should be entrusted to a competent gas engineer. For further guidance check the earlier panel on Gas Engineering Qualifications.

Space heating appliances

The open burner gas fire is no longer used in motorcaravans for safety reasons. Apart from the risk of something falling on to the exposed flames, the system takes oxygen from the living space. Fumes are discharged into the living area as well, which in extreme cases means there could be a risk of carbon monoxide poisoning.

That is why the appliances are now referred to as 'space heaters' rather than 'fires' and they have to be 'room sealed'. This means the burners are housed in a compartment completely sealed from the living area. Combustion air is drawn directly

into this sealed enclosure from outside and in a similar way, exhaust gases are subsequently returned via a flue.

Heat generated in this combustion chamber then has to be directed into the living area. This is achieved by directing the hot air through a heat exchanger which is designed to release its heat as efficiently as possible. Many heat exchangers are thus manufactured with moulded fins – rather like the fins on an air-cooled motorcycle engine.

In other words it's the heat exchanger which warms the living space rather than the gas flames. To assist in the distribution of heat, many appliances also have a fan which drives the

The heat exchanger in a room-sealed appliance usually has fins moulded on its casing to release its heat efficiently.

This display using a Truma room-sealed space heater shows how both the combustion air intake and the exhaust flue are ducted directly to the outside.

warmed air along a network of ducts. Outlets in the ducting then ensure that heat is released at key points. Rooms normally closed off from the main living spaces, such as the shower cubicle, thus receive a share of the warm air coming from a space heater.

Many older motorcaravans were fitted with a wall-mounted Carver space heater matched with the 12V Fanmaster air distribution system. The Fanmaster has a 1.5 amp, 18 watt motor fused at 5 amps.

In addition, a Fanmaster incorporates a mains-operated electrical element that draws 8 amps at 2kW; in other words the product does more than distribute warm air. It also warms the air using independent integral electric elements. This system produces heat at manually switchable output levels from 0.1 to 2kW. The temperature is regulated using a wall-mounted controller and it's important to note that gas and electrical heating should not be operated at the same time.

Carver products were deservedly popular but Truma subsequently purchased the gas appliance division in Autumn 1999 and products like the Fanmaster were discontinued. However, Truma undertook to sell spare parts for most of Carver's products for several years beyond that date.

The operation of the Truma Ultraheat is very similar to the Carver products, although this appliance can operate on gas and its 230V element simultaneously. A further distinction is that the 230V element is bolted directly to the heat exchanger instead of being part of the fan on the rear of the casing. Its output is:

• 500, 1000 or 2000w from the electric element
• 3.4kW from the gas burner
• 5.0kW from the combined systems.

For quick warm-up both gas and electric systems can be used; when the heater reaches 2kW the electric heating element is switched off automatically. This is a safety feature of the Ultraheat system. However, Truma points out that

to enjoy the full benefit of the 230V option, you need to stay on a site where the hook-up offers a minimum supply of 10 amps – which is quite substantial.

Many practical owners add a ducting system to their motorcaravans and, using Truma components, this task can be fairly straightforward. Hiding the ducting discreetly is the main challenge, although it is possible to obtain specially reinforced sections to take routeways beneath the floor without too much loss of heat.

Large motorcaravans sometimes have wet systems which use radiators. The 3000 Compact central heating system from Alde, for example, has been installed in Buccaneer motorcaravans. This motorcaravan also incorporates the Alde 2968 engine heat exchanger which operates in conjunction with a Fiat engine's heating system.

In small motorcaravans, compact heaters are more suitable. These are completely enclosed (apart from the air intake, air distribution outlet and flue) and an integral fan distributes the warm air. One great benefit of these products is that they can be mounted in lockers and small wardrobes.

Models made by Truma are long-established and operate with remarkable efficiency. Ignition is electronic and in spite of its compact size, the heat output from a Trumatic E2400 model is a noteworthy 2.4kW. Heat from the unit is transmitted through ducting and, like all room-sealed heaters, it can be left on all night. Output is thermostatically controlled to ensure that warmth remains at a consistent level.

Similar products include the Propex unit and the Carver P4 compact blown air unit. The P4 is a self-contained unit featuring a low profile side wall flue. With 1.2kW or 2.2kW output settings, the specification includes automatic ignition, thermostatic control, and operation on either butane or propane. However, it is no longer available and spare parts will be increasingly difficult to obtain.

The control panel of a Truma Ultraheat space heater offers three output levels when the 230V mains option is switched on, though ideally this requires at least a 10 amp supply.

Popular for many years, the Truma E-series blown air heaters incorporate a balanced flue/air intake and their compact size means they can be fitted in very small spaces.

Heating appliances

- There are no servicing tasks on gas heating appliances that an owner should attempt to carry out.
- Space and water heating appliances must be checked by a qualified gas engineer in accordance with the manufacturer's instructions – a task which should be carried out as part of an annual habitation service check.
- In addition to checking an appliance, its flue will also be given a safety and efficiency check.
- Ensure that you are given a written and dated account of the servicing work that has been completed.
- Space heaters usually have an automatic cut-out which comes into operation if they overheat. This can occur if all the outlet ducts are closed off or accidentally obstructed. However, on a Carver Fanmaster there's a re-set button which owners can activate themselves. Firstly you wait for the appliance to cool down, then open all the outlets and disconnect the mains supply at your consumer unit. Then you re-set the trip button situated on the side of the fan casing, bearing in mind that in some motorcaravans access to this part of the unit isn't easy. Then switch the mains supply back on. Truma products have similar overheat safety devices.
- Many space heaters used to have a piezo ignition system where you depress a button to create a spark at the burner. Today, electronic ignition systems have taken over and there's usually a wall switch which triggers the spark. Regarding compact heaters, the Truma E-series has employed electronic ignition since the 1980s.
- Most ducted systems have two main branches serving opposite ends of a motorhome. However, many owners do not realise that if there's an imbalance in the heat flowing down these branches, the heat distribution can be adjusted using the control lever on the back of a wall-mounted appliance.

The Truma Ultrastore water heater is used in many motorcaravans and it can normally be run on both gas and mains electricity.

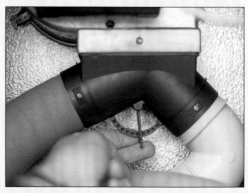

If an overheat situation arises on a Carver Fanmaster, the system shuts down. Later the reset button needs activating.

On some of the space heaters from Carver and Truma, the distribution of warm air released into the ducts can be easily adjusted by means of a control lever.

Servicing and safety check

Like cooking appliances, space heaters need an annual safety check and service. This is not something the owner can tackle.

Several tasks need to be carried out and one is to check the shape of the gas flames. A problem in motorcaravans is that there are periods when gas appliances might not be used for an extended spell. This is when dust and cobwebs can accumulate. Even a spider can upset the operation of a gas appliance; filaments of a web across a pilot light can distort the shape of the flame and this sometimes prevents the main burner from igniting.

It's the same with a flue. Even a spider's web spun across a flue at the roof outlet can sufficiently upset the exhaust efficiency to prevent a space heater switching from pilot to main burner. So general cleaning is one of the elements of servicing and the charge for this is modest.

Water heating appliances

Availability of hot water is a great asset and few motorcaravans are built without the inclusion of a water heater. There are two main types:

1) Storage water heaters (Carver Cascade, Rapide GE, Maxol Malaga, Truma Ultrastore).

2) Water heaters integrated with a space heater (Trumatic C range, Atwood Confort 3, Alde 3000 Compact).

Note:
- *American manufacturer Atwood ceased marketing products in Europe in 1997. Spares are now difficult to obtain.*
- *The National Caravan Council (NCC) has recommended that old instantaneous water heaters with exposed burners should be replaced by an approved storage heater.*

Storage water heaters

These appliances are usually mounted inconspicuously in a cupboard and operated from a remote control panel. Their balanced flue is discreet, too, and recent models incorporate a mains heating element either to take the place of the gas burner or to supplement it when you want to speed up heating time.

Integrated space and water heaters

Combined heaters are often fitted in larger vehicles. For instance the Alde 3000 with its radiator system was fitted in Buccaneer's 1998 models. The Atwood Confort C was fitted to the Murvi Morello in 1996 and 1997 models.

The Trumatic C Combi heater has been fitted in several Swift coachbuilt models such as the 2002 Gazelle F63 High. All the operating functions of this sophisticated appliance are monitored electronically. The combined space and water heater is also fitted with a release valve which empties the water heater reservoir automatically when air temperature drops to 2°C, although this can be over-ridden when necessary.

Whereas the water heater runs on both gas and mains electricity, some of the Combi systems do not offer alternative 230V space heating. Some owners find this out too late, with considerable dismay. Normally it's an optional extra which can only be specified at the time of purchase.

Owner care

It is important that a water heater is cleaned and checked as part of an annual habitation service. Together with other gas-operated appliances, servicing and repair work fall outside the scope of DIY endeavour. Draining-down work, however, is different.

Frost can seriously damage a water heater so steps have to be taken if you do not use your motorcaravan for extended periods in the winter.

There are two ways to protect the system from frost. One is to drain down the entire system and leave it empty until the cold weather is over. The other is to fill the water system with a purpose-formulated non-poisonous anti-freeze – but check first that your appliance manufacturer approves this.

Prior to a lay-up period, filling a water system with special anti-freeze is seen as a seasonal

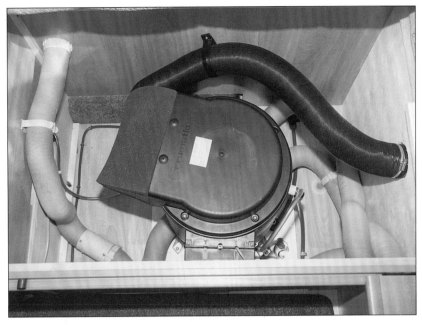

task in the United States and an American winterising product called 'WinterBan' is available in the UK under the Camco accessory range and is available from Recreational Vehicle (RV) specialists such as ABP Leisure. You merely have to pump the recommended quantity of this fluid into the system and to leave it there until you are ready to use your motorcaravan again.

The other option of draining down a system is described in the manufacturers' literature. With a Truma Ultrastore the instructions are:

1) Switch off the water pump.
2) Open all taps; in the case of lever types, make sure the lever is raised and left in its central position.
3) Open the appliance's safety drain valve and leave in the vertical position.
4) Water now drains to the outside; be careful if it is still hot.

Early Carver Cascade heaters may take an hour or more to drain completely. Later models have an air release screw on the top left of the external frame to speed up the process.

Draining a Carver Cascade water heater is easy, although on older models it takes a long time to release all the water.

The Trumatic C Combi heater is fitted in many large coachbuilt motorcaravans; however, the space heating facility on some models works only on gas.

Diesel-fuelled heating systems

Eberspacher heating systems used in boats and long distance lorries have recently been re-engineered for motorcaravans. Murvi helped with this development work and an Eberspacher system was shown on a Murvi motorcaravan at the annual Earl's Court Exhibition in 1998. Since then it has become the preferred choice of heating by most people ordering a Murvi. Other manufacturers fitting Eberspacher products include Autocruise CH, Auto-Sleepers and Romahome.

Eberspacher's hydronic system provides both space and water heating. To explain how it works, it's helpful to liken the product to the heating system fitted in a car. Water heated by the engine is diverted to a small radiator mounted behind the dashboard and fitted with a fan. When the driver operates the blower switch, the fan pushes air through the small radiator (often called a heater matrix) and then directs it to screen outlets, face vents or footwell outlets, according to requirements.

In a hydronic system, it's the same idea except that additional pipes take engine-heated water to similar fan-operated radiators which heat the living area. However, another flow and return pipe is directed to a small copper cylinder, storing water for domestic use. Hot water from the engine is passed through a coiled pipe running down the centre of the cylinder, thus heating the domestic water around the coil. Many of us have a similar water-heating cylinder in our homes – usually fitted in an airing cupboard. The two gallons of water in an Eberspacher cylinder become extremely hot and a blender valve is fitted to mix cold water into the supply automatically.

From the description so far, you will note that this system can operate only when the engine is running. In fact you don't have to drive far before the domestic water in a motorcaravan is hot; equally, the living area can be heated via the additional heater matrix units while you are driving.

However, it stands to reason that the heating operation described must cease as soon as the engine is switched off. So an Eberspacher Hydronic installation includes a small oil (or petrol) fuelled heater which is mounted under the floor or low down in the engine compartment. This is smaller than a shoe box and its fuel is drawn via a small pipe which has been connected into the vehicle's fuel tank. You switch this unit on when required and it performs the same heating functions as the engine.

A digital control panel provides a wide range of options. This can be programmed so that the heating comes on automatically for a selected period of time, and it can do this on up to three occasions during a 24-hour period and on any chosen day(s) of the week. This rolling operating timetable is very helpful when a vehicle is laid-up in winter.

In the summer, you can disregard the space heating function altogether and just select the water heating option. Incidentally, although water heating is normally achieved through the engine or the diesel heater, the hot water cylinder also has a 230V immersion heater which can be wired into your mains system.

An Eberspacher installation can also be linked up with a base vehicle's original cab and screen heater, thus augmenting the heat output from the other Eberspacher heater outlets in the living area. That is useful in motorcaravans whose cab forms part of the living space but there is also a benefit from coupling-in the screen vents. It means you can get the system to defrost the screen in advance of a departure time and you can also select an engine pre-heat programme for easy starting.

To derive the full benefit from these many facilities, a remote control unit can be fitted and if you leave the fob by your bed, you can switch on the heating whenever you want during the night. Equally, if you park your motorcaravan outside your home, the remote control is powerful enough to activate the heating and the screen defrost facility from inside the house – even while you're having breakfast.

The control facilities are unusually versatile, but no less important is the low fuel consumption of these heating systems. Even with the largest 5kW hydronic heater working with maximum fan speed and heat demand, the consumption is listed as a frugal 0.62 litres of diesel an hour. Gas is then only needed in a motorcaravan for cooking and refrigeration. However, the weight saving on gas cylinders has to be offset against extra battery weight, as a leisure battery with a higher than usual Ah is needed to run the heater matrix fans.

It is also appropriate to point out that an externally fitted hydronic oil-fired heater is considerably noisier in operation than a gas appliance. In fact it could be regarded as unreasonably noisy by anyone sleeping in a small tent on a neighbouring pitch. However, improved silencers are being developed.

In addition to Eberspacher's hydronic 4kW and 5kW water and space heaters, the company also supplies compact oil-fired warm-air heaters which are fitted by several manufacturers including Romahome and Auto-Sleepers. These are referred to as Airtronic units; there are 2.2kW and 4.0kW output versions currently available, and they can be discreetly installed in a blanket locker. They provide precise temperature control and, again, a digital timer offers seven-day programming possibilities.

Eberspacher leads the diesel and petrol motorhome heating developments in Britain, although other manufacturers also work in this field. For instance, Webasto products are used in several German motorcaravans. In addition, an efficient space heater manufactured in Japan and used in small boats, is being promoted at motorcaravan shows.

So whereas gas heating has much to commend it, diesel and petrol systems are now providing motorcaravanners with an intriguing alternative.

One or more compact radiators fitted with a fan – similar to those mounted in a car's dashboard – will be installed in the living area of the motorcaravan.

The hydronic system heats domestic water stored in an insulated two-gallon copper cylinder (this also includes a 230V immersion heater).

This compact diesel-fueled heating unit is mounted low-down in the engine compartment or underneath the floor, and takes over the task of providing heat when the vehicle engine is off.

A digital control panel gives complete control over an Eberspacher system and its seven-day timer can be programmed to run the system automatically.

Oil-fired heating hydronic 12V system

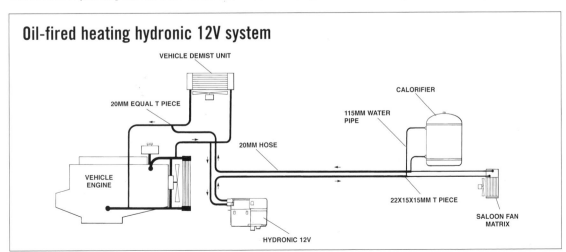

Water supply and waste systems

Motorcaravans have two separate water systems. One is concerned with the supply of fresh water: the other removes waste water from a sink, wash basin or shower tray. Their operational success depends on several components.

Water systems in motorcaravans vary in a number of ways. The type of pump, the taps, the refilling arrangement, the filter system and the waste water facility all differ from model to model.

The supply system

Even the arrangements for supplying fresh water and collecting the waste can vary. Most motorcaravans have fixed water tanks, but a few models use portable receptacles instead.

Portable containers

It's not unusual to find camper vans built without fixed water tanks simply because they take up too much space. This is particularly true in respect of micro-van conversions and adapted multi-purpose vehicles. Instead, portable water containers are used – one for fresh water and one for waste. Examples of models using this system include conversions from Reimo, la strada and Wheelhome.

In a similar way, a few motorcaravanners adopt

Some van conversions, like this model from la strada, are equipped with portable water containers rather than fixed tanks.

the system used by owners of touring caravans in which fresh and waste water containers are placed on the ground alongside the van. The use of portable containers in this manner certainly makes sense on sites which lack a service point. Indeed it's the surprising lack of good motorcaravan service points on sites at home and abroad, which prompts many owners of motorcaravans fitted with on-board tanks to carry a length of hose, a plastic water container and a bucket. Poor access to a tap often makes it necessary to top up a tank from a portable container; equally a full waste water tank may have to be emptied in stages, using the bucket.

On-board water tanks

These problems aside, the majority of motorcaravans are built with on-board tanks – one for fresh water, and the other for waste. Incidentally the word 'waste' in this context refers to water discharged from a sink or wash basin. Some people refer to it as 'grey water'. Only large American motorhomes have a special holding tank for sewage as well, and that's often described as 'black water'.

With regard to tank location, there are two options: either to mount the tanks below the floor, or to install them inside. Some manufacturers, such as Auto-Sleepers, usually mount both tanks under the floor in order not to take up internal space. But there's a disadvantage with this arrangement. In winter, the water in externally fitted pipes and tanks soon freezes and this has severe implications if you want to use your motorcaravan during the colder times of the year.

It is for this reason that many motorcaravans have a fresh water tank mounted internally. The panel opposite also describes a good way for dealing with waste water in freezing temperatures.

Fortunately, all is not lost if your motorcaravan has an under-floor tank system. Some owners

The water tanks on many motorcaravans are mounted under the floor, which can lead to problems in freezing weather.

If you intend motorcaravanning in the winter, look for a model which has a fresh water tank installed inside the living area.

rig up an alternative supply in which fresh water is drawn from a portable container placed in the shower tray. A submersible pump is lowered into this container and an alternative connection is made to feed water into the normal supply pipe. It is an involved modification and Carver used to sell a special winterising kit before the Company's withdrawal from the motorcaravan market. However, a specialist like Caravan Accessories Kenilworth (CAK) can supply all the components needed to make this kind of modification. Alternatively, CAK also supplies electric immersion heaters for fitting inside underfloor tanks.

Moving to the matter of emptying, the water level in waste and fresh water tanks needs checking and it's customary to have a gauge fitted in the living area as shown on page 59. In practice, a system fitted inside a waste tank can sometimes get upset by water-borne food particles which affect its reliability. However, it is also possible to install a waste tank fitted with sensor studs instead of long probes, as shown in the accompanying photograph.

If a motorcaravan waste tank isn't fitted with a level indicator, you need to adopt the discipline of emptying it every time you add fresh water. Then it cannot get over-full.

On the subject of emptying waste tanks, water must be emptied into a purpose-made gully or inspection chamber. Emptying on to a grass verge is unacceptable. However, there's no doubt that

Some water tanks are fitted with sensor studs which send a reading to a water level display panel.

Tanks and frost

Freezing tanks can make life very difficult in winter and not many motorcaravans have a heated double floor system as described in Chapter 4. However, if an exposed under-floor fresh water tank freezes, at least it is possible to bring in water using a kettle, saucepans, plastic bottles or a portable container. In contrast, if a waste container and its linking pipes freeze, a situation is reached where waste water cannot be released from the sink, washbasin or shower tray, which is rather more inconvenient.

To prevent water freezing in a waste tank, it is better to leave its drain outlet open, so that discharged water runs straight through it and into a bucket or portable waste water container. These will need to be emptied regularly but at least the tank itself should remain clear.

Mindful of these problems, the Nova from la strada is built with two waste tanks of roughly half normal size. One is mounted in the warm interior; the other is mounted underneath. A controlling isolation tap keeps them either connected or separate. This is how it works:

In summer the isolation tap is kept open and both tanks receive waste water. However, in winter, the tap is closed. This means that waste water flows to the interior tank, which benefits from heat in the living space and doesn't freeze. The outside tank – which would be likely to freeze – remains empty. When the interior tank needs emptying, the isolation tap is opened together with the main release tap and water discharges straight through the outer tank into the emptying facility. The isolation tap is then closed once again, leaving the under-floor tank empty.

Another strategy adopted by several manufacturers, such as Auto-Trail, is to wrap externally mounted tanks in a silver 'insulating blanket'. This certainly delays freezing, but in really cold weather the contents will eventually succumb to low temperatures. That's when an insulating blanket becomes a disadvantage. When external temperatures eventually rise, the insulating material hinders the thawing of water inside the clad tank.

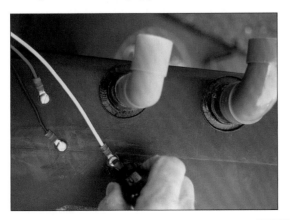

the availability and quality of motorcaravan service points in Britain and the rest of Europe is not as good as it ought to be.

Waste water disposal facilities are found on well-equipped sites like this one at Crystal Palace.

On this self-built motorcaravan, a deep water trap under the sink ensures that smells from the waste tank cannot enter the living space.

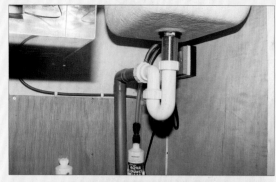

Welded outlets can be mounted closer to the bottom of a tank than fittings which are secured with plastic lock nuts.

To empty this tank completely, the drain-down pipe is coupled into a low level portion that has been specially moulded in the tank.

A good tank will be manufactured with an inspection and cleaning port.

Letters to magazines reveal that many motorcaravanners are inconvenienced by unpleasant drain odours. These occur when smells from stale water in the waste tank enter the living space via sink, wash basin or shower tray outlets. This is usually attributable to a poorly designed system.

After all, the problem doesn't happen at home because under sinks, baths, or in the bottom of a toilet pan, there are deep water traps. The water held in the trap creates a barrier which prevents smells from sewer pipes getting into our houses.

Motorcaravans built by the author have similar deep water traps together with 30mm (1.25in) domestic waste pipe. It is an inexpensive arrangement which was also used in Vanroyce touring caravans; what a pity that motorcaravan manufacturers seldom follow this example. Smells do not reach the living area and the wide bore pipe ensures that water runs out of a sink far faster than it does when a narrow bore ribbed hose is fitted. But why are there smells in the first place?

The problem is usually caused by a poorly designed waste water tank. It occurs, for example, if the emptying outlet is formed using a 'nutted' connector instead of an outlet nozzle which has been 'plastic welded' to the tank. The trouble with outlets held by nuts is that they cannot be fitted as close to the bottom of a tank's side wall as a welded outlet. This means that a tank which an owner believes to be empty is really retaining an inch or more of water in the bottom. What's more, this water often holds rotting food particles which have been flushed down the kitchen sink. That's where most of the smells originate.

It was pleasing, therefore, to see that in 2002 some manufacturers, such as Auto-Sleepers, started fitting tanks built with a moulded low point in the tank design. In addition, CAK has also found a way to release residual water if your tank has a red cleaning cap on the underside. This represents the lowest part of a waste tank and CAK supplies fittings which can be coupled into a hole drilled in this red cap. The revised waste outlet, thus formed, is now at the lowest point and it takes the place of the original one.

Sadly, some manufacturers cut cost by fitting tanks which don't have a cleaning port and screw lid on the underside. If intolerable smells arise from one of these waste tanks, the only answer is to fit a better-designed tank in its place.

Installing tanks

An experienced DIY enthusiast is unlikely to find the installation of a replacement water tank particularly difficult. It's an awkward exercise if you cannot elevate a vehicle, but apart from the inconvenience of wriggling around underneath, the task isn't technically challenging. Tanks are sold by Amber Plastics, CAK and Fiamma. In fact, in CAK's 'must-have' catalogue, there are illustrations of 156 tanks in different shapes and sizes, all of which are made at the Warwickshire factory.

When placing an order it is advisable to specify the inclusion of a large port with screw cap for cleaning the inside. Several other associated components will also be needed, such as outlet unions, couplings, pipe, stop cocks and level gauges – all listed in the CAK catalogue.

Water level gauges are also distributed by Plug-In-Systems and Zig, whose products are commonly seen in British-built models. The light-emitting diode indicator fitted in Murvi motorcaravans is supplied by Calira of Germany.

Taking the Plug-In-Systems product as an example, the fitting leaflet shows clearly what is involved. Probes from the sender unit come in several lengths to suit different tank depths and these can be cut to meet your requirements. Alternatively a tank ordered from CAK can be fitted with stainless steel bolts which have to be coupled up to an LED 12V gauge.

As a final warning, before tackling a tank installation project, always spend time reflecting on the merits of different locations. Water is heavy stuff: a litre weighs 1kg (2.2lbs), or if you prefer imperial measures, a gallon weighs 10lbs; so a large container inappropriately located isn't going to help the rear axle loading limit.

Many motorcaravanners fill their tanks to the brim prior to leaving a site and this obviously affects the payload. On the other hand, a part-

filled tank might affect the braking. It's true that some tanks feature a rudimentary baffle in their moulding, but a sudden surge of water might still hinder braking efficiency if you have to carry out an emergency stop.

This is one of the many tank kits manufactured by CAK of Kenilworth.

Comparing tank systems

Few people buying a motorcaravan enquire about the tank system, and many find later that it isn't as good as it might be. So check:

■ The emptying procedure. Are the outlet and release cock easy to reach? Is there a flexible drain-down hose retained with unsatisfactory clips? Several models are poor in this respect.

■ Is the fresh tank easy to fill when you cannot drive close to a site tap? Would you need a funnel when topping up with a portable container? To avoid heavy lifting, some models (such as recent Swift KonTiki coachbuilts) have a 12V socket alongside the filling point to accept a 12V Whale submersible pump. This is lowered into a portable container which can be left on the ground as shown alongside.

Some motorcaravans are fitted with poorly designed and insecure drain-down hoses such as this.

This Swift motorcaravan has a 12V socket to run a submersible pump.

Here the pump is lowered into a portable water container.

The feed hose is inserted into the fresh water inlet to top-up the tank.

At high-class British sites, you will often find full service pitches which provide an individual tap and emptying point.

Direct supply and waste provision

In America, many 'camping grounds' offer visitors a direct link between their 'recreational vehicle' (RV) and the site's drainage and supply facilities. On pitches offering this opportunity, fresh water, waste water and sewage service points are coupled up to the vehicle's holding tanks using purpose-designed connectors.

This provision is seldom seen in Britain, although 'Superpitch' points offering this facility have been installed on a number of sites for several years. However, British motorcaravans are not usually fitted with Superpitch connectors. Instead, the trend here is to offer 'full service pitches'. On these pitches, the user has a personal water tap and an emptying point for basin/sink (but not toilet) waste. This is especially helpful for the touring caravanner who can dispense with a portable water container and use a Whale Aquasource instead. A direct coupling system features a pressure reducer so that a permanently

The inside surface of this convoluted waste pipe has a smooth lining to improve the flow of water.

plumbed-in connection can be made with the tap – which is left on all the time. However, motorcaravans usually have a built-in fresh water tank and you cannot adopt this arrangement without modifying the system and by-passing the tank. Nevertheless, as long as you carry a short length of hose, you can top up your tank in the usual way without having to drive the van to the service area. Equally, you might be able to rig up a coupling pipe from the waste tank's outlet in order to release water directly into the gully.

Pipework

In some respects, the general plumbing in many motorcaravans is surprisingly disappointing. Some manufacturers have made improvements in the last few years but many owners will share the author's misgivings reported here.

Waste water systems

It is disappointing to find that in many motorcaravans, water empties from a sink or washbasin at a decidedly slow rate. The narrow bore of the pipe is partly to blame for this and sometimes there are up-turns which slow the flow.

If that isn't bad enough, some manufacturers fit a convoluted plastic pipe which has ridges around it. On the better versions of this pipe, there's a smooth surface lining on the inside to enhance the flow rate. But many manufacturers have been fitting a cheaper convoluted pipe which has ridges on the inside as well. On gentle gradients, these ridges trap food particles which soon stagnate. Add to this the lack of a deep-seal water trap under a motorcaravan sink, and you can see another reason why smells often seep into the living quarters. The panel opposite shows how to solve this problem.

Fresh water systems

Like waste systems, many fresh water supply systems are equally disappointing. For instance, flexible hose and clip systems are still fitted in a surprising number of motorcaravans.

The trouble with flexible hose is that over a prolonged period, kinks often develop so that on older models it's not unusual to find that the fresh water flow rate is disappointingly slow. Typically the pump gets the blame, but a closer investigation often reveals a constriction in one of the feed pipes where it turns a sharp bend or bears against a sharp edge. Once a section of flexible hose develops a kink, it is very hard to get it to regain its former shape.

There's also the problem of leaking joints. In a motorcaravan, a remarkable number of hose clips are needed to couple up branch pipes and appliances. Worm-driven clips are not always fault-free and any hint of weakness is aggravated by the movements sustained when driving on bumpy

Improving a waste water system using domestic pipe

In a motorcaravan, a waste water system can be made quite easily using domestic 30mm (1.25in) PVCu waste pipe sold at builders' and plumbing merchants, as well as many DIY Superstores. This is the type of 'plastic' waste pipe many of us have under our sinks and washbasins at home.

When connecting up the pipe, all joints are formed using a proprietary adhesive weld sold for the purpose. With a brush mounted on the screw cap, it's easy to apply; but preparation is important. The collar of each coupling and the end of the pipe should be perfectly clean. If you rub the surface with a light grade of abrasive paper, the mildly roughened surfaces will 'key-in' successfully.

During construction, the inclination of flatter pipe runs should be checked with a spirit level to ensure that whenever the vehicle is parked level, there is a distinct fall throughout the system. The job demands patience rather than a high level of skill, and water will flow along the pipes at speed.

In some motorcaravans, making modifications to the entire system isn't possible without embarking on serious alterations. Pipes are often hidden and there's also the problem that the waste outlet on sinks and basins is too small for coupling up to domestic waste pipe. However, in one of the author's improvement projects, most of the system was converted to 30mm PVCu pipe, while the original narrow convoluted pipe fitted to a sink was retained but cut about a foot (300mm) from the waste outlet. This 'tail' of original ribbed pipe was then inserted around 8in (200mm) into the larger domestic pipe thus giving sufficient overlap to prevent a leak. Foam (sold in aerosol cans at builders' merchants) was used to seal the small gap around the thinner ribbed pipe.

Manufacturers are reluctant to use 30mm domestic waste pipe in spite of its obvious benefits.

roads. It's no surprise that a joint occasionally fails, and if the faulty coupling is hidden behind a panel, effecting a repair can be quite difficult.

With this in mind, the case for installing semi-rigid pipe with push-fit couplings instead of a hose and clip arrangement is a very strong one. This type of product has proven reliability; for instance it has been used to pump beer in many pubs for over 30 years. Curiously, it has been used by motorcaravan manufacturers only in recent years.

Admittedly, there are some occasions where, in a tight squeeze, it's easier to run a length of plastic hose. However, that doesn't mean that you need to fit flexible hose throughout the entire supply because there are adaptors to link both types of pipe.

Similarly there are unions which enable a length of semi-rigid pipe to be terminated with a threaded coupling nut. A threaded coupling is usually needed when connecting semi-rigid pipe to a diaphragm pump.

A particularly innovative item in the John Guest range of semi-rigid pipework components is a short length of plastic channelling which has a moulded 90-degree bend. This is used where a length of semi-rigid pipe has to be led around a sharp corner. Without this component, the pipe would kink irreparably, but when a section is

Adaptor couplings can be purchased in order to combine sections of flexible hose with semi-rigid pipe.

Laying-up tip

When leaving a motorcaravan for a prolonged period, remember to put plugs in the sink and basin outlets. This prevents smells from the waste water system creeping into the living space. Buy a spare plug for the shower tray as well.

This 90-degree support channel ensures that semi-rigid pipe doesn't kink when turning a sharp bend.

In order to form good connections with semi-rigid pipe, this tool from Whale ensures the ends are cut squarely and cleanly.

pressed into the angled channelling its sidewalls are supported.

Semi-rigid pipe is also distributed by Whale and the range includes a pipe cutting tool which ensures that a measured section of the 12mm or 15mm (outside diameter) pipe is cut cleanly and squarely. This is important when forming a joint.

Hose and clip plumbing

· When replacing a failed joint, don't be tempted to re-use the old worm-drive clip – buy a replacement. (Worm-drive clips are often known as 'Jubilee clips', which was the original brand name.)
· Buy good quality clips, even if they cost a little more. Poor quality imitations often have a ridged drive which is all-too-easily deformed when the clip is tightened.
· Prior to fitting a new clip, apply a small drop of oil on the worm wheel and also on the ridges of the tightening strip.
· Make sure the end of the hose is trimmed neatly and squarely.
· To ensure the hose is flexible, immerse the end in very hot water for several seconds. If you work quickly, you'll find the Jubilee clip will pull more tightly into the warmed hose.
· Some clips may have a sharp edge which can split a hose if over-tightened.
· Most clips don't over-compress, but if you're connecting up to a rigid plastic tube on a component (such as the coupling nozzle of an in-line water filter) be careful not to crack it.

To create tight joints in a hose and clip system, dip the ends of hose in boiling water before fitting the clip.

Push-fit semi-rigid plumbing

· Forming a joint is extremely easy with a push-fit system. Make sure the pipe is cut cleanly and squarely, then insert the section into the coupling and push it fully home. A water-tight connection is immediately achieved. Take care as sometimes it seems that the inserted pipe has been pushed fully into the coupling, whereas there's still a bit further to go.
· Inside each coupling there's a small collar known as a 'collet'. This can be removed if you want to see what it looks like – but it is normally left in place, and it shouldn't be taken out when forming a joint.
· The collet grips the outside of the pipe, so if you try to pull the joint apart, the collet is driven against the surface of the pipe with increasing force. Disconnection by muscle-power is virtually impossible.
· Notwithstanding the grip achieved by the interaction of these key components, the joint can be disconnected by holding the exposed part of the collet firmly against the coupling itself. While pushing the collet towards the coupling, the pipe will disconnect when pulled in the opposite direction.
· To ensure a coupling isn't accidentally disconnected by pressure on the exposed part of the collet, some systems have cover caps which are pushed over the finished joint to prevent unintended disconnection.
· Whale recently made minor improvements to its push-fit products and the latest couplings don't always match-up with earlier components. In consequence, some couplings are inclined to jam.

When fitting a coupling to semi-rigid pipe, always make sure you push the pipe fully home.

Technical tip

A winter drain-down is recommended by water system and motorcaravan manufacturers – as discussed in the accompanying text. However, an alternative strategy was discussed in the section on water heaters in Chapter 5. This involves pumping a purpose-made, non-poisonous motorcaravan anti-freeze into the system prior to a winter lay-up. The practice is commonplace in the US and among British boat owners. This anti-freeze product for motorcaravans is sold in the Camco range and called 'Winterban'. It is imported from the US and can be purchased from ABP Accessories.

System requirements for both types of fresh water system

Irrespective of the pipe system and connectors installed, there are several components that may also be needed.

Non-return valve

Once pipes are primed, it would be a disadvantage if water drained back to the tank or water supply vessel every time a tap was turned off. Where a diaphragm pump is installed (as described under *Water pumps*), its mechanism doesn't permit water to drain through its chambers when the motor isn't operating, so a non-return valve isn't normally needed.

However, motorcaravans fitted with a submersible pump are different. When a submersible pump stops operating, water held in the pipes sometimes drains back to the tank (through gravity) because it can flow unimpeded through the pump's casing. If the supply pipes lose water like this, there will be a delay in the delivery of water when a tap is next operated. To prevent this, a non-return valve is usually fitted inside the pipe near the water supply container or tank. This ensures that residual water is held in the pipes.

Drain tap

Retaining water in the supply pipes is beneficial, but if a vehicle is going to be unused during periods of low temperatures the system needs to be drained down to prevent frost damage.

It's true that some owners never drain down their entire system, and the pump, pipes or water filters manage to avoid damage. Flexibility in plastic components can sometimes cope with freezing water and the attendant pressure build-up if there's only a light frost. However, that's taking a risk and certainly where water heaters are concerned, draining them is absolutely essential, (as discussed in Chapter 6).

It's therefore disappointing to find that some motorcaravan manufacturers don't fit drain taps for releasing water from the supply pipes. Accordingly, one of the hose or pipe connections has to be

This drain-down tap from the Whale range is designed so that it can be easily coupled up with semi-rigid pipe.

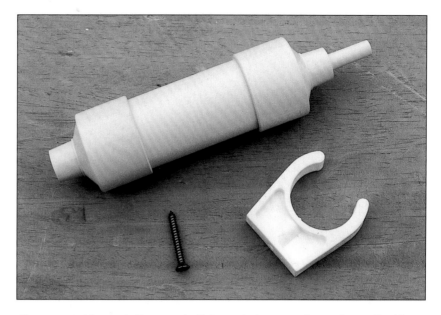

A surge damper fitted in a fresh water supply system helps to prevent a pump from operating with a pulsing action.

disconnected instead. Fortunately, fitting a drain tap isn't a difficult job for a practically-minded owner, even though it ought to have been installed when the motorcaravan was originally built. A tap, or taps, should be located:

a) Where it is easy to catch the drain-off water
b) At any low points in the system
c) At a point (or points) 'upstream' of a non-return valve or a diaphragm pump since these components prevent water passing through.

Surge damper

Where a diaphragm pump is fitted, it is sometimes found that the motor operates with irregular pulses. This is usually solved by fitting a small chamber within the pipe feed known as a 'surge damper'. Several motorcaravan manufacturers now fit one of these as standard. But don't let the shape confuse you – this is not an in-line water filter which sometimes has similar dimensions.

Note: *Some surge dampers have to be mounted vertically with the connection at the bottom.*

Water pumps

Motorcaravan water pumps fall into two categories: models that need priming and models that don't.

Some products are unable to start the pumping action until water is introduced into the casing of the unit, thus expelling the air; this is what is meant by 'priming'. Typically a pump that needs priming is made with a small impeller or paddle wheel that spins around, pushing water through the casing and along the pipes. This is known as a centrifugal pump.

In contrast, a self-priming pump usually incorporates pistons that move up and down within sealed chambers; this type of pump will start to draw water along an empty pipe even when the chambers are empty. To most people

This Shurflo diaphragm pump in a blanket locker is connected with flexible hose on the left and semi-rigid pipe on the right.

the perception is that the pump is able to 'suck' water up from a water container rather than merely pushing it along the pipe. A physicist might politely point out that it's not a matter of suction but of vacuum creation and pressure. The subtle difference is not important to our understanding here. More important is to state that the self-priming devices fitted in motorcaravans are called diaphragm pumps.

Examples of the two types are:

■ *Non-priming pumps* – Whale GP74 (seldom seen today), submersible pumps (made by a number of manufacturers).

■ *Self-priming pumps* – Fiamma models, Shurflo models, Whale Evenflow Pumps, Whale Clearstream Pumps, Whale Universal.

This section will focus on submersible pumps and their more expensive counterparts: diaphragm pumps. However, irrespective of the type used there has to be a switching arrangement.

Pump switching

Before an electric pump can deliver water, the tap has to be opened and the 12V electric motor switched into operation. One of three switching methods can be used:

1) Manual switch

A 12V switch could be mounted in a kitchen to operate the pump once a tap has been turned. Foot-operated push switches are available as well as conventional finger-operated rocker switches. Neither of these is fitted these days although they *could* be installed as a temporary cure if a fault were to develop elsewhere.

2) Microswitch

These tiny units are mounted in the body of a tap so that the motor is switched into action as soon as the tap top is turned. Damp is their enemy and if water or condensation gets inside their casing,

Confirming if a microswitch is faulty

If your water pump isn't working it might be because of a faulty microswitch. Firstly check that you've got microswitches in your taps by looking for the pairs of cables under each tap's mounting point. Detach these cables and with the pump switched on at the control panel, touch the terminals on the cables together. If the switch is at fault, the pump motor should start. If it doesn't, the fault is elsewhere in the system.

Alternatively if your motorcaravan has microswitches and the pump motor won't stop running, similarly disconnect the cables on all of the taps (including the shower control) and you will probably find that one of the switches is failing to interrupt the flow of power. It has probably got damp inside.

electricity can track across the tiny gap between the switch contacts. When this happens, the microswitch needs changing – a topic covered later under *Taps and shower systems*.

3) Pressure-sensitive switch

This type of switch can be mounted:

a) In-line, within the feed pipe itself
b) Integrally within the body of a diaphragm pump
c) As part of the water inlet socket of a submersible pump system – as in the Whale Watermaster product more commonly fitted on touring caravans.

A pressure-sensitive switch recognises that when a tap top is turned or an operating lever is raised, an 'opening' appears in an otherwise sealed system of pipes. The switch mechanism is then activated thereby bringing the pump motor into action. Unfortunately, if there's a small leak in any of the pipe connections, this can cause the motor to start as well. So it's not unusual to hear a pump clicking in and out very briefly because of a drop of pressure in the system. This is especially

A pressure-sensitive switch is sometimes fitted in the supply pipe; this Whale example includes a pressure adjusting control.

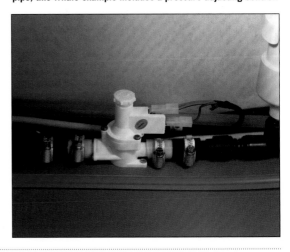

disturbing in the night so motorcaravans usually have a separate over-ride switch on the 12V control panel. Indeed it becomes a habit to switch off the pump last thing in the evening – or even during the day if false switching occurs often.

Over-frequent false switching can be resolved by altering the sensitivity of a pressure switch and most units feature an adjuster screw to fine tune the system. However, if there's a leak at a coupling, this should be repaired promptly to prevent water damage.

Further information on switching systems is mentioned in the subsequent sections on diaphragm pumps and taps.

Submersible pumps

Whilst the submersible pump is an example of a non-priming pump, the device normally achieves a state of prime as soon as it's dropped into a water container. Water fills the casing, air is expelled, and as soon as the motor is set into motion, water is pushed along the system by an impeller.

Submersible pumps have been fitted in smaller motorcaravans (such as the Swift Mondial) although they are also fitted in some large German models.

Another example of a submersible pump is the Whale Superfill 80 which is often supplied with large coachbuilts to lift water from a portable container in order to fill an onboard tank. This can equally be used to fill the independent flushing reservoir of a cassette toilet. In both cases, a 12V connector will have to be mounted on an outside wall, as shown in the photograph on page 95.

On a small motorcaravan which uses external water containers, an input has to be fitted to the wall of the vehicle. This has two functions. It couples the supply pipe into the motorcaravan system. It also connects the two feed wires that operate the pump's motor. These wires are usually hidden within a section of the plastic tubing.

Submersible pumps are also used in Thetford toilets fitted with a power flushing facility.

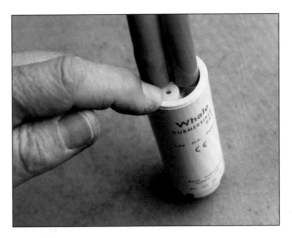

The Whale 881 submersible pump has an anti-airlock hole in the top of the casing.

Advantages
- A well-designed submersible pump achieves a good flow rate.
- Good-quality models are sturdily built.
- A submersible pump is much cheaper than a diaphragm pump.
- Noise level is low during operation.
- Recent Whale submersible pumps incorporate an anti-airlock hole in the top of the casing.

Disadvantages
- When the mechanism fails, a submersible pump cannot be repaired.
- If the casing cracks, water will penetrate the motor compartment and cause a short in the 12V system. If this occurs, a fuse in the pump circuit will blow, thereby ensuring that damage isn't caused elsewhere.

In view of the 'throw-away' nature of the less expensive submersible pumps, owners whose water system relies on one of these units know the wisdom of carrying a spare.

Diaphragm pumps

These well-engineered products are widely fitted. Their mechanism is elaborate and there is nothing an owner should attempt to repair inside. If something goes wrong the importers or manufacturers offer an overhaul and repair service. However, there are a number of tasks an owner should carry out – such as cleaning the filter.

The mechanism of a diaphragm pump can be badly damaged by grit and its filter must be kept clean as shown in the photographs on page 103.

Advantages
- Very good output and flow rates.
- Well engineered products.
- Powerful ability to lift water – the Whale Clearstream 700, for example, is able to lift water up to 100cm (39in).

Disadvantages
- When the mechanism fails, the pump usually has to be sent away for repair.
- These products are expensive.
- Some models are inclined to be noisy.

Airlocks in submersibles

If a submersible pump doesn't deliver water after it has been dropped into a water container, there are probably air bubbles caught in the casing.
- **To expel air bubbles, disconnect the feed pipe from the motorcaravan. Keep the pump under the water and swing the feed pipe so that the unit bumps several times against the side of the water container. This dislodges air bubbles, some of which may be seen rising in the water. Alternatively air is dispelled through the upper end of the hose.**
- **To reduce the likelihood of air bubbles getting caught in the pump casing, more recent products (such as the Whale 881) feature an air release hole on top of the casing.**

Pump problems

• If a diaphragm pump fails, first check the in-line fuse which is often fitted alongside the unit.

• If water delivery is intermittent, the sealing 'O' rings inside the mechanism may have failed, allowing air into the system. Eventually the water flow will fail completely.

• Excess noise is sometimes caused because the mounting screws are so tight that the rubber feet underneath the unit are compressed. The base then acts as a sounding board and amplifies the noise. Loosen the screws, or if necessary, replace the rubber feet.

• If the pressure-sensitive switch needs adjustment on a Whale Evenflow model, the adjusting screw can be found hidden under a blob of white silicone sealant.

• On other models the adjustment may be more conspicuous. On the Whale Clearstream 600 it is accessed by removing a protective blue cap. On a Shurflo pump there's a turn screw.

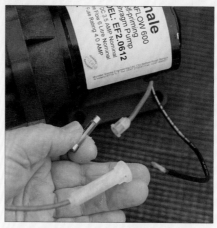

If a pump fails to operate, the first step is to check whether the fuse has blown.

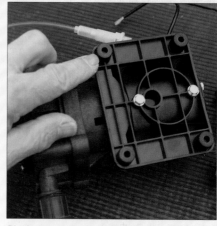

Diaphragm pumps can become noisy if the mountings are over-tightened.

The pressure-sensitivity adjuster is hidden below white sealant on this Whale Evenflow pump.

On a Whale Clearstream pump, the pressure-sensitivity adjuster lies beneath a blue cap.

Adjustments are made on this Shurflo Trail King pump by turning the centre screw.

Pump replacement

Anyone who carries out DIY repairs will find that pumps from Fiamma, Shurflo and Whale are supplied with clear installation instructions. Of course, consideration must be given to the way that the pump is going to be switched, and the options of micro-switching or pressure-sensitive switching have already been discussed.

If you are fitting a diaphragm pump, these usually have an inbuilt pressure switch and you merely need to couple up live and neutral power feeds to the unit. But make sure that you fit cable of the correct gauge. For instance, Whale diaphragm pumps require 2.5mm^2 cable (cross-sectional area) which achieves a continuous current rating of 21.5 Amps. Cable selection was discussed in Chapter 5, and the manufacturer's specification must be followed to ensure efficient operation of the pump.

Also make sure that you don't screw the unit down too tightly to its mounting board. It has already been mentioned that if the rubber feet are over-compressed, noise from the pump is amplified by the board.

As regards the hose coupling points, you may need to get an adaptor to suit the type of pipe fitted in the motorcaravan. And check the arrow which is usually marked on the casing to confirm the inlet and outlet ports.

Filter systems

There are three types of water filter:

■ A grit filter (such as those fitted on diaphragm pumps)

■ The taste filter (such as the in-line Whale filter)

■ A filter which also purifies water (such as the Nature-Pure from General Ecology).

GRIT FILTERS

When a diaphragm pump is fitted, it is most important to have a grit filter installed on the in-flow side of the unit. The photographs on page 103 show the filters fitted on three different pumps. The Evenflow and Shurflo filters can be dismantled for a thorough clean, or you can run water through the casing in a reverse direction under a running tap.

The grit filter on a Clearstream 700 pump is located below a tightly fitting cap.

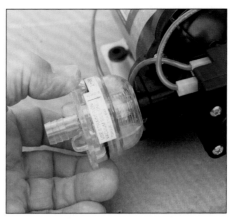
On this Shurflo pump, the grit filter is screwed onto the water inlet as shown.

The gauze strainer on a Whale Evenflow filter is held within a tight-fitting enclosure.

TASTE FILTERS

These products help to remove water-borne particles but their main function is to improve water palatability. Similar charcoal filters are often used in kitchens at home. While they improve the taste, they do NOT purify contaminated water.

It's usually quite easy to fit a taste filter in a motorcaravan and these are generally fitted in a pipe run as close as possible to the drinking water tap. The in-line filter from Whale is especially compact and installing one of these in the supply pipe to a sink or basin is an easy task for a practically-minded owner. But don't forget to replace the filter at frequent intervals. An average user could reasonably expect a filter to last a season, but some motorcaravanners leave them

in place for several years. Quite apart from failing to achieve its objective, an old taste filter might become a health hazard.

WATER PURIFIER

Few motorcaravanners drain down their fresh water tank at the end of every trip, so the wisdom of fitting a water purifier is clear. This is why many owners of motorcaravans, cabin cruisers and narrow boats fit a Nature-Pure Ultrafine water purifier. This removes tank taste, traps chemicals such as pesticides and solvents as well as removing disease bacteria, pathogenic cysts with disease toxins, parasites and so on. In fact this purifier is so effective that a boat owner could even draw water from a canal and convert it into clean, clear drinking water.

This American-manufactured product is not cheap, but it is sturdily constructed and isn't difficult to install either. The job involves diverting water from the supply pipe serving the fresh water tap on the sink to the Nature-Pure treatment unit. The purified water can then be coupled to a purpose-made supply tap provided in the kit, or diverted to your existing tap. It's also possible to take it to the cold outlet of a mixer tap, although this might not be quite so good. For instance, if the mechanism which separates (or blends) hot and cold water is poorly engineered, treated cold

An Aqua Source Clear taste filter is narrow enough to be fitted even where space is restricted.

The filter used in the Nature-Pure Ultrafine water purifier from General Ecology is housed in a strong plastic casing.

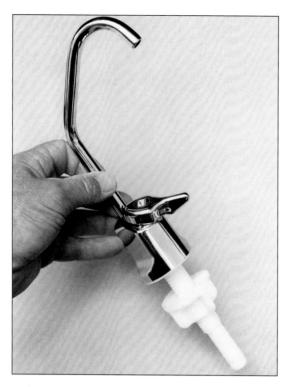

A dedicated fresh-water tap is supplied in an Ultrafine water purifier kit.

water might be affected by small quantities of non-treated water coming from the hot supply. If the purifying element is critically important – for instance in an expedition vehicle travelling in undeveloped countries – it's best to fit the separate Nature-Pure tap which is provided in the kit.

The Nature-Pure Ultrafine has much to commend it, but as with a taste filter product, you must change the high-specification cartridge filter at the intervals recommended by the manufacturer.

Taps and shower systems

The design of taps and shower heads has changed significantly over the last decade. Moreover, to the disenchantment of many owners, some taps have proved extremely unreliable and these are usually cheaply-built imported products.

One response by manufacturers has been to fit domestic-style mixer taps instead, and these often suit a large motorcaravan. Unfortunately, the rate of flow from a 12V pump sometimes looks rather feeble after the more familiar output from domestic taps fitted at home.

As explained in the earlier section, some taps are fitted with a microswitch which triggers the pump into action. These need to be accessible and it's always wise to carry a spare, if damp causes a microswitch to fail. However, on some imported taps, the microswitch is not accessible because it is sealed within the casing and if a tap develops a fault the entire unit has to be thrown away.

On Whale's recent taps like the Elegance and Modular models, changing a microswitch is fairly easy, as the accompanying photographs show. The main problem is reaching them and it certainly

Changing the microswitches on Whale taps

1

Feeling in the dark under your sink, locate a plastic collar clip.

2

Ease the clip away from the switch mounting point.

3

Gently pull the microswitch from its two locating pins.

4

Replace the switch with a new one and reverse the operation.

1

Working from above the tap, prise out the hot/cold plug to reveal the tap lever attachment screw.

2

Remove the tap lever, then lift off the switch activating plate, noting its position carefully.

3

Gently prise up the microswitch from its cradled location with the aid of a small screwdriver.

4

Pull the switch clear to disconnect the terminals; then replace it with a new microswitch.

helps to be a contortionist when working under a kitchen sink. In addition, remember to turn off the tap completely before starting the work. It's also wise to switch off the 12V supply.

The job is even easier on Whale's Elite mixer taps because everything is done above the sink. However, these models are sold in two versions – either *with* or *without* microswitches. If there are

wires coming down underneath their mounting, then they have a microswitch inside and the procedure for changing this component is shown in the sequential illustrations. But be warned. Be careful not to let the mechanism flick out when you remove the operating lever; it can be very difficult trying to work out where all the dislodged components are meant to fit!

Taps and winter precautions

When you lay-up a motorcaravan in frosty weather, you must leave all taps and shower controls OPEN. When residual water freezes it expands and this introduces pressure in the pipes which can split the couplings. Leaving all taps open provides a pressure relief facility. But take note. If you have lever-operated mixer taps, you must make sure that the lifted lever is in its CENTRAL POSITION in order to give pressure relief to both the hot AND cold supply pipes. Whale now fits warning stickers on Elite lever taps because a number of owners have

experienced frost damage when a lifted lever hadn't been centralised. I was one of those owners, as the photograph here reveals. . .

The lever on this shower control wasn't left lifted in its central position, and the subsequent pressure build-up from freezing water completely split its casing.

Whale now fits warning stickers on lever taps and shower controls to ensure that frost damage is avoided.

8

Refrigerators

In a motorcaravan, the refrigerator makes one of the most important contributions to comfortable living. However, successful operation can only be achieved if an appliance is correctly installed and regularly serviced.

The refrigerators installed in motorcaravans work by circulating a chemical around a network of pipes. The chemical is described as a 'refrigerant' and when it circulates it changes state from a liquid to a gas and back again. This change of state needs heat, which is duly drawn from the food storage compartment via the sliver fins that you can see at the back of the fridge. That's how it grows cooler inside, and it stands to reason that the cooling efficiency of a fridge will be lost if these fins are obstructed.

In the cooling appliances used in our homes, the refrigerant is circulated by a compressor pump and you'll often hear the motor spring into life when a thermostat recognises a need for further cooling. The system works well but it is only recently that appliances adopting this operating principle have been installed in motorcaravans.

This 65-litre compressor refrigerator is one of several popular products from WAECO.

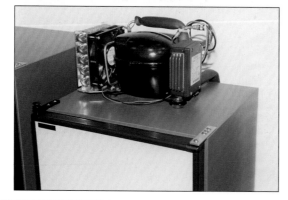

The unit shown here employs a compressor pump to circulate the refrigerants.

The more common type of motorcaravan refrigerator has a cooling unit whose refrigerant is circulated by the application of heat. An appliance of this type is referred to as an *absorption refrigerator* and the heat needed to create this all-important circulation comes from one of three sources:

• A 12V DC heating element
• A 230V AC heating element
• A gas burner.

Notwithstanding the availability of compressor refrigerators for leisure vehicles, absorption refrigerators are fitted by all but a few motorcaravan manufacturers. This is because compressor refrigerators are wholly reliant on electricity and cannot operate on gas.

Of course, both types have advantages and disadvantages, and their respective suitability is linked to the way in which you use your motorcaravan. For instance, if you park a motorcaravan for extended spells on sites which are not equipped with mains hook-ups and then use a bicycle, scooter or support car for touring locally instead of driving the motorcaravan, an absorption refrigerator is the preferred product. That's because it can be run on gas, whereas a compressor refrigerator used in conditions like this would soon discharge the 12V leisure battery from which it derives its power.

So let's compare the two types of product:

Absorption refrigerators

Advantages

■ The operating system is silent and this is important in the compact living area of a motorcaravan.

■ There's a choice of operating mode. On the road, 12V is used. On a site with a mains hook-up, the appliance can be run on 230V electricity. On other sites or when camping in the wilds, gas operation can be selected.

Disadvantages

- Ventilators have to be installed on the external side wall of a motorcaravan (alternatively the lower one can be fitted in the floor).

- An absorption refrigerator may perform poorly if the motorcaravan builder hasn't fitted the appliance in accordance with the fridge installation instructions. Indeed, some manufacturers have taken shorts cuts in the past – but that's not the fault of the appliance.

- These products are comparatively costly.

Compressor refrigerators

Advantages

- Products are usually less expensive than similarly-sized absorption refrigerators.

- There's no need to fit external ventilators and the installation task is less involved.

Disadvantages

- Noise from the compressor pump can be irritating.

- A significantly greater demand is placed on the leisure battery. Letters published in magazines have revealed that many owners find this a serious limitation.

As long as these points are noted, a compressor refrigerator has its merits, especially if you're on the road a lot so you keep your leisure battery well charged. However, the majority of motorcaravans are equipped with absorption appliances with models from Electrolux, Dometic and Thetford. For this reason, most of this chapter focuses on absorption refrigerators.

Operation

All three operating modes on an absorption refrigerator achieve efficient cooling, although the mode to choose depends on circumstances. For instance, if mains electricity is provided at a site, it is logical to use the 230V supply. Alternatively, on sites not equipped with mains hook-ups, you would select the gas operating mode. The 12V mode can only be used when the vehicle is being driven because it would otherwise discharge a battery very quickly.

A fridge would also run on gas while a vehicle is being driven, but this is potentially VERY

Product identities

For many years, the refrigerators fitted in leisure vehicles were manufactured by Electrolux. However, in 2001, the leisure appliance division of Electrolux became an independent company and the name Dometic was adopted. This had been a brand name in the US for a number of years.

In 2003, many appliances were still bearing both Dometic and Electrolux badges which was rather confusing. However, in 2004 the licence to use the Electrolux name expired. In this chapter both names are used because thousands of motorcaravans are fitted with products previously manufactured by Electrolux. Only more recent models have appliances bearing the Dometic badge, and because many of the Company's staff worked in the former Leisure Appliance Division of Electrolux, aftersales advice covers both products.

Norcold is another manufacturer of absorption refrigerators. These products were launched in the UK in 2002 and are being marketed by Thetford. As a further development, compressor fridges from Waeco are being installed by several van converters, such as Bilbo's.

The van conversions from Bilbo's usually have a compressor fridge.

dangerous. Moreover, it is illegal to enter a filling station with a gas appliance in operation – an explosion could have terrible consequences. So before taking to the road, always turn off the gas at the cylinder and select the 12V setting.

Some owners are misled into thinking that 12V operation is not very efficient. But that's wrong. Provided a vehicle's alternator achieves a good output and as long as the electrical connection is made using cable of the correct gauge, cooling is good. The only disadvantage with the 12V option is that the level of cooling cannot be altered; the fridge works at a steady rate, irrespective of where you set the cooling control on the control panel.

Procedures for changing the operating mode of a fridge are explained in owner's handbooks and when you use a motorcaravan frequently, the task of switching over becomes a matter

Example of controls and their functions on a late 1980s and early 1990s electronic ignition fridge.

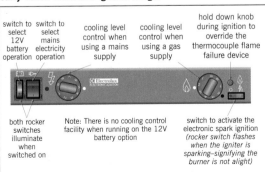

Example of controls and their functions on a mid and late 1990s electronic ignition fridge.

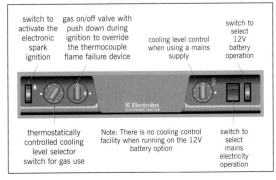

Although some American RV fridges are designed to run on gas when on the move, it is strongly recommended to turn off a gas supply at the cylinder before taking to the road. On Electrolux refrigerators made prior to 1992, the burner flame is not extinguished just by turning the temperature control to its lowest setting. If your fridge has a red ignition push button on the fascia, it is one of these earlier appliances. Only more recent Electrolux fridges activate a gas shut-off valve when the temperature control is set to zero.

This is why earlier models can sometimes be accidentally operated on both a 12V and gas supply simultaneously. The user wrongly presumes the gas option won't work because the control has been set to zero, and also hasn't remembered to turn off the gas at the cylinder before starting the engine. Apart from the danger of having a naked flame when driving, the use of two supplies at once doesn't do the fridge a lot of good.

Merely turning the gas control knob to its lowest setting does *not* extinguish the gas flame on early Electrolux models which are fitted with a red ignition button.

of routine. However, if you haven't used your motorcaravan for a long time and it has one of the more complicated control panels, it's not unusual to forget the steps you have to follow. That is why Electrolux AES refrigerators, first introduced in the UK during 1995, have a clear advantage: they choose the most appropriate operating mode on your behalf.

Automatic Energy Selection

Automatic Energy Selection (AES) employs an electronic source selector. Twelve seconds after the fridge has been switched on, the device selects the most appropriate operating mode in accordance with a programmed priority system. The priority order is:
1) 230V mains
2) 12V supply
3) Gas.
For instance, if the fridge identifies the availability of a 230V supply, the unit will automatically operate on mains in preference to gas or a 12V supply; however, when parked on a site offering no mains hook-up, the appliance will choose the gas operating mode – provided the cylinder is switched on. Lastly, as soon as you start the engine, the refrigerator chooses the 12V operating mode.

Note: *Never start the engine when the mains hook-up cable is connected. On many motorcaravans, a fuse is likely to blow.*

An AES refrigerator is very convenient although when you take to the road, you still must remember to turn off the gas supply at the cylinder for safety reasons. If you forget to turn off the gas, an AES model still selects 12V operation when you start the engine. But what happens when you turn the engine off?

During the development of AES products, it was realised that if an owner had forgotten to turn off a gas cylinder, the fridge would subsequently return to gas operation whenever the vehicle's engine was switched off. When stopping at a filling station, this would be illegal and highly dangerous.

So the manufacturer programmed a 20-minute delay into the automatic selector; but note that this time lapse *only* takes effect in the transition from 12V to gas operation. The switchover delay effectively resolves the filling station problem – presuming that a vehicle can be re-fuelled and driven away within 20 minutes. But the issue doesn't arise if you always turn off your gas cylinder before driving the vehicle.

Getting the best from a refrigerator

Several courses of action will ensure you get the best results from a motorcaravan fridge:

Prior to departure

Before leaving home, it helps to pre-cool the food storage compartment. Do this by adding several items such as bottles of mineral water and cans of drink; then operate the appliance for around three hours. If you can hook up to a mains supply you'll save gas, but an adaptor is needed in order to connect a motorcaravan's industrial-style hook-up plug into a household 13 Amp socket. You should also fit a portable RCD device in the socket to offer protection to anyone working near the trailing lead. These safety devices can be purchased in DIY stores.

The following points should be observed:
• Only transfer perishable items like butter, meat and milk when the temperature has dropped
• Avoid packing food so tightly that air cannot circulate around the storage area
• Freshly washed lettuce or other damp vegetables should always be packed in a bag
• Never completely cover the silver cooling fins inside the food storage area. Cooling efficiency is often impaired when an owner stows a shrink-wrapped pack of beer cans hard against the fins at the rear of the food compartment
• Before taking to the road, *always remember to secure the door catch.*

A refrigerator can hold many items, but avoid packing the food so tightly that air is not able to circulate inside.

On-site use

Several points should be noted to ensure your refrigerator performs efficiently:

Ignition problems

If initial attempts to ignite the burner are unsuccessful, this is often caused by air in the gas line. However, repeated attempts usually purge the air quite quickly. Should there be continuing difficulty, it is probably time to have the appliance serviced. As part of the service work, the ignition electrode will be cleaned and realigned as explained later in this chapter.

Ventilators obscured

Ensure that the ventilators on the outside are not obscured. For instance, in hot weather, refrigerator cooling is impaired if a motorcaravan's door completely covers the vents when it is left fully open. **Note:** *Compressor fridges don't normally have external wall ventilators; these appliances usually vent into the living space instead.*

Voltage loss

On crowded sites, particularly abroad where electrical standards might not be as strict, power from a 230V hook-up is often reduced. It can fall as low as 190V and cooling is seriously affected as a result. Under these circumstances, you should switch back to gas operation because this will achieve better cooling. However, if your motorcaravan is fitted with an AES fridge, this switches to gas automatically whenever its power module detects a significant drop in voltage.

Some refrigerators are fitted with a false door front which unfortunately hides the control panel.

Packing tip

Leave some of the cooling fins at the rear of the food compartment exposed as they are the means by which the operating system at the rear of the casing draws heat from the food compartment. Also be careful not to dislodge the thermostat capillary tube which is sometimes clipped to these fins, particularly on refrigerators manufactured before 1996. This would cause the thermostat to make false readings and the appliance would then over-cool the provisions.

Never completely cover the fins in the food compartment; they create cooling and often provide a mounting for the thermostat's capillary tube (indicated).

Cooling loss

Open the fridge door as briefly as possible. Regrettably, some refrigerators are fitted with a false door front which completely hides the fascia controls. Admittedly this cosmetic addition allows the fridge to match adjacent furniture, but it also means that a refrigerator has to be opened simply to alter the cooling control or energy selection switches. This inevitably causes a loss of cooled air from the food compartment.

Over-cooling

If you use your motorcaravan in the winter, low outside temperatures may bring the reverse problem – over-cooling. It's not unusual to find that your milk, cucumbers, and yoghurt are frozen solid. In reality, this is only likely on models fitted with a gas valve such as the RM212, RM4206, RM4230 and RM4200. It doesn't occur on refrigerators fitted with a gas thermostat like the RM2260, RM4237, RM4271 and later models.

Winter covers

If your refrigerator over-cools in low temperatures, both Dometic and Electrolux have manufactured winter covers which clip on to the ventilators. These plastic shields reduce the flow of air across the rear of the appliance. You are recommended to fit winter covers whenever outside temperatures fall below 10°C (50°F).

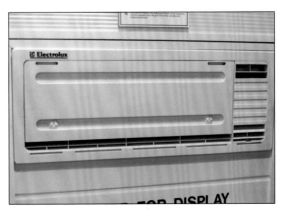

A winter cover from Electrolux should be fitted when outside temperatures fall below 10°C (50°F).

Catches which hold a door ajar during a storage period, like this example on a Thetford refrigerator, are often rather fragile.

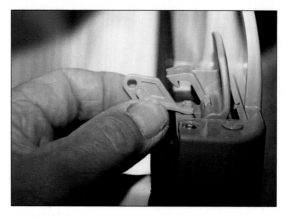

Ventilators from other manufacturers may not accept winter covers, so a makeshift answer in cold conditions is to cover some of the fins with cooking foil. In practice, this is not easy to achieve and under no circumstances should the flue outlet be covered.

Note: *Winter covers are not draught excluders. If wind blows into your motorcaravan through the outside vents, the refrigerator has been incorrectly installed. See Ventilation, page 111.*

On returning home

On completion of every trip, remove foodstuffs and leave the door partially open – fridges usually incorporate a catch that holds the door slightly ajar so that air can circulate and prevent mould from forming inside. On a few models, such as early examples of the Powerfridge, the manufacturer did not fit a catch with a storage setting.
Note: *Of all the design challenges, creating a two-position door catch has proved to be one of the toughest. Many examples will be found and some are fragile. A door often flies open if you drive off when it's clipped in the part-ajar storage position.*

At the end of a season, clean the inside of your refrigerator. Electrolux recommended using a weak solution of bicarbonate of soda, by mixing a teaspoonful into half a litre of warm water. Other cleaners are NOT recommended – some types have led to cracks developing in the cabinet lining several weeks after the cleaning operation.

If you lay-up your motorcaravan, you should also consider having the refrigerator serviced by a specialist before the annual rush begins at the start of every new season.

Installation

The following information provides guidance for DIY motorcaravan converters, but it also provides a point of reference for anyone buying a motorcaravan or for existing owners whose fridge performance is disappointing.

Choosing a location

A refrigerator is a heavy appliance, especially when fully loaded, so its position in the living quarters may have an effect on the suspension, particularly if it is situated at the extreme rear of the vehicle. And whereas a tall fridge-freezer or a conventional fridge installed at chest-height are particularly convenient to use, the higher centre of gravity inevitably contributes to body roll when cornering. Finally, if the chosen position results in its ventilators being obstructed when the entrance door is fully opened, cooling efficiency might be impaired.

Levelling

Since the circulation of the refrigerant in an absorption fridge is hindered if a fridge isn't level, the installer should first park the motorcaravan on level ground. A spirit level should then be used when installing the refrigerator so that its level position coincides with that of the vehicle.

On Electrolux refrigerators, the reference point for verifying a level plane is usually the shelf in the small freezer compartment. Of course, a very short spirit level is needed to take a reading here. An exception is the RM123 which has a sloping shelf; on this model the spirit level should be placed on the base of the food storage cabinet.

Note:
*1) All Electrolux refrigerators manufactured before 1986 had to be level to operate and cooling won't occur if there's a tilt in excess of 2-3 degrees. Since this date, all higher specification models are described as 'tilt tolerant'. Some models will operate at an angle of 3 degrees (eg RM122 and RM4206), while others operate at 6 degrees from a level plane, (eg RM4217, RM4237, RM4271 and RM6271).
2) On the road, a fridge will seldom be level, particularly when driving along a carriageway with pronounced camber. However, as long as a level position is achieved periodically – which is the case on normal roads – chemical circulation will take place and cooling will occur.*

Structural fixing

When on the road, the living quarters in a motorcaravan receive a considerable shake-up, especially on bumpy country lanes. To resist this, a refrigerator needs to be carefully secured. It is prudent, for example, to fit small wooden blocks on the floor at the rear of the unit. Normally, blocks are not needed at the sides because support is afforded by the adjacent kitchen units to which the appliance is anchored.

Side anchorage used to be achieved by driving screws through furniture on either side and directly into the metal casing of the appliance. As long as they penetrated no further than 12mm (½in), the interior plastic lining wouldn't be damaged; however, models like the RM2260 and RM2262 were manufactured with a projecting flange around the front which incorporates fixing points.

In addition, Dometic refrigerators and Electrolux models made since 1994 incorporate holes in the sides of the food compartment. This means

Stain removal

To remove stubborn stains from the interior of a Dometic or Electrolux refrigerator, use a very fine wire wool pad, lubricated with water to reduce its abrasive effect. If applied gently, this will remove marks without damaging the plastic lining material.

More recent Electrolux refrigerators have side mounting points – plastic caps hide the heads of the screws.

that long screws can be driven from the *inside* outwards, thereby achieving anchorage from adjacent structures – usually kitchen cupboards. The heads of the screws are then concealed by a white plastic cap which matches the food compartment lining.

Whichever method is adopted, three objectives must be achieved:
• The fridge should be in a level position when the vehicle is parked on level ground.
• It must not shake loose when driving on rough roads.
• The appliance should be easy to remove for servicing.

Ventilation

In both the heat of summer and the cold winds of winter, an owner whose motorcaravan is fitted with an absorption refrigerator will experience problems if the installation doesn't meet the ventilation requirements specified by the manufacturer.

Sealed ventilation path

To ensure efficient operation, the refrigeration unit fitted on the back of the casing must be kept cool. When this is achieved, a well-maintained absorption refrigerator operates effectively in air temperatures as high as 38°C (100°F). However, if a motorcaravan is parked in a non-shaded spot on a hot, sunny day, temperatures inside the vehicle can rise to considerably higher levels. That's why the rear of the casing must be completely sealed off from the living space.

Additionally there must be a ventilation facility in which air gets drawn from the outside, passes over the cooling unit fixed to the rear of the casing by convection and is then directed back outside via an upper ventilator. To facilitate discharge of the warmed air, a deflector shield has to be fitted on top of the casing as shown in the accompanying diagram.

To help installers create a sealed ventilation path, Electrolux manufactured an aluminium shield, complete with deflector, for mounting

Installation method

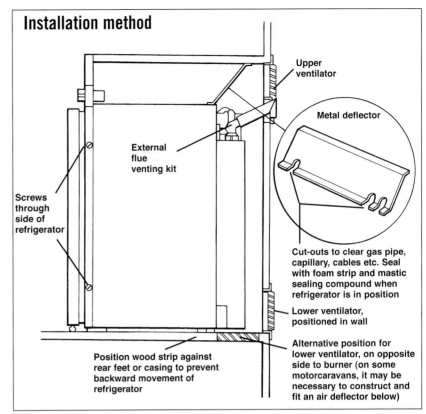

Upper ventilator

Metal deflector

External flue venting kit

Screws through side of refrigerator

Cut-outs to clear gas pipe, capillary, cables etc. Seal with foam strip and mastic sealing compound when refrigerator is in position

Lower ventilator, positioned in wall

Position wood strip against rear feet or casing to prevent backward movement of refrigerator

Alternative position for lower ventilator, on opposite side to burner (on some motorcaravans, it may be necessary to construct and fit an air deflector below)

between the appliance and the side wall of the vehicle. This was referred to as the IK1 Kit. Alternatively, a custom-made shield can be formed using aluminium sheet and this is often preferred when an enclosure has to be shaped to fit closely against the curving profile of a side wall in a van conversion. As said earlier, creating a ventilation facility which is wholly sealed from the living area is very important.

It is therefore most regrettable that some motorcaravan manufacturers disregard this requirement in spite of the fact that it is clearly described in refrigerator installation manuals. If the ventilation pathway at the rear of the appliance is not kept entirely separate from the living space, two problems arise:
1) A refrigerator does not operate to its maximum potential in hot temperatures.
2) In cold weather, draughts blowing through the wall vents will penetrate the interior.
Note: *It is wrong to resolve the draught issue by applying adhesive sealant around an installed*

Correct installation is important and the need to fit a metal shield deflector at the rear is emphasised by the manufacturer.

In this DIY installation, an aluminium deflector is screwed down to wooden strips bonded to the refrigerator.

Checking that a ventilation facility has been sealed off from the living quarters.

If a work top over a refrigerator gets hot, this is a certain sign that the ventilation facility hasn't been properly sealed.

When the upper ventilator was removed, it was clear that this installation had a deflector shield as specified by the manufacturer.

This motorhome had a useful chopping board, but when it was removed, you could see the light through the upper fridge ventilator. The installer had clearly not followed the fridge manufacturer's instructions.

fridge – a practice seen in some German and Italian-built motorcaravans. This makes it extremely difficult to remove a refrigerator for routine servicing work.

If your refrigerator doesn't cool as well as you think it should, feel the work top or draining board directly above the refrigerator. If it gets hot, then warmed air from the rear of the cooling unit isn't being correctly deflected to the outside via the upper ventilator. Then remove the upper ventilator from the outside wall and look inside. If you can see into the living space, the installation is at fault. Equally if you remove drawers and open cupboard doors in the kitchen and can then see directly through one of the ventilators, the installer has most definitely disregarded the fridge manufacturer's instructions.

Ventilation components

If a sealed ventilation path has been constructed correctly, there is no need for an electric fan to accelerate air movement over the rear of the appliance (except on a large fridge-freezer). Nevertheless, motorcaravanners who frequently visit hot regions often fit a compact 12V-operated fan. These can be obtained from dealers and

some types are designed to attach to the inside face of the upper ventilator.

The size of ventilators also contributes to performance. On models with less than 60 litres (approximately 2 cu ft) storage capacity, the ventilators should provide at least 240cm^2 of free air space; models offering more than 60 litres storage need ventilators achieving at least 300 cm^2 free air space. Unfortunately the effective area is significantly reduced if a vent is fitted with an insect mesh.

The A1609 and A1620 ventilators formerly made by Electrolux meet these requirements but they are quite expensive. This is why some manufacturers fit other types – some of which lack the rain-proof design of Electrolux units. Equally, some of the less-expensive ventilators cannot accept winter covers, although earlier types of Electrolux ventilator present problems, too. Some owners decide to upgrade their ventilators. The A1620 version incorporates the flue outlet; in previous models the flue was a separate fitting.

The position of ventilators relative to the appliance is also important. The top vent should be located so that its lower edge aligns with the top of the appliance. This ensures that the upper edge will be at least 55mm above the refrigerator.

The lower vent can be positioned in either

Some owners fit a fridge fan to the upper ventilator to enhance air flow in hot weather conditions.

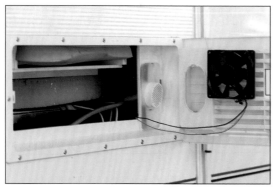

Later products from Electrolux incorporated the flue outlet in the upper ventilator as shown here.

the side wall or in the floor. If the latter option is preferred the vent should be situated as far away from the burner as possible so that draughts do not extinguish the flame. A deflector shield might also need to be fitted under the floor so that road dirt doesn't get into the enclosure when you're driving.

The refrigerator flue

The provision of a flue is necessary in order to disperse the products of combustion when an appliance is operating on gas. This is nothing to do with the ventilation requirement. The fact that the flue outlet is accommodated in the latest ventilators is purely for tidiness. On older installations the outlets were entirely separate.

The assembly of the flue pipe supplied with a refrigerator is straightforward and is clearly explained in the fitting instructions. These should be carefully followed and the tubing supplied must not be lengthened since this could lead to an imbalance in the gas/air mixture at the burner.

Large fridge-freezers from Dometic do not have a flue outlet as such and the entire area offered by the upper ventilator is used to discharge combustion fumes to the outside. For this reason it is critically important that the ventilation facility at the rear of the unit is effectively sealed from the living space.

Mains connection

Like most home appliances, motorcaravan refrigerators are now supplied with a moulded 13 Amp plug that needs to be connected up to a mains supply socket. Typically there's a dedicated point for the fridge which will be protected by a miniature circuit breaker on the mains consumer

The fridge freezers from Dometic do not have a separate flue outlet; all the combustion waste is discharged through the upper ventilator.

unit as described in Chapter 5. The mains plug for a fridge should be fitted with a 3 Amp fuse.

Low voltage connection

One problem with 12V operation is that there's a voltage loss if the connecting cables are too long and of insufficient gauge (thickness).

In most refrigerators the operating supply is taken from the base vehicle's battery, albeit via a relay that prevents the supply being available until the engine is running. A second supply for operating the electronic spark igniter is usually taken from the leisure battery – as shown in the diagram.

The 12V connection to an Electrolux refrigerator must follow the manufacturer's specifications to avoid a voltage drop.

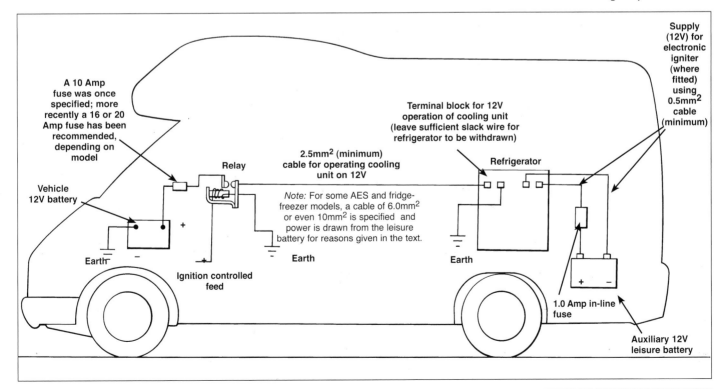

A 10 Amp fuse was once specified; more recently a 16 or 20 Amp fuse has been recommended, depending on model

Vehicle 12V battery

Earth

Relay

Ignition controlled feed

2.5mm² (minimum) cable for operating cooling unit on 12V

Note: For some AES and fridge-freezer models, a cable of 6.0mm² or even 10mm² is specified and power is drawn from the leisure battery for reasons given in the text.

Earth

Terminal block for 12V operation of cooling unit (leave sufficient slack wire for refrigerator to be withdrawn)

Refrigerator

Earth

Supply (12V) for electronic igniter (where fitted) using 0.5mm² cable (minimum)

1.0 Amp in-line fuse

Auxiliary 12V leisure battery

Connection to a 12V supply uses a block that is fastened behind the fascia control panel.

However, in the case of an AES refrigerator, both the operating supply and the electronic igniter supply are taken from the leisure battery rather than the base vehicle's battery. There's a reason for this. On an AES fridge you can drain your battery if you omit to switch off the appliance using the fascia control when the vehicle is parked. Even if you've turned off the gas supply, disconnected a mains supply and the engine isn't running, the 'computer' responsible for automatically selecting the operating mode will still draw electricity. The current drain is small, but over a long lay-up period it could completely discharge a battery – and discharging a leisure battery is the lesser of the two evils. That's why you should always switch off the appliance at the refrigerator's fascia control.

Key elements in a 12V supply are:
• A 16 or 20 Amp fuse (depending on the model) which must be fitted close to the positive terminal on the supply battery. **Note:** *At one time a 10 Amp fuse was specified but this recommendation has been revised.*
• A relay – this is an electric switch which ensures that a refrigerator will only run on a 12V supply when the engine is running and the battery is receiving a charge from the alternator. That's because the drain on a battery is considerable – a fridge draws at least 8 Amps when running on 12V. Suitable relays are available from both Lucas and Hella.
• Cable of the correct gauge (explained in Chapter 5). To ensure minimum loss of current, Electrolux (and now Dometic) recommend connecting cable of at least 2.5mm² gauge where the total cable run (live and neutral) does not exceed 10.5 metres; connecting cable of at least 4.0mm² gauge where the total cable run (live and neutral) does not exceed 17 metres; and connecting cable of 6.0mm² or 10mm² gauge for some AES and fridge-freezer models.
• Connection to the appliance. The live and neutral feeds are coupled to a terminal block on top of the refrigerator casing, just behind the control

fascia. The polarity IS important on the AES models, but not on other models.
• A 12V feed to the electronic igniter for the gas burner (where this form of ignition is fitted). This is a separate supply needing 0.5mm² (minimum) cable and a 1 Amp fuse; it is normally taken from the leisure battery.

Gas operation

Requirements for the gas supply include:

• An independent gas control tap in the supply to the fridge – usually situated in a kitchen cupboard.
• Copper feed pipes usually of 6mm (¼in) outside diameter (OD) – the final connection to the appliance must never be made with flexible gas hose.
• A flue arrangement – this is *entirely different* from the ventilation system as described earlier. On the outside of the vehicle, the flue cover plate used to be separate from the ventilator grilles. In 1994, however, Electrolux introduced the A1620 grilles which incorporated both the flue outlet and the upper ventilation outlet. However, freezer-fridges use the entire upper vent for the discharge of combustion fumes.
• An ignition system – in the 1960s and early 1970s, the gas burner had to be lit with a match. However, push-button igniters that use a piezo crystal to generate a spark replaced this system. In the mid-1980s, electronic ignition was introduced and this is now much more common. In order to create a light at the burner, the spark gap has to be set to 3mm and the components should be free of soot.
• Where an older A1609 wall ventilator has been fitted, a low level 'drop out' hole of 40mm (1⅝in) has to be formed in the floor to allow escaping gas to discharge to the exterior. The A1609 vent cannot act as an alternative escape route because it would be completely obstructed when a 'winter cover' is fitted. However, current Dometic ventilators **can** afford an accepted gas escape facility as long as the lowest louvre is below floor level. This portion of these later vents remains unobstructed even when a 'winter cover' as been attached..
• The union for coupling to the gas supply is often situated just behind the control fascia. On more recent models, however, it is more conveniently fitted at the rear where it can be easily reached by removing a wall vent.

Note: *Many aspects of refrigerator installation could be tackled by a DIY enthusiast. However, making the final connection to a gas supply should be entrusted to a competent gas engineer. The joint will be made using an approved threaded coupling and a jointing compound e.g. Calor-tite, will be applied to the threads. A generous length of copper pipe should be left on the top of the appliance so that the unit can be drawn slightly forward from its housing when removing the appliance for servicing.*

It was easy to remove this refrigerator for servicing, but some models take several hours to withdraw from their housing.

Servicing

As with any gas appliance, periodic servicing is important. Not only does this ensure efficient operation, it is a safety element too.

Despite this, some motorcaravanners *never* have their fridge serviced and it seems to run well, season after season. Unfortunately nothing is more annoying when it finally fails on holiday, especially in hot weather.

Recognising different levels of use, manufacturers have recommended that servicing should be carried out every 12 to 18 months. The task itself doesn't take long but it is sometimes time-consuming to remove the appliance from the motorcaravan. On some models it might only take 20 minutes to remove and reinstate a refrigerator, but in extreme instances it can take a full day. This is allegedly the case on a recent Laika coachbuilt model. It's true that on some of the latest refrigerators quite a lot of the components which need cleaning and adjustment can be reached by removing the wall ventilators. But to do a thorough job most specialists prefer to transfer an appliance to a work bench.

The servicing tasks must be carried out by a competent, experienced and trained refrigerator specialist and the job must not be tackled by an untrained DIY enthusiast. On the other hand, a labour charge might be reduced if the owner were able to remove the fridge from its housing. Reinstatement could also be considered, although the gas should only be reconnected by a qualified gas specialist.

The main servicing operations are as follows:

With the fridge on a bench, the angled flue connection fitted to the top of the burner tube is removed. This tube is effectively a chimney clad in insulating material. Wrapped within its insulation are the 12V and 230V heating elements.

A baffle is lifted out of the burner tube. This is a twisted piece of metal sheet suspended on a wire, and its position within the tube is critically determined by the length of this wire. One servicing task is to clean off any carbon deposits from the baffle. This component helps to retain heat in the lower part of the burner tube.

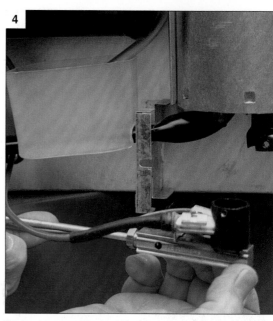

A protective shield is removed to gain access to the burner assembly.

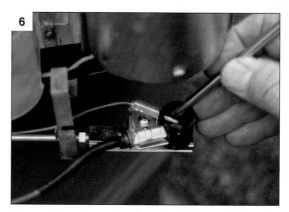

The burner assembly should be unscrewed and pulled away from its normal position to prevent soot falling on to it when the flue above is cleaned.

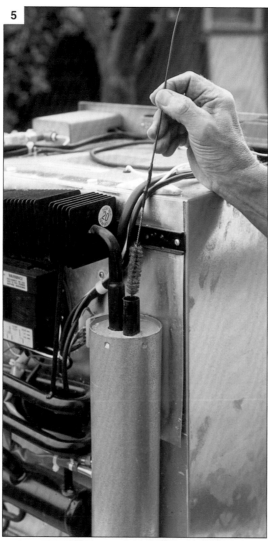

A special wire brush is manufactured by Electrolux for cleaning soot from the burner tube.

The screwdriver is merely used to point to the end of the thermocouple; soot on its tip will be removed. A service engineer will then adjust the adjacent ignition probe to achieve a 3mm clearance spark gap.

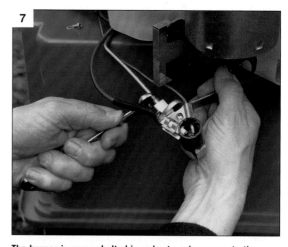

The burner is now unbolted in order to gain access to the small, removable gas jet. This has to be replaced; under no circumstances should the original jet be cleaned because the size of its aperture is critical.

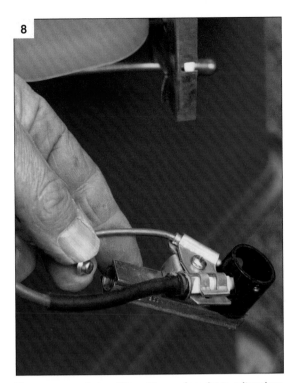

There are around nine different types of gas jet to suit various models in the Electrolux range. A new one must be fitted; it's an inexpensive component.

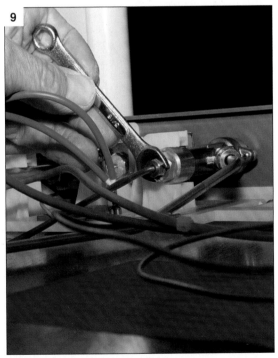

The thermocouple in the burner flame is part of a copper conductor which is coupled to the gas control behind the fascia. Its attachment nut is checked; if it shakes loose, the flame won't stay alight.

After a general inspection of the appliance, a bench test is carried out, including checking the burner flame. For example, on Electrolux RM 4200 and 6200 series models, the maximum flame height should be 50-60mm and the minimum flame height 15-20mm. On a fridge freezer, the maximum flame height is 30-40mm and the minimum height 10-15mm.

Flame failure device (FFD)

Gas only flows to the burner when the tip of the thermocouple has warmed up and the operating valve has automatically opened. During the warming-up period, you have to hold the valve open by depressing the gas control knob for a few seconds. The way a flame failure device works is described on page 85 of Chapter 6, and the operation of the FFD on a fridge is checked during a service. The latest 2004 models have a more sophisticated system.

Other types of refrigerator

In very small motorcaravans, there may not be space for a fixed refrigerator and semi-portable cool boxes are often fitted instead. Most of these offer three-way operation like an installed absorption fridge. But there are also compressor type versions from manufacturers such as Waeco.

Portability is certainly an asset and some motorcaravanners who already have a fixed fridge, purchase a cool box to keep in an awning or to take to the beach. As stated at the beginning of this chapter, 'in a motorcaravan, the refrigerator makes one of the most important contributions to comfortable living. . .'

Problem solving

If a refrigerator doesn't work on gas, check:

- The fridge's selection switch is set to gas operation
- The gas cylinder isn't empty and its control is switched on
- The gas control valve near the appliance is switched on
- If it has been serviced in the last 18 months.

If a refrigerator doesn't work on 12V:

- Ensure the fridge's selection switch is set to 230V operation
- Remember that this option only works when the engine is running
- Check all fuses related to the 12V supply
- Get an electrician to check that a 12V supply is reaching the fridge's connector block.

If a refrigerator fails to work on 230V check:

- The fridge's selection switch is set to 230V operation
- The mains is connected and the consumer unit's RCD and MCBs are switched on
- The refrigerator 230V plug is in the socket and the switch is on
- The fuse is intact if a 13 Amp plug is fitted.

Furniture and furnishings

The interior design of a motorcaravan is important to an owner. It is not just a matter of the layout or the number of beds; the styling is important, too. In fact the design of the furniture and the choice of fabrics is one of the first things you notice when entering the living area.

We all have individual preferences when it comes to interior design. Moreover, we all have different reasons for using a motorcaravan. Some owners, for example, enjoy passive leisure activities and prefer a traditionally-styled motorcaravan fitted with deep pile carpet, velvet curtains and florid fabrics. However, 'carpet-slipper' comfort isn't everyone's preference and this type of interior is hardly appropriate if you enjoy outdoor pursuits.

Many of the people designing British motorcaravan interiors haven't recognised that a lot of owners are interested in cycling, fishing, walking, or taking children to the beach. But that is starting to change. Today, fewer models adopt ornate styling and there's a shift away from fitted carpets, costly curtains, plush pelmets, and illuminated cocktail cabinets fitted with decorated 'plastic glass' and padded velvet interiors.

At last the designers are more mindful of the realities of weather and the nature of campsites, both of which impose a need for practicality. For instance, a smart fitted carpet looks fine in a showroom but it's far too 'precious' when it's raining, your shoes are muddy and the site owner's mower has left a lot of grass cuttings in the camping field. That's when a vinyl floor covering, with or without removable sections of carpet, is much more practical. So are surfaces which are easily cleaned.

Having said that, practical and contemporarily styled interiors are most likely to be found in van conversions, with models from Bilbo's and Murvi leading the way. Now the latest 2004 Trident from Auto-Sleepers has also joined this world of modern styling. But these are van conversions. In contrast the coach-built motorcaravans built in Britain still tend to adopt traditional design features. These observations are certainly worth noting, especially if you're planning to purchase a new or pre-owned motorhome; the accompanying pictures illustrate these contrasts.

Having made the point about different interiors, the rest of this chapter is concerned with the realities of ownership. To begin with you would want to keep your upholstery clean. Then there's

Removable carpet sections laid on a vinyl floor covering combine comfort with practicality, being much easier to clean after a stay at a muddy campsite.

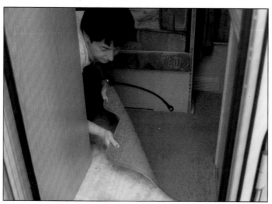

This 1994 Auto Sleepers model with its ornate styling, fitted carpet and florid fabrics might be fine for passive leisure but is hardly suitable for outdoor sports enthusiasts.

In complete contrast, this 2004 Auto-Sleepers Trident has clean lines, easy-clean surfaces and a vinyl floor covering – just what active owners need.

Notwithstanding the contemporary styling seen in many van conversions, British coachbuilts tend to have more traditional interiors.

the ever-present possibility of accidents in which a stain is left on the cushions or chewing gum gets trodden into the carpet. These problems are discussed as well.

After maintenance, there are improvement issues. Advice is given on upgrading the upholstery as well as seating in the cab. And there's guidance on furniture construction with ideas for improving a bed.

Interior cleaning

For routine cleaning when you're away from home, portable vacuum cleaners are very useful. Many of these are cordless rechargeables, whereas others run from a cigarette lighter socket.

Of course, you'll periodically need to undertake more thorough cleaning work and it's often worthwhile transferring seats and seat backs to a work bench outside. You can then use a proprietary product and it's often surprising how dirty a cloth becomes when wiping away a cleaning fluid.

Many domestic cleaning shampoos are suitable for motorcaravan furnishings and products from specialists such as Stain Devils are popular. Also take a look at vehicle upholstery cleaners. Products such as Auto Glym Car Interior Shampoo are suitable for use on most motorcaravan fabrics, including velour covers. With this product, the cleaning process entails:

- Spraying the Auto Glym cleaner directly on to the fabric
- Stippling the fabric gently with a soft brush to agitate the fibres
- Wiping the material with a clean cloth. Be warned – the cloth often gets much dirtier than expected!

If you do this work outdoors, cleaning fumes disperse easily and you avoid the problem of condensation forming inside the vehicle. So it's wise to wait until the weather's warm – but don't delay a cleaning operation if it involves removing stains.

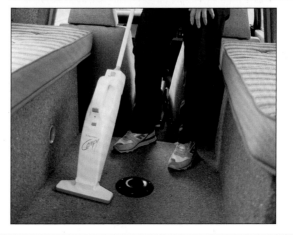

For use at sites, several rechargeable vacuum cleaners and hand-held portable units are available.

Using Auto Glym Car Interior Shampoo

First spray the shampoo onto selected areas of the fabric that needs to be cleaned.

Then agitate the fibres to work in the shampoo by stippling the fabric with a soft brush.

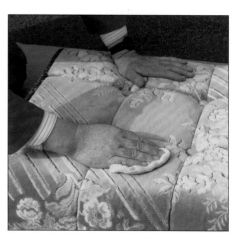

Finally, wipe the material with a clean cloth, which in turn lifts off the dirt.

Cleaning loose covers

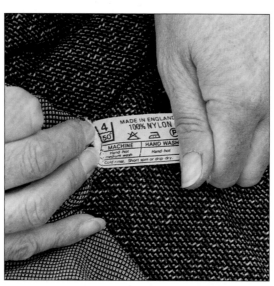

Many loose covers are machine washable, and if this is the case it should be indicated on the label.

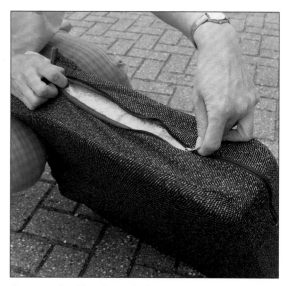

Covers made with a zip can be fastened more securely and are better than covers held on with tapes.

Dealing with stains

Everyone has the occasional accident, but if there's a regular risk of stain damage – perhaps from dogs or young children – it may be wise to have some loose-fitting protective covers made for selected seats. These are usually machine-washable as the label will confirm. The subject of covers, however, is dealt with in greater detail later.

It's also useful to keep a small container of general-purpose stain remover as a permanent item in your motorcaravan, but bear in mind that a 'do-everything' cleaner is seldom as successful as a cleaner made specifically to deal with a particular blemish.

Alternatively there are a number of kitchen products which can be used for removing stains

and a useful cleaning kit can be made up using the following:

• Absorbent white cloth
• Spray mister bottle
• Blunt, round-bladed knife
• Nail brush
• Salt
• Lemon juice
• White methylated spirits
• White vinegar
• Household ammonia
• Biological washing powder
• Glycerine
• Borax.

Many common stains can be removed using these household products as the panel opposite explains.

Other points to keep in mind:

· Treat a stain as soon as possible; the longer it is left, the harder it can be to remove.

· When applying a treatment, use a clean, white, cotton cloth – an old sheet is ideal. This is because the dye in a coloured or patterned rag can sometimes seep into the fabric you're cleaning.

· Always remove stains BEFORE submitting a fabric to the dry-cleaners.

· Identify the cause of a mark before applying a cleaner. An incorrect product can sometimes set a mark permanently.

· Before applying a treatment, always try it first on an inconspicuous corner of the fabric to make sure there's no unexpected reaction.

· Where there's a surface deposit, scrape away any remnants with a blunt-bladed table knife before applying a cleaning chemical to prevent the stain from spreading.

· Be gentle – fibres can be damaged by rough, scrubbing actions.

· If removing a mark from a velour seat cover, work in the direction of the pile to avoid causing damage.

· Be sparing with liquids, blotting periodically to avoid penetration into the foam below the cover.

· Remove all traces of cleaning fluids afterwards – some compounds leave a mark of their own.

· A final application of water is best done using a mist spray – the atomiser bottles sold at garden centres are ideal.

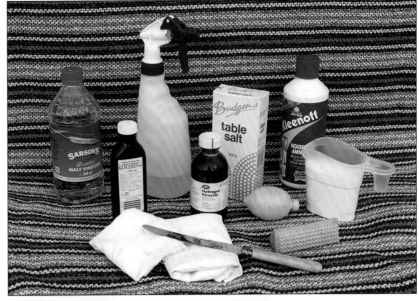

A very effective stain removal kit can be made up using products taken from the kitchen.

Safety

· Cleaning chemicals sometimes have an unpleasant odour; when working inside, open doors and windows to ensure there's good ventilation.
· Some proprietary cleaning fluids are inflammable; ensure there are no naked flames.
· Keep cleaning chemicals in labelled containers and store them away from children and pets.
· Don't experiment by mixing chemical cleaners together; results could be explosive.
· Wear protection when advised to on an instruction label; gloves are obvious but eye protection is sometimes needed, too.

Chewing gum

Freeze using ice cubes packed in a polythene bag, then tap away the brittle gum with a knife handle. Alternatively use Scotch 3M Clean Art – this comes from stationery specialists and removes deposits left on book covers by gummed-back price tickets. It can be similarly used to dissolve chewing gum.

Grass stains

Remove using a mixture of two parts white methylated spirits with one part water. Spray with water mist then dry.

Coffee stains

Soften using glycerine and leave for 25 minutes. Sponge away with clean water.

Tea stains

Treatment for coffee often works for tea as well. Alternatively sponge the area with a mixture of 1.5ml of Borax added to a half-litre of cool water.

Blood

Sponge with salt water solution followed by a mild ammonia and water mix. Blot at every stage, finish with clean water, and allow it to dry without applying heat.

Vomit

Sponge area with water to which drops of ammonia have been added. Then apply washing powder and water mixed into a dense paste, leaving it for 30 minutes. Brush this away before finishing with fresh water.

Wine

Remove colour using white vinegar and water. Alternatively make a mix of lemon juice and salt, then apply a washing powder paste as described for 'vomit'.

Sauces and ketchup

Soften with glycerine and remove excess. Sponge with an equal mix of white vinegar and water. Biological washing powder mixed to a paste may help to shift the final dye marks, but remember that some sauce stains are very resistant.

Worktop stains

Lemon juice is often successful in removing a discolouration.

Refrigerator staining

See Chapter 8, page 110 for dealing with stains inside the food compartment of a fridge.

Improving the soft furnishings

Being able to sit and recline in comfort is important. However, being seated during a journey is quite different from using a seat when parked on a site. Moreover, we all have different preferences when it comes to cushion resilience and improvements are often easily accomplished.

Foam failure

In some motorcaravans, seat foam loses its resilience surprisingly quickly. Usually this is because a cheap product was specified and the foam soon starts to 'bottom out'. This means you abruptly hit the under-base when sitting down firmly. Fortunately, many cures are available from upholstery specialists. These include:

Top-up foam

Since the original foam has compressed slightly, there's often room within the cover to add a thin layer (typically 25mm/1in) of high-resilience foam. Although the cover has to be opened to insert the top-up layer and then re-stitched, this is soon done with factory machinery and the cost is usually quite reasonable.

Foam replacement

Replacing the foam with a high-resilience product is obviously the best answer and several specialists provide this service. However, a good quality foam is quite costly, so get hold of some samples first in order to check their characteristics.

Specialist upholsters are able to cut foam to any size you want and it's equally straightforward to bond additional sections to create special shapes. Making a 'knee roll' (the raised front portion of a bench seat that gives support behind the knee) is also a simple task.

Creating a multiple-layered foam

A number of specialists are also able to bond two or three layers together to produce a composite foam; for example, a harder foam is often preferred as an under layer, with a softer product bonded on the top. Specialists such as the Caravan Seat Cover Centre of Bristol can even create a 'his 'n' hers' mattress in which the two halves of a double bed are made using bonded foams of different resilience to suit individual preference.

If you decide to have a new foam core, the finished job is even smarter if a final 'fibre wrap' is added. This is a white fibrous synthetic material often used as padding in quilted jackets and the

Replacement foam

Suppliers can cut upholstery foam to any size or shape and angled cuts are achievable too.

If extra sections are needed, these can easily be bonded together using special adhesives.

The forward edge of a seat can be fitted with a 'knee roll' for added comfort if required.

Foam offering different levels of resilience can be bonded together where needed.

Fibre-wrap or a layer of thin, resilient foams helps to round off sharp corners on a cushion.

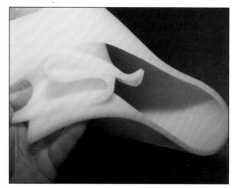

Replacement foam can be bought by mail order, but a template helps to ensure the size is correct.

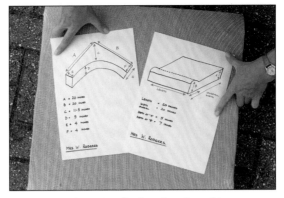

Diagrams showing unusually-shaped sections of foam are helpful when ordering by post.

effect is to round off the angular corners of block foam. Alternatively a thin layer of softer foam can be used to achieve this.

Most owners would prefer to have the refill operation completed professionally; however, mail order services are available for owners wishing to pick open a cover and later re-stitch it up again. If you order foam by mail order, it is usually wise to make some clear drawings of cushion shapes and to provide paper templates as well.

Spring interiors

These have been used for several seasons in more expensive motorcaravans; they can also be specified if you're having re-upholstery work done.

For the mattress on a bed, a spring interior is the preferred choice of many owners. However, on a bench seat used while you're travelling, a spring interior cushion can produce a bouncy ride. Equally there are instances where the forward edge of this type of seat is inclined to collapse, thus reducing leg support. Good support on a travel seat, together with safety belt security, is especially important.

So the case for preferring this type of core isn't completely straightforward. It partly depends on whether it's for a bed base or a seat used when travelling.

Cures for under-mattress damp.

If you use a motorcaravan in cold weather, it's not unusual to find damp patches developing on the underside of mattresses. This is especially prevalent if a mattress is supported by a table top or a solid ply base; it is far less frequent when a bed has a slatted base as described later in this chapter.

To facilitate the movement of air under a mattress – which helps to prevent the build-up of condensation – several underlay materials are available. For instance a 15mm non-slip, rubberised coir pad is available from The Natural Mat Company, Ventair 5 is sold by Dynamic Systems International, and Calypso Aqua Stop can be dispatched to the UK by E-Con Consulting GmbH & Co.KG and purchased via the web-site www.calypso-schlafsysteme.de.

Cover fabrics

Moving on to the cover fabrics, a cost-effective way of improving appearance is to fit loose covers. These are sometimes made with stretch fabric and a zipped version is undoubtedly better than one that uses tie tapes. Some loose covers are machine washable and these are a great help to parents whose children are at their 'sticky

In some situations a spring interior product is needed and these can be supplied by upholstery specialists.

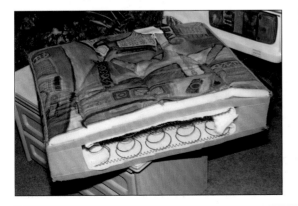

The 15mm non-slip, rubberised coir underlay from The Natural Mat Company helps reduce damp forming under a mattress.

New cushions bought from end-of-the-line models can be purchased from Magnum Caravan Surplus.

Surplus upholstery products are often on sale at outdoor shows.

'finger' stage. However, a problem with loose covers is the fact that they sometimes slip around the cushions.

Alternatively if you are refurbishing an elderly model but don't want to spend large sums of money, specialists like Magnum Caravan Surplus sell cushions which are bought-up from leading manufacturers when a model is coming to an end. You will also see surplus products on sale at some of the Outdoor Motorhome Shows. Finally there are caravan/motorhome breakers, some of whom dismantle insurance write-offs which are only two years old or less. For instance, reclaimed upholstery is racked and sold at The Caravan Centre in Pontypool.

Needless to say, there's an element of luck involved when trying to track down suitable products in this way. If you're renovating a

motorcaravan but are prepared to spend a reasonable sum on the upholstery, having new covers made professionally will achieve a stunning transformation. Caravan, Motorhome and Boat upholstery specialists are equipped to make unusually-shaped cushions, including split folders which open like a book for use when making-up beds or bunks.

Provided you pre-arrange your visit, several motorcaravan upholstery specialists can sometimes make and fit covers while you wait at their factory. However, with a large coachbuilt model this is likely to be a full day's work.

Prior to booking an appointment, send for fabric samples; the range of suitable materials is remarkable. Not only are there hundreds of

Features of professional re-covering services

Motorcaravan upholstery specialists can make unusual cushions like these 'split folders' which open up to form additional beds.

Here decorative ruche is stitched around the edges, but there are various alternative products to consider including piping, cord and tape.

A rotating table and specialised machinery is used by this professional upholsterer to stitch the top, side panels and ruche to a mattress.

Some skilful owners make their own covers, but with thicker fabrics you really need to have access to an industrial sewing machine.

A professional upholstery re-covering service will be able to make up attractive buttons using matching or contrasting material.

A thick needle is passed through a mattress, the 'T' tag is held flat in its eye, and then it is pulled back to secure an upholstery button.

patterns, there are also tweeds, velours and printed cottons to consider. In addition, you need to choose the edging trims. These include:

• *Taped edges* – usually a budget alternative, often used on a cushion base where the backing fabric is stitched to the main material.
• *Piping* – either made in matching material or in a contrasting colour.
• *Ruche* – decorative, woven tape that gives a smart appearance.
• *Cord* – used in a number of recent models, often with spiralling striped colours in the lay of the cord.
• *Cut ruche* – a fluffy edging that suits more ornate interiors.

These trims are usually applied on a rotating table top linked to a machine which stitches the main fabric to the edging trim and encapsulates the foam in a single operation. On the other hand you may prefer the covers to be made with a zip, which makes dry cleaning at a later date a feasible proposition.

Some indefatigable owners tackle this kind of refurbishment themselves, but if they don't own an industrial sewing machine, the results aren't always successful. Moreover, a specialist will make up matching upholstery buttons to prevent a cover from slipping around the foam. These are pulled through both the fabric and its foam core using an industrial needle. Careful use of an opened metal coat hanger and some insulation tape achieves the same result. Tags on the back secure each button, but if you want to remove the cover for laundering, the securing tape has to be cut.

Cab seating

Nearly all motorcaravans built in Britain are based on a light commercial vehicle (LCV). Compared with commercial vehicles manufactured 15 or more years ago, the current models have refinements like power steering and efficient heaters. But they are still principally designed for commercial use and in a few areas they lack the level of refinement appropriate for leisure accommodation vehicles. The seating is a case in point.

Swivelling seats

To begin with, it makes sense to use a cab to augment the space available in a living area. This can be achieved by fitting swivels to the seat mechanisms. There are also more comfortable seats on the market with padded head restraints and arms on both sides. And from the appearance point of view, the plastic lining material used on the inside of most doors can be easily covered using a fabric to match the rest of the interior.

The installation of seat swivels is a fairly straightforward job as the accompanying photo-sequence indicates. However, there are two points to keep in mind. Firstly, the addition of a swivel

Installing a low-level seat base and swivels

Crash-tested approved turntables are supplied by many automotive seat specialists.

The safety belt buckle was originally fitted to a lug on the sliders. This had to be sawn off and the buckle was then fitted to the swivel assembly.

The original Fiat seats were removed first and then the high base was unbolted from the floor.

The sliders are bolted to the swivel, though it's slightly different on the driver's side because there's a rise and fall mechanism on this seat.

The lower bases from TEK are made to fit the shape of a cab floor; cross brackets are also supplied.

The finished Fiat cab. Now it's possible to swivel the front seats round once parked and bring them into use as part of the living area.

In modern motorcaravans, covers have to possess a resistance to cigarette or match ignition and new models carry a label verifying their integrity. Sometimes, however, the resistance is lost after dry cleaning and the manufacturer should be consulted about this. Fabrics can often be re-treated to reinstate their fire-resistance.

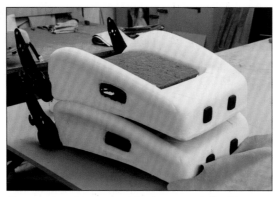

If you want to change your style of seat, specialists like Speedograph Richfield and TEK can supply new products.

When you visit the TEK factory, you'll often see fabrics that you recognise from the latest motorcaravans.

Conversion to Aguti seating

The Aguti seats which are fitted to high-quality motorcaravans can be supplied with an integral swivel system.

Aguti seats can be specified with arm rests whose height can be adjusted with a knurled wheel.

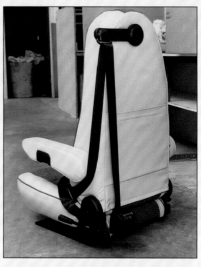

In this project, two additional 'occasional' removable seats were needed, and these featured integral crash-tested safety belts.

The high backs, leather edging, dark piping and contrasting fabric panels of these specially trimmed Aguti seats are a notable improvement.

The original plastic-covered door panels of this Fiat Ducato betrayed the commercial origins of the vehicle.

mechanism will raise the height of a seat and for taller drivers, this means that their line of vision is lifted inconveniently close to the top of the windscreen. This can be overcome by fitting lower seat bases. TEK Seating supplies replacement bases for Fiat Ducato, Peugeot Boxer, and Citroen Relay models; bases to suit other vehicles are also being designed. However, if your motorcaravan's leisure battery is stowed under a cab seat, you need to check its dimensions to confirm it can still be accommodated in a low-profile base.

Secondly, the steering wheel often limits clearance and prevents a driver's seat from swivelling through 180 degrees. Fitting a removable steering wheel will overcome this and these devices add a useful security benefit as well. Unfortunately, vehicles with a steering wheel fitted with an airbag cannot have this conversion carried out, although it has been reported that efforts are currently being made to find an answer to this.

Upgrading the seats

Some motorcaravans have matching fabric covers which merely fit over the standard commercial seats. However, these can sometimes pucker and slip so it's best to have the original seat properly re-upholstered. This is a job for a fabric trimmer and the addresses of A Baldassarre, Speedograph Richfield and TEK are given in the Appendix.

If you want to improve the quality of seat, both TEK and Speedograph Richfield carry stocks of moulded seat units, some of which you can try for comfort at the factory. High quality versions like Aguti seats – fitted to top motorhomes – are also imported by TEK.

TEK also supplies many of the British manufacturers and if you arrange to visit the factory, you will often recognise fabrics from the latest models. Not surprisingly, when the company is tackling a large order, it stands to reason that a one-off job for a private owner will have to wait for a week or so. However, that's the case with any

At TEK, door panels can be covered with upholstery fabric which is bonded to the original plastic and stapled around the perimeter.

upholstery specialist working in an industry with seasonal peaks.

Nevertheless, when the author wanted to achieve a top-class finish in his self-build motorhome, securing the services of TEK was worth a few week's wait. In the project shown alongside, four Aguti high-back seats with arm rests were needed. Two were to replace the original Fiat seats and two further seats with special swivelling plinths and built-in crash-tested safety belts were required to offer occasional seating for two more adults. The secondary seats had to be easily removable from floor mounting points because on most occasions, the vehicle is only used by two adults.

The four Aguti seats were trimmed in light grey leather with contrasting panels using a good quality automotive fabric. Extra fabric was also ordered to create matching bench seating in the lounge and some scatter cushions. Finally, the plastic door liners were trimmed with this matching material to disguise even further the commercial origins of the Fiat base vehicle.

Furniture construction and repair

Considerable skill is shown by the cabinet makers who construct and fit furniture in motorcaravans. Three objectives have to be met:

1) Structures have to be strong enough to withstand the rigours imposed by bumpy roads and uneven surfaces
2) The entire structure has to be light
3) The finished product should look attractive.

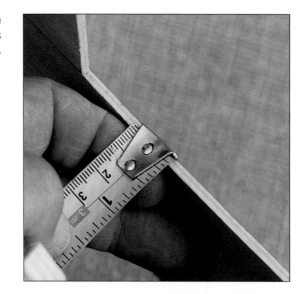

The print-faced decorative ply used in motorcaravans is only 3mm thick.

Hollow panels, door frames, tables and other components from major manufacturers are sold at Magnum Caravan Surplus.

Products, suppliers and building techniques

There's no doubt that many amateur converters with joinery experience are successful in producing smart, strong furniture, but some fail to keep the structures light. Even if you just want an extra shelf, you need to be mindful of weight-saving strategies. For that reason, the decorative veneered chipboard used in our homes is far too heavy for a leisure vehicle.

Conventional plywood is also too heavy, so for major structural work, motorcaravan manufacturers use Vohringer 15mm (9/16in) lightweight plywood which is usually faced with a plastic veneer. The importer's address is given in the Appendix and there are suppliers around the country.

Apart from Vohringer's products, the decorative faced plywood used for motorcaravan furniture and shelving is only 3mm thick and it's remarkably light. Unfortunately, 3mm faced plywood is seldom available from DIY stores and it may have to be purchased from a motorcaravan manufacturer's aftersales department. Alternatively, dozens of patterned boards are held in stock at the premises of Magnum Caravan Surplus in Grimsby. This Company has an arrangement with a number of major motorcaravan manufacturers to buy surplus stock whenever a model is replaced.

Ceiling, wall and mock-woodgrain boards for cabinets are held in stock. But bear in mind that the wood effect is generally achieved using a mock veneer printed on paper and stuck on to light grade plywood. The result looks convincing, but on no account should it be rubbed down with abrasive paper, as the paper veneer will simply rub off.

To achieve a smart finish, hardwood trim is often used as a surround moulding. This is the only concession in the weight-watching

As a small concession in the quest to save weight, the frames of cupboard doors are often made from solid wood.

To get a clean edge, 3mm lightweight ply is best cut to shape using a woodworking knife and a large rule.

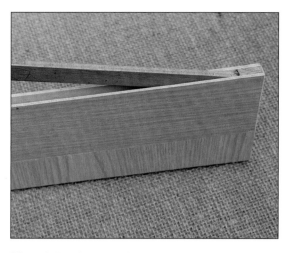

When a hollow door is cut down to reduce its dimensions, a spacer has to be glued into the void.

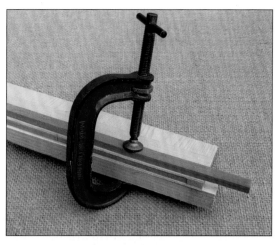

A 'G' cramp holds the assembly temporarily in place while the woodworking adhesive is setting.

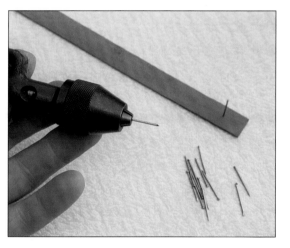

A slender veneer pin is used in a hand-drill to prepare pilot holes in the edging strip.

In this task, a grooved lipping piece is used to give strength to the edges of a 3mm plywood shelf.

battle. Hundreds of surplus furniture boards and cupboard door frames are stocked by Magnum Caravan Surplus. Whilst the frame of a roof-level locker door might be made in English Ash, for example, the main body of the piece is often just a thin plywood sheet. Alternatively a door may be hollow and built using two pieces of faced 3mm ply held apart by spacer blocks or a honeycomb of corrugated paper. Hardwood lipping around the edges adds the finishing touch and makes the unit look heavy and strong. It's only when an unhinged door is lifted up that you suddenly appreciate the clever weight-saving strategies.

Once this has been recognised, a skilled DIY woodworker can undoubtedly copy the techniques used by manufacturers. Using a steel edge and a sharp woodworking knife, it is easy to cut 3mm ply with several passes of the blade to achieve a clean edge.

Normally the fixings used by a home constructor would be rust-resistant woodscrews together with an appropriate adhesive – instead of staples which are often used by a converter for speed of construction. However, if you buy an electric staple

gun, you will find the abrupt impact often causes less damage when assembling a structure than repeated blows with a hammer.

Another point to remember is that the dimensions of a hollow door bought from surplus stock will probably need altering. The photographs above show how a hollow door was reduced in size and an insert slipped into the core to act as a spacer. A wood adhesive (Evo-Stik Resin W) was applied before introducing the spacer piece to create a good bond. A 'G' cramp held the assembly temporarily in place for 24 hours, using scrap timber to protect the surface of the workpiece from direct pressure and to extend the zone of compression.

The exposed edge is finally covered with a thin lipping cut on a circular saw bench. Veneer strip is an acceptable alternative but because it's so thin it is less bump-resistant. The lipping is held in place with an impact adhesive but additional strength can be achieved using veneer pins. Panel pins are too thick and a thin veneer pin is much less conspicuous. However, you will need to drill pilot holes to prevent the lipping from splitting

These hollow worktop sections were surplus stock which was being sold at an outdoor show.

This waste bin was mounted in a Woodfit lift-out, self-assembly drawer which slides on wheeled runners.

and the pin from bending. Some woodworkers nip off the pointed head of veneer pins which helps to overcome this problem, but it's better to drill a pilot hole.

If you don't possess slender twist drill bits, use one of the pins themselves. Cut off the head with pliers so that the pin seats well in a hand-drill chuck, then offer up the pointed end and keep the drill turning quite fast. It gets hot as it penetrates the lipping, but it does the job well.

Another recommendation if you want to strengthen a small shelf made from 3mm ply is to cut some 8mm (or thicker) hardwood lipping and prepare a groove in it on a saw bench. Alternatively use a combination plane. As the accompanying photograph shows, this is glued and slid onto the edge of the ply to add surprising

strength to an otherwise flexible, lightweight sheet. However, if it's hollow worktop material which you need, this is often sold by surplus specialists and the products shown here look very much like worktops fitted by the Swift group.

As regards furniture catches, hinges and handles, specialists like Woodfit supply a whole range of items including self-assembly drawer kits with roller rails; this company's catalogue is well worth obtaining. In addition, stays, ventilators and plastic turn-buttons used in the caravan trade can be purchased by mail order from CAK of Warwickshire or by using the huge 1150-page Häfele catalogue and mail order service.

Improving beds

It is surprising that so many bed bases have been constructed using solid plywood to support the mattress or seat cushions. It was mentioned earlier that if there's no free-flow of air under a mattress, damp patches from condensation will soon appear, especially in cold weather.

Softwood slats help to solve this but they lack resilience and contribute very little to comfort. Slats made with a camber from solid beech or a laminated construction are much better. Provided the ends of each slat are retained within a sleeve to permit movement, these products add to the resilience provided by the mattress.

However, this can be further improved if each slat is mounted within a cushioned end cap as shown alongside. This arrangement permits even greater flexibility and bed kits of this type are obtainable from The Natural Mat Company. Having created a double bed using two of these kits, the author is able to report that the arrangement affords extremely good comfort, even with a mattress as shallow as 100mm (4in).

Taking the idea even further, a German manufacturer is now offering the Calypso system where slats are supplied to suit a double-width bed. Whereas slats of this length had always flexed too much at mid point, the Calypso product includes sprung plastic supports which prevent this from happening.

In both systems, the ends of all the slats need to be supported on a rail, but they are free-fitting and are not fixed in place. So if it were necessary to lift the assembly of sprung cross members, this could be easily achieved. Anyone wishing to upgrade a motorcaravan bed could certainly have one of these products installed. The length of each slat will need to be cut to length to suit the particular location but the result would be well worth the effort involved.

In Germany the developments in bed systems have proceeded even further. Good though slatted systems may be, an assembly of wooden struts and fittings can be fairly heavy. This has led to the development of the Froli and Lattoflex systems which have been used in motorcaravans manufactured by la strada and Knauss.

The Froli components which provide support for a mattress look rather like the heads of flowers. They can either be mounted individually on a base board or clipped to flat strips of interlocking plastic. Then there's a clever feature whereby coloured inserts can be added in the centre of selected units to limit the spread of the 'petals', thus creating a firmer support. It means that individual zones can be firmed-up for anyone wanting to create extra support in particular places.

Today there are six or more variations on the basic design and it is fairly easy to construct a bed base using Froli components. They can be purchased from Froli Kunstoffwerke Fromme GmbH and further information appears (in English) on the website www.froli.com. A similar system is sold under the Calypso brand name, and there's also a further variation on the theme. A hybrid system of springing comprises sprung wooden slats to which the builder adds Calypso plastic

units to create even more flexion.

The CarWinx system from Lattoflex is different again and the accompanying photograph shows the plastic cross bars and their circular plastic supports. Resilience is derived from both the flexion of the bars as well as the supports and the system is certainly light. The photo here was taken on a fixed rear bed on a 2001 la strada Nova, and CarWinx products were also used on Knauss Traveller models of the same year. Provided there is a suitable base, a CarWinx system can easily be fitted as part of an upgrading project. Further information on the product is available from Thomas GmbH & Co Sitz und Liegemöbel KG, or the website www.lattoflex.com.

Beds in many motorcaravans are not as comfortable as they ought to be and the introduction of new systems like the ones described here is certainly welcome.

Different bed systems

Cambered wood slats from The Natural Mat Company are mounted in end caps which offer additional springing.

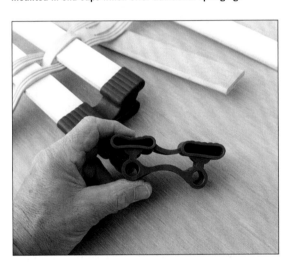

The extra-long slats in a Calypso double bed kit include flexible supports which are fitted at the mid-point.

The Froli system has removable units which also accept coloured inserts to firm-up selected parts of the bed.

The CarWinx system from Lattoflex is now being used in a number of German-built motorcaravans.

10
Contents

Motorcaravan accessories

Fire extinguishers, security products, cycle racks, TV aerials, awnings and many more accessory items are included in this chapter. However, the most important of all are those concerned with safety and security.

The first accessory items discussed in this chapter are probably the most important of all. Whereas recent motorcaravans are fitted with a smoke alarm as standard, owners are left to purchase their own fire extinguisher and fire blanket.

Fire precautions

Fires can develop in a number of areas of a motorcaravan and the first concern is to get everyone out of the vehicle. Whether a fire can be extinguished depends on the circumstances, but having the right equipment can buy sufficient time to make sure everyone is out of danger. So what sort of extinguisher should you buy?

There are different types of fire and safety equipment is manufactured with this in mind. Fires are classified as:

Class A: Solid materials, especially those of organic origin (such as paper, wood, fabrics).
Class B: Liquids (such as oil, petrol, alcohol, fat).
Class C: Flammable gases (such as butane, propane, hydrogen).
Class D: Unusual substances including metals (such as aluminium, lithium).
Class E: Electrical products (such as burning mains cable).

Fire extinguishers

The measures to adopt vary depending on these different types of fire. Whereas a bucket of water is sufficient to extinguish flames, the effect on a fat fire can be devastating. Similarly, water is entirely inappropriate where electrical components are on fire; even a jet of foam directed at a mains supply cable can lead to electrocution. Manufacturers therefore offer a range of products which meet the

A fire extinguisher should be easy to reach but it must never be fitted where it might be in the path of flames from a cooker.

A fire blanket is an essential item for dealing with fat or pan fires.

requirements of current European Norms (formerly covered under BS 5423).

In the context of motorcaravanning, where the living area is relatively confined, a dry powder extinguisher is recommended as the most appropriate all-round type to purchase. This can deal with wood, fabric, burning liquids and gases; in addition it can be used on an electrical fire.

With older types of dry powder extinguisher the contents sometimes got compacted – so the casing had to be inverted and given a good shake. This tendency has largely been overcome and the latest formulation is less likely to suffer from caking up.

Having bought one you need to:
- Consider the extinguisher's proposed location
- Keep note of the date on the casing – all extinguishers have a shelf life
- Check the pressure gauge, where fitted. This is a useful feature to have
- Be familiar with the way the extinguisher is withdrawn from its rack
- Ensure you know how the trigger is released and activated.

Fire safety is important and advice on procedures and precautions can be obtained from the caravan clubs. It is also prudent when arriving at a caravan site to familiarise yourself with the equipment provided. Fire is not a subject to be taken lightly.

Fire blankets

The method for dealing with a chip or frying pan fire is to smother it with a fire-retardant cloth in order to cut off the oxygen. In some instances you can achieve the same result using a metal tray. Nevertheless, a 'fire blanket' complying with EN 1869 is a worthy purchase.

Smoke detectors

In theory these are useful warning devices but in the enclosed confines of a motorcaravan, they are easily activated when you're cooking. The fact that many owners remove the battery is testimony to the problem but you should check if this action would invalidate the insurance or warranty of the vehicle. The practicality of these devices is partly dependent on the size of motorcaravan and the detector's location.

Installation tip

When fitting a fire extinguisher or fire blanket to an item of furniture built from thin plywood, a piece of 9mm (³⁄₈in) ply should be fixed on the reverse side of the mounting point. However, on a wall lined with plywood the material is too thin, so add 9mm ply on its face. This reinforcing plywood can be fixed using an impact adhesive like Evo-Stik or an adhesive sealant like Sikaflex 512 Caravan Sealant together with several short screws. When the extinguisher framework is then installed, the fixings benefit from a total thickness of 12mm (¹⁄₂in) of solid material.

Safety regulations

To comply with safety regulations, upholstery fillings in *touring* caravans built on or after 1 March 1990 have 'combustion modified' foam in the cushions, mattresses and seat backs. Motorcaravans fall outside these regulations because they are classified as motor vehicles, thereby coming under different legislation. Nevertheless, fumes emitted from burning upholstery foam can cause severe respiratory problems, so it is wise to have the foam upgraded.

In a touring caravan, all upholstery covers also have to possess a resistance to cigarette or match ignition, and new models carry a label confirming this. A motorcaravan can be treated similarly; this resistance, however, will be lost after dry cleaning – re-treatment by a specialist is then needed.

Security products

Mechanical security products, electronic alarms and tracking devices all help protect a motorcaravan against theft and break-in.

Storage and parking protection

When comparing security systems, it is important to appreciate the difference between alarming a vehicle parked in town, and one that is parked for an extended period in an unattended storage compound. The battery which provides the power will eventually lose its charge.

Similarly when comparing wheel clamps, it should be recognised that light products intended for use on a site are very different from the heavy duty models needed in an unattended location.

Security tests

With so many security products on sale it can be quite difficult to ascertain the level of protection they provide. However, this has been helped by the establishment of test houses. For instance, in Britain the Sold Secure initiative provides manufacturers of security devices with an opportunity to have their products evaluated by independent testers.

The tests are strictly timed and conducted in a closely controlled manner, thereby standardising the procedures. A remarkable armoury of destructive 'tools' is at the disposal of the experienced examiners, and the attack tests employ anything from crude wrecking bars to the very latest lock-picking tools. To pass the Silver and even more stringent Gold standard tests, products have to be good. If they fail, their manufacturers are advised where further development is needed. Different procedures are used for testing electronic alarms, although the tests are no less searching.

Obviously this is a useful benchmark although it doesn't necessarily mean that a Sold Secure Approved Product cannot be beaten. Equally there are other good products on the market which

Don't be tempted to fit a fire extinguisher and fire blanket too close to a likely problem area (such as adjacent to a hob). If the equipment falls within the path of flames, it becomes a hazard to reach.

When using a fire blanket, grasp it first and then turn your hands so that the edge of the fabric covers your fingers, protecting them from flames. Alternatively, some models are fitted with tapes so you can keep your hands at a safe distance.

might not have been submitted for assessment. Nevertheless, it is very useful for members of the public to be able to find out – free of charge – which products have passed Sold Secure tests.

Types of security product

The accompanying photographs show both mechanical products and a Strikeback electronic system from Van Bitz being installed.

Removable steering wheels provide space for rotating a driver's seat so that it can be put to use in the living area. Moreover, the lack of a steering wheel is certainly a discouragement to anyone intent on stealing a vehicle. On the other hand, recent vehicles now have air bags mounted within their steering wheels and this has led to a decline in sales of these security products.

The illustrations of wheel clamps also show two contrasting examples. There are certainly a lot of wheel clamps on sale for cars and caravans, but only a few fit the larger wheels of commercial vehicles. The photographs show one of Bulldog's lighter clamps for use on holiday; the PGR clamp could similarly be used on a campsite but is a heavier product more appropriate for use in storage situations.

As regards electronic security systems, there's an ever-growing array of tracking devices which reveal the movements of a motorcaravan *after* it has been stolen. There are also plenty of

The removable steering wheel on this Auto-Trail motorcaravan is not just a security feature; it also allows the driver's seat to swivel round so that it forms part of the living area seating.

electronic alarms for cars, but very few purpose-designed alarms for motorcaravans. The Van Bitz Strikeback Alarm is the exception and versions are made for both small/mid-sized motorhomes and American RVs. Free booklets provide useful information about these sophisticated systems. One of the installations will even call your mobile phone if the motorcaravan is being tampered with, and there's also a facility for setting your alarm by phone. Strikeback security systems are used by many motorcaravan owners although they're too sophisticated for DIY installation.

On another note, Strikeback is one of several

Bulldog manufactures several types of wheel clamp and this one is conveniently compact to stow in a motorcaravan.

This sturdy PGR wheel clamp which has passed Sold Secure tests is suitable for use during extended storage periods.

A Strikeback Alarm system can incorporate many features, including bike and rack protection and telephone paging.

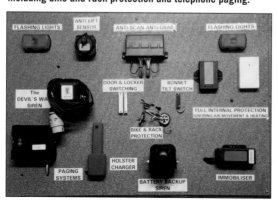

Because of the sophisticated electronics used in a Strikeback alarm system, it has to be fitted by an experienced installer.

Gas attacks on sleeping motorcaravanners parked in lay-bys abroad have led to increased sales of gas alarms.

Plastic trackway sections from Fiamma help to prevent the driving wheels from sinking in soft ground.

manufacturers supplying gas alarms. These detect a butane or propane gas leak in a motorcaravan but that isn't their only purpose. There have been reported instances where owners who have parked at night in service stations on the Continent have been gassed and robbed. Slender tubes delivering ether have been fed through window rubbers or other apertures by thieves intent on breaking in without waking the occupants. The Van Bitz Strikeback alarm thus serves a dual purpose.

Pitch parking

To achieve a level parking position, wheels may need elevating and motorcaravanners often carry short lengths of wood to achieve this. The alternative is to buy purpose-made blocks and chocks. Portable plastic ramps from Fiamma are popular and a double-width version is available to

suit motorcaravans with twin wheels.

A more expensive model from Fiamma is the Level System ALU. This includes a chock to keep the wheel firmly on its slope. Serrated surfaces reduce slipping and Fiamma's ALU product is undoubtedly more suitable when motorcaravanning in wet or wintry weather.

Levelling aids are an essential part of a motorcaravanner's equipment. However, on muddy ground sinkage is another hazard and to avoid getting well and truly stuck, plastic trackway sections from Fiamma are available from most dealers.

Awnings and roller blinds

When based on a site for several days, an awning increases the living space and also stakes a claim to a pitch when a motorcaravan is away from the site. Roll-out blinds cannot do this of course, though they're much speedier to set up. If a blind is preferred, remember that some models accept side panels to create a complete enclosure. However, these panels have to be detached prior to withdrawing the blind.

It should also be recognised that a blind cassette mustn't project dangerously beyond the side of a motorcaravan. This installation challenge was neatly solved by Auto-Trail which mounted the cassette in a moulded channel which had been

The roll-out blind fitted to this Auto-Trail Mohican is both simple to use and quick to set up.

Additional front and side walls have been added to this Omnistor roll-out blind.

The idea of fitting a roll-out blind in a moulded channel has been adopted here.

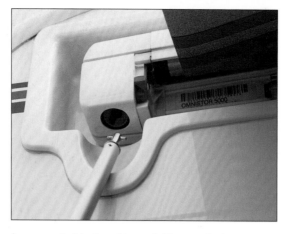

Awning cleaners

Try to avoid erecting an awning under trees; some species are notorious for releasing sap.

If you have a problem removing sap, or other unusual marks, awning cleaners are available. An example is Camco Awning Cleaner, available from ABP Accessories. This American product is specially formulated to remove sap, mould, mildew and grime.

On this Ventura awning, the valance achieves an effective coupling with a variety of different motorcaravans.

incorporated in the side wall. The product was shown in 1998 and many other manufacturers have since employed this arrangement.

However, channelling like this cannot be easily incorporated in a panel van conversion and in acknowledgement of the curving surfaces that often make it difficult to attach a cassette unit, a range of brackets is available from specialists like Fiamma and Omnistor. Without doubt, a roller blind has much to commend it.

Free-standing motorcaravan awnings need to have a zip-up fourth side to provide total closure when the vehicle leaves the pitch. Unlike touring caravan awnings, these structures have to be self-supporting and a valance is intended to create a weatherproof coupling with the motorcaravan's door. The success of this varies simply because it's difficult to design a universal coupling when the body profiles of vehicles vary so much. However, the latest models in the Ventura range have a valance coupling which is particularly versatile.

A further problem for the awning designer is the variation in vehicle heights. Some awnings (such as Apache) are therefore available in high and low versions. It's also important that a hinged motorcaravan door doesn't chafe against the roof panel when it is opened.

A recent development in awnings is the manufacture of modified tunnel tents which are

made to link with the door of a van conversion. Their flexible hooped poles are light and the extra living space is surprisingly capacious. Examples are illustrated in the catalogues of Just Kampers and Reimo.

When comparing awnings, bear in mind the merits of different materials:

Poles

Steel tubing

Strength is the point in steel's favour; weight is its disadvantage. A resistant anodised finish is used on higher quality awnings, whereas less expensive products soon rust when the coating gets damaged.

Aluminium

Though less common, aluminium is light and resistant to corrosion, but aluminium tubing lacks the rigidity of steel poles.

Glass fibre tubing

This is strong, light, and it neither rusts nor oxidizes. Its disadvantage is its flexibility and a winter motorcaravanner watches vigilantly when it snows. The weight of snow can flex glass fibre poles so much that a structure can subsequently collapse.

Glass fibre rods

These are used for tunnel tent/awnings. Misuse will lead to fractures and metal sleeves should be taken to effect temporary repairs.

Fabrics

Cotton

Though usually less expensive than a synthetic fabric, cotton has the advantage of breathability. In consequence it doesn't suffer from the condensation problems associated with impervious synthetics. However, cotton is less tolerant of ill treatment. If packed damp and left for several

Sturdy anodized steel poles are a feature of this quality awning.

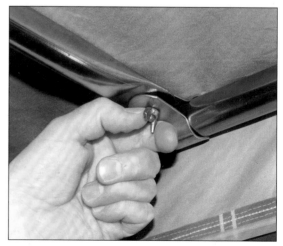

Many awnings are made with a protective PVC panel which is designed to counter splash-up marks.

days, the material soon suffers from mildew stain which is one of the most difficult marks to remove. If left for longer, the fabric will start to rot.

Synthetic

There are many types of synthetic material and some are as soft as cotton but more resistant to wear. Good synthetic fabrics are expensive and many types are not breathable – so venting is essential to disperse condensation. Damp surfaces soon form on the inner surface of a non-breathable material, especially if an awning is used for cooking or as a drying room.

Mixed materials

Some roofs consist of a weather-resistant coated polyester fabric, while the main part of the wall is cotton and the lower section – approximately 30cm (12in) – is PVC. The PVC copes with splash-up damage in downpours and spray damage from canine leg-lifters.

Design Details

Awning accessories include:

- A pocket panel for storing holiday items
- An inner tent which offers additional sleeping space
- Storm guys
- Zip-on side extension rooms.

The benefit of having a ground sheet should be taken into consideration, too. Traditional plastic sheets damage a grass pitch, so there are meshed carpets which are breathable. These can often be cut from a roll to meet specific requirements.

Repairs and spares

Several repairers advertise their services in motorcaravan magazines and spares suppliers often attend outdoor rallies. Awnings can be expensive, but with spares and repairs they can last a long time.

Roof racks

Awkward but light items such as folding camp chairs can sometimes be conveniently transported on a roof rack. However, it is unwise to stow heavy equipment here because it can seriously upset a vehicle's cornering capabilities.

Unfortunately it has become fashionable to fit a semblance of a roof rack on many vehicles. These are cosmetic appendages rather than serviceable carriers. In many instances, tying points are missing and the roof cladding is exposed instead of being protected by load-bearing support rails running across the roof.

Bicycle and motorcycle racks

Heavily laden roof racks are not the only creators of instability. The carriage of heavy items on the rear of a motorcaravan can also affect road-holding as well as adding significantly to the weight being carried by the rear axle. Some

Two bicycles, a satellite dish and a top box carried on a motorcaravan with a long rear overhang could easily lead to an over-laden rear axle.

Bike rack fixing points

- To ensure owners fit a bike rack securely, models like the Auto-Roller Arabella are made with factory-fitted mounting plates.

- On a number of Auto-Sleepers GRP coachbuilt models, 12mm plywood strengthening sections are bonded into the rear panel to provide sound mounting points. Auto-Sleepers' dealers are sent information sheets which show the precise location of these strengthening pads.

- Problems are often more acute on van conversions because the steel panels lack reinforcement. A metal door skin can flex badly when a rack is laden, so installation is often best left to a skilled bodywork specialist.

If it isn't fitted correctly, a cycle rack mounted on a van door imposes considerable stress on the steel panels.

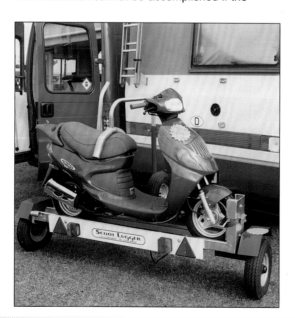

The Scoot Lugger sold by TOWtal offers an alternative way to transport a scooter.

On the rear wall of this Auto-Roller coachbuilt, fixing brackets fitted during production are all ready to receive a cycle rack.

owners seem oblivious to the stated loading limit of their motorcaravan's rear axle, but exceeding the maximum weight is not only dangerous – it's a criminal offence. The effect of carrying a heavy motorcycle, particularly when a motorcaravan has a large rear overhang, must be checked on a weighbridge. So must the integrity of a rack's fixing points. There have been several instances where detached racks loaded with bicycles have fallen in the path of following vehicles. Self-tapping screws are no good at all: rack fixings must be bolted right through a body panel and fitted with a plate on the inside.

Mindful of this, several Italian coachbuilders manufacture motorcaravans with standard factory-fitted fixing brackets. Some Laika models also include a chassis modification which incorporates a slide-out motorcycle rack and number plate/lighting board.

Equally impressive are motorcycle racks from AL-KO Kober which are purpose-designed for installing on motorcaravans built on an AL-KO chassis (as described in Chapter 4.) However, the installation cannot be accomplished if the

Slide-out racks are designed as an integral part of the chassis on several Laika motorcaravans.

motorcaravan manufacturer has extended the body *beyond* the rear-most cross member of the chassis, as some do.

One way of overcoming these problems is to carry motorcycles or scooters on a purpose-made trailer, and examples are sold by companies such as TOWtal. However, don't forget that your permitted maximum speeds are reduced when towing and it is illegal to use the outside lane of a three (or more) lane motorway.

Of course, if you want to tow a trailer you'll have to have a tow bracket fitted. On that note, if it's a flanged bolt-on towball, you can install some bike racks as well. For example, mounting plates on racks manufactured by Witter use the towball's attachment bolts. The product allows you to carry bikes even when a trailer is attached – provided you exceed neither the maximum permitted nose weight of the towing bracket nor the rear axle's weight limit.

Storage boxes

External storage containers are another way to increase stowage space. Products from Omnistor and Fiamma are stocked by most dealers and several smaller suppliers are involved as well.

Few roof boxes have a shape likely to facilitate fuel economy and to re-state an earlier point, heavy loads should never be carried on a roof because it can seriously affect stability. Then there is the matter of roof structure and an earlier panel has drawn attention to this matter.

If you are desperate to have more space for stowing light but bulky items, a rear-mounted storage box might be better. The Bak-Paka from Premier Glassfibre is made of GRP; back boxes in

ABS plastic are manufactured by Omnistor. These are easier to reach than roof boxes. However, you need to be mindful of the security of the contents, the effectiveness of the mountings, and the matter of rear axle loading limits.

Noise reduction

Recognising that the majority of motorcaravans are built on light commercial vehicles, it's hardly surprising that the cabs are inclined to be noisy. More surprising is the fact that few owners seem to complain about this. It's certainly a hindrance for anyone wishing to listen to quieter passages of music.

However, now that noise reduction products are available for motorcaravans, expectations might change. After working on sound reduction in cars for a number of years, Noise Killer Acoustics UK has recently developed products for the motorhome market as well. For example, Teflon-coated engine blankets are available for muffling engine noise. But that's only a start. Also available is a special lining for the bonnet lid and the company sells waterproof-foil-faced material which is self-adhesive and easily cleaned. There's also an open-cell Class 'O' acoustic foam used to absorb engine noise.

The cab doors are another contributor to noise inside and a full installation carried out by Noise Killer Acoustics includes attention here as well. Products are also available for DIY installation.

Less easily solved are wind noises created from a poorly designed overcab moulding which occurs on some coachbuilt models. Another common problem is noise caused by poor sealing around the cab doors. Nevertheless, it is likely that this is an area which will receive increasing attention in the future.

Cab window blinds and covers

Many motorhomes are fitted with cab curtains which often get caught on their rail and usually fall foul of the seat belts. They certainly do little to curb the loss of heat in the winter and that is one of the reasons why Silver Screens were launched by J & M Designs nearly 20 years ago. Today there are several models in the Silver Screens range, all of which are made to fit the cabs of most motorcaravans. There's also a version which accepts a mesh panel as well. This lets in light but still affords a measure of privacy during the day. Velcro enables its interchangeable panels to be attached as required.

More recently, there has also been a Seitz roller blind on sale which will fit in a variety of motorcaravan cabs. It uses attachment points already available in vehicles and the product can be installed in minutes. When unrolled it simply hooks over the sun visors. However, it is a Remis

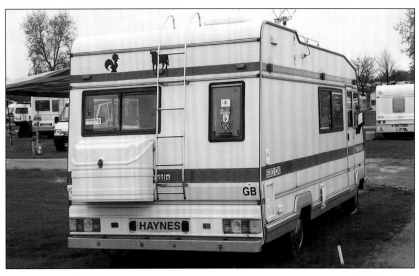

product which goes one step further by including privacy blinds for side windows.

The Remis system was first fitted to 2004 models and is easy to install on many existing Fiat, Mercedes and Peugeot cabs. A DIY installation of this product is straightforward and it is only the side window frames which call for some drilling work. The front and side blinds can be bought separately or as a set.

Rear storage boxes are a good alternative to roof boxes because they keep the weight lower down.

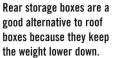

Products from Noise Killer Acoustics UK are often on display at outdoor motorcaravan shows.

Recent Silver Screen products include covers which are made of interchangeable mesh and silver-insulated panels.

Fitting Remis
screen and side
window cab blinds

The Remis concertina blind pulls up from the fascia and runs along hinge-up trackways on either side of the screen.

To secure the side trackways, push-fit catches are mounted on this Fiat Ducato's screen pillars using the original trim screws.

Six self-tapping screws attach each of the moulded plastic side frames securely to the doors.

When the concertina side blinds are extended and secured with their magnetic catches, total privacy is assured.

TV equipment

Many motorhome owners take a TV set on holiday in order to watch terrestrial programmes. If you usually avoid sites with mains hook-ups, remember that monochrome TV sets take considerably less power out of a battery than a colour TV. However, few people want to watch black and white images.

Whichever type of set you use, two further items are needed:

• An aerial
• A signal controller.

Aerial

The majority of motorcaravans are fitted with an omni-directional aerial. These saucer-like units need no adjusting because, as the name implies, they capture signals from all directions. At least that is the intention. In reality, their performance is often disappointing, especially in areas where the reception is poor in the first place.

A directional aerial provides much better reception – as long as it is pointed towards the

transmitter. Its elements also have to be set either in a vertical or a horizontal plane to suit the signal transmitted from the nearest station. In addition, the traditional directional aerial with its assembly of metal elements is rather ugly and wouldn't be permanently mounted on the roof of a road-going vehicle. However, the Status 530 directional aerial is different.

The Status 530 has its elements enclosed in a streamlined plastic casing. There are two versions, the 530/10 with its metre-long mast, and a short-mast version, the 530/5. Once these products have been permanently mounted, they can be rotated, raised, lowered, and angled either horizontally or vertically from inside the living area. Their performance is also very much better than a Status omni-directional aerial.

The mast has to be lowered before you take to the road so the 530/10 version has to be installed where its metre-long pole can slide down into a wardrobe, cupboard or purpose-made enclosure. If the layout inside makes this difficult, the 2004 version of the 530/5 is sufficiently short for the mast to slide down into a typical roof locker.

The accompanying photographs show a new installation in progress, although it is also fairly easy

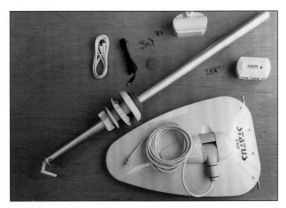

The installation kit includes a complete mast assembly, the signal controller and all the fixings needed.

A pilot hole was drilled in the roof to confirm that the mast position would be suitable for the layout inside.

A 45mm hole was then formed in the roof to accept the mounting foot; the aerial is assembled and ready.

The mounting foot permits a degree of tolerance in roof slope but the mast needs to be set in a vertical plane.

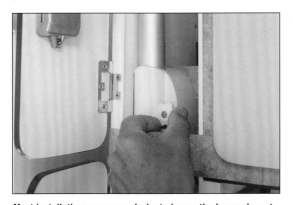

Most installations use a wardrobe to house the lowered mast and clamp but this cupboard was purpose-made.

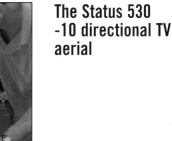

Before driving off, the aerial is lowered and aligned fore and aft; the VHF antennae shown here then needs to be withdrawn.

to fit a 530 directional aerial as a replacement for a Status omni-directional one. With this in mind, the manufacturer, Grade (UK), can supply a special cover plate that seals the original attachment holes left behind when an omni-directional type is removed. The plate can be fitted using an adhesive sealant like Sikaflex 252 or Sikaflex 512 Caravan Sealant. Then a fresh 45mm hole can be drilled in the middle of the cover plate to accept the 530 mast collar. Alternatively, there's nothing to stop you fitting it elsewhere on the roof as long as the structure is sound and there's somewhere inside where the lowered 800mm section of mast can be appropriately accommodated.

When it comes to signal gain, the longer masted 530/10 is obviously the better of the two. However, both have a folding handle on the bottom of the mast for altering the inclination of the aerial. Equally you can rotate both 530 models while checking picture quality from inside the living area. You only need to go outside to withdraw the telescopic VHF antennae if the aerial is going to be used to receive FM radio.

Signal controllers

Whether you have a directional aerial or an omni-directional model, the quality of picture also depends on the proximity to a television transmission station. This is why most manufacturers of motorcaravan aerials supply a signal control box. Using a battery-powered amplifier, a weak signal can thus be improved. On the other hand, you might be too near to a station. The Caravan Club Site in South London is situated directly below the TV transmission mast at Crystal Palace. In this instance the signal is too strong and most control boxes include an attenuation control that will reduce its strength.

Satellite TV

Motorcaravans can also be fitted with satellite dishes, some of which are notably compact. On the other hand, if you want to receive all UK television stations in a wide range of countries abroad, a dish no less than 1.2m in diameter is normally recommended.

Several specialists supply the necessary equipment, and satellite TV is much liked on account of its picture quality, range of available channels, and the fact that you can visit many other European Countries and still receive the programmes you watch at home.

This is a fast-developing medium and in some respects it is a complex subject. Nevertheless, further guidance on receiving satellite TV in motorcaravans can be obtained from specialists such as Grade UK and Maxview. Also particularly helpful are the guidance pages on Satellite TV in RoadPro's catalogue.

Tables

It is surprising that many manufacturers fit unsatisfactory tables in motorcaravans. In a number of German A-Class motorhomes, for example, clumsy and surprisingly heavy tables are fixed permanently to the floor, thereby impeding movement around the living space.

In many British motorcaravans, notoriously unstable pole tables are installed and a small nudge leads to a wobbling table top and spilt drinks. Movable tables are better and can be used outdoors; but some of the folding leg assemblies are heavy and have a nasty habit of causing pinched fingers.

Mindful of these problems, the Dutch company Zwaardvis, known by many boat owners, has now introduced its products to motorcaravan manufacturers. Its pole systems are notably rigid because hitherto they've been used to support seats in sports boats. Out of necessity, the support pole hardly deflects at all – even though it is removable – and telescopic versions are fitted with a gas strut-assisted rise and fall mechanism. Their suitability for motorcaravan applications is very obvious and this was recognised a few seasons ago by some German manufacturers including la strada and Knauss.

Apparently Zwaardvis is Dutch for 'swordfish' and there are many variations in the company's pole systems, floor mounting plates, table-top slide mechanisms and bases which allow a table to be used as a free-standing unit outside. All you then need is a top to complete a table.

In the Mystique motorcaravan, described in the next chapter, this was accomplished using lightweight Vohringer-faced ply (discussed in Chapter 9), together with some edging trim. The accompanying photographs show some of the Zwaardvis products, and it is interesting to learn that several British manufacturers are now considering these products with a view to installing them.

Zwaardvis table fittings

With a telescopic pillar and a special base, this Zwaardvis table may be used outside and its height can be raised or lowered as needed.

When installing the table inside a motorcaravan, most builders fit either a raised or flush base, together with a single length pole.

This convenient Zwaardvis assembly fitted under a table top allows the table to rotate as well as slide from side to side on tracks.

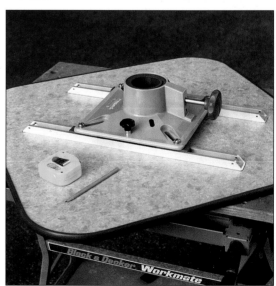

Air conditioning

Whilst a motorised fan can be helpful on a sunny day, an air-conditioning system brings particular benefits to the traveller in hot regions. There are two types of air conditioners:

• Water evaporative units
• Refrigeration units.

Water evaporative products

A simple experiment helps to show the principle behind a water evaporative system. On a hot day take a clean handkerchief, soak it in cold water, put a single layer of damp fabric over your mouth and breathe in deeply. It is immediately apparent that air being inhaled is unexpectedly cool and this phenomenon continues until the handkerchief is dry.

Water evaporative systems like the roof-mounted Webasto Bycool Camper and the Trav-L-Cool, distributed in the UK by CAK, employ this principle, albeit in a more sophisticated manner. These products are very light and the Trav-L-Cool weighs only 8kg (17.5lb).

Whereas a water evaporative system may not lower temperatures as remarkably as a refrigeration device, Trav-L-Cool products are well respected and have been optional extras on some Hymer motorcaravans. As part of the installation, water supply tubing has to be connected to a water reservoir – normally discreetly fitted in a locker or wardrobe base – and this is duly fed to the filter on the roof.

A double-acting slow-running diaphragm pump circulates the cold water, some of which evaporates during the air cooling process. In temperatures around 30°C, water consumption is half a litre an hour and the 20-litre water reservoir keeps the Trav-L-Cool operating for around 40 hours between top-ups. In contrast the Bycool Camper draws its water from the fresh water supply tank.

Advantages include:

• The light weight of the appliances
• The easy installation; both products fit a standard-sized roof light aperture
• The vent on the outer casing acts as a warm air extractor while a motorcaravan is being driven
• The products operate from a 12V supply.

Only in places where there are high levels of humidity will this cooling system be ineffective.

Compressor refrigeration products

Air conditioners using compressor refrigeration principles are better known and have a higher cooling capacity than water evaporative units. They also operate when the weather is humid and lower the humidity level within the living space as well as cooling it.

A disadvantage is the fact that the rate of consumption of these appliances is in excess of

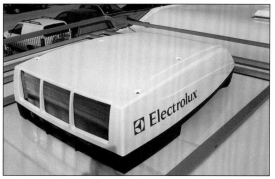

When there's already a sky-light aperture in a roof, an air conditioning unit like this can be fitted in less than an hour.

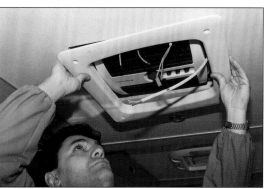

On the inside, the frame is soon fitted around the controls and outlet vent; providing a hidden 230V supply can take longer.

1000 Watts and therefore you need either a 230V mains hook-up or a high-output portable generator. Moreover, on closely-packed sites, these air conditioners are often quite noisy.

Models bearing the names Blizzard, Electrolux, and Telair are commonly seen on the roofs of motorhomes; they are usually easy to install and efficient in use. Unfortunately these appliances are also heavy, typically weighing 25 to 40kg – and that weight on a roof is not a helpful contributor to a vehicle's stability. It also needs a strong roof to support the unit physically.

Having said that, the installation is usually relatively easy because the units are designed with a conventional roof-light aperture in mind. According to the model chosen, this usually means a cut out is required of either 350 x 350mm or 400 x 400mm. Fitting a discreet power supply is often one of the harder tasks, although on some motorcaravans, such as Mobilvetta models, the cabling is put in place when the motorcaravan is originally manufactured. That aside, if an aperture is already available, a model like the Blizzard can often be installed in an hour or less.

An alternative point of view is that the best place for a compressor air conditioner is low down, and that's the thinking behind the Frostair models from Truma. Several manufacturers make similar products and these are normally fitted in a blanket locker. Instead of cooled air from these units being introduced at ceiling level, it is usually ducted around the interior and directed where considered most appropriate.

For anyone who regularly visits hot countries, the products described here are a great contributor to comfort. But the total price of an installation, especially if it includes a generator, is more than many owners are willing to spend.

11

A surprising number of people decide to build a motorcaravan themselves.

Self-build projects – case histories

Although there are many fine motorcaravans on the market, a number of spirited enthusiasts prefer to build their own. The challenge proves irresistible and the reward and feeling of accomplishment on completing a major project is certainly hard to measure.

Previous chapters have been concerned with choosing and using motorcaravans. In contrast, this final chapter is about self-building because a surprising number of people decide either to renovate an old motorcaravan or to build one from scratch.

In some ways this may seem a misguided enterprise. After all, if you consider the number of new motorcaravans built in Britain, plus the imported models and the thousands of pre-owned models offered for sale, the choice is legion. In the data listings published in recent magazines, the number of different motorcaravans available added up to 753 models! This remarkable total is made up of 263 products built by major manufacturers in the UK, 405 European imported models, and 85 American RVs.

Then there are specialists who build one-off models for customers. In other words, if mass-produced models do not meet your specific requirements, you can even have a motorcaravan constructed to an agreed design. With all these

different products available, why do so many prospective owners decide to embark on a self-build project?

The self-build approach

In the last 50 years, DIY has become a flourishing leisure activity. In a few cases it has even led to more elaborate enterprises than self-build alone. For example, when the late Siddle Cook completed a DIY caravan in 1963, it was so well-received that he decided to build a few more touring caravans. A new company was established which used his name spelt backwards and even though the marque is now under different ownership, Elddis caravans and motorhomes are still manufactured near Siddle Cook's first small factory in Durham.

This is not an isolated case either. In the motor industry, the origin of several large manufacturers can be traced back to an entrepreneurial individual. An irrepressible eagerness to explore new ideas is why some individuals go it alone, and it would be a great loss if the spirit of DIY enterprise was stifled.

Then there's the quality issue. Most modern motorcaravans are extremely well-made but you'll occasionally find surprising design mistakes – and even examples of poor construction. A recent Motor Caravan Quality & Reliability Survey undertaken by The Caravan Club drew attention to several areas of weakness. In reality, it's unlikely that many amateur builders are in a position to create better products than those constructed by experienced professionals. But there's nothing wrong with trying.

Another motivating element is cost related; the prices of new models start from around £20,000 and this is more than many people want to spend. Whether a private builder is able to construct

The quest to own something different is a matter of prime importance to some self-build enthusiasts.

One of the advantages of a self-build project is that you can design an interior exactly in the style you like.

an equivalent motorcaravan any cheaper than a manufacturer who can buy components at bulk discount prices is questionable. But at least the costs can be spread over a long period because parts only need to be purchased as and when they're needed. It's also possible to save a lot of money by buying parts from quality breakers' yards. Most of the recycled items are old, but The Caravan Centre in Pontypool also dismantles written-off caravans less than a year old; that's because road accidents have deemed them uneconomical to repair. Quite often the appliances inside these wrecked structures are unmarked.

So in a quest for individuality, cost-saving and a variety of other reasons, many would-be owners embark on improvement or self-build projects. Indeed, several of the technical matters discussed in the earlier chapters of this book should be noted by DIY builders.

To summarise this self-help approach to ownership, the following points should be recognised:

Advantages

- A finished DIY motorcaravan can reflect an individual's precise needs.
- The DIY builder's flair and design skills can be put into practice.
- Personal preference in elements like the layout can be planned from the outset.
- The interior styling and choice of soft furnishings can meet individual taste.
- Costs can be controlled at every stage and spread out over the building period.
- Additions can easily be made at a later date when extra funds become available.
- DIY maintenance and repairs are so much easier on a vehicle you've built yourself.

- There's great satisfaction in completing a major project of this kind.
- Unlike a manufacturer, you have no expenditure on advertising, marketing, labour, factory overheads and so on.

Disadvantages

- Getting hold of components can be particularly difficult.
- Some products, such as decorative 3mm ply, are not available from the usual DIY retailers.
- Selling a DIY motorcaravan isn't always easy.
- Safety elements such as installing sufficient ventilation can be inadvertently overlooked.
- The Maximum Technically Permissible Laden Mass of a vehicle can all too easily be exceeded.
- Insuring a DIY vehicle can sometimes be difficult.
- Future legislation may impinge on the freedom enjoyed by self-builders.
- Some site owners are unwilling to accommodate unusual conversions.
- A radically altered base vehicle will have to pass the Single Vehicle Approval inspection test.

Different degrees of self-help

An important thing to remember in any major DIY enterprise is to avoid trying to do EVERYTHING yourself. You can't be good at ALL the skills involved in complex construction work and many DIY projects are spoilt when a key element has been bodged rather than entrusted to an expert.

To illustrate this in respect of the Mystique, the author's most recent coachbuilt motorcaravan described later, specialists carried out work extending the chassis, designing a towing

To avoid a large overhang at the back, the Fiat Maxi chassis was extended *between* the axles.

bracket, installing a computer-controlled reactive air suspension system, extending the length and upgrading the weight limit of the rear axle, and carrying out all the fabric trimming/upholstery work inside.

That still left many tasks to complete. But it makes the point that self-building work should involve expert assistance where needed. You should also take account of the different strategies which a self-builder can adopt.

Several specialists are able to supply and fit a high-top roof on a van you want to convert.

An elevating roof can also be fitted before a DIY conversion begins.

These include the following:

■ Conversions on customer-purchased vehicles

One way to reduce the cost of ownership is to buy a base vehicle yourself and get someone else to carry out the conversion work. For instance, some owners import a vehicle purchased abroad at an attractive price, and then appoint one of the smaller motorcaravan manufacturers to convert the interior. In the case of Concept Multi-Car in Kent and Motor Caravan Conversions in Manchester, these specialists use Reimo interiors which are designed and constructed in Germany, then assembled and installed in the factories here. The catalogue shows all the layouts available and the sophisticated assemblies of flat-pack components. In addition to these specialists, many other converters will carry out a conversion which fulfils your particular requirements.

■ Conversions using older vehicles

More money can be saved by converting a second-hand base vehicle. Again there are manufacturers who will convert a pre-owned vehicle, too, and this includes specialists like AVA Leisure, Nu Venture Campers, Nu Venture Motor Homes, Rainbow Conversions and Young Conversions, just to mention a few. However, if you want to purchase a suitable pre-owned light commercial vehicle but have doubts about your ability to choose one which is mechanically sound, Mike Young of Young Conversions runs an advisory/purchase service for potential customers. He will track down and short-list suitable vehicles, and pass his recommendations on to the client.

■ Installing high tops, elevating roofs and windows

If you're planning to build a van conversion and want a specialist to fit the windows or install either a glass fibre (GRP) high top or a Reimo lift-up elevating roof, this work can be carried out by AVA Leisure near Gatwick, Concept Multi-Car (Reimo) in Hythe, and Motor Caravan Conversions (Reimo) in Manchester. Elevating roofs are installed on VW Type 2 Brazilian imports by Danbury Motor Caravans. High tops and windows can also be fitted by specialists such as Autocraft Motor Caravans (near Chesterfield), Country Campers (near Dartford), and LeisureDrive DIY (Manchester). Similarly, a complete high top roof installation which includes a fitted lining can be undertaken by Young Conversions.

■ Part-build work

There will also be some prospective owners who have specific qualifications and plenty of the appropriate tools. A number of owners, for example, feel confident undertaking cabinet construction and installation work. On the other hand, a confident joiner might feel very uneasy about the prospect of undertaking electrical work. So that aspect of a project should be handed over to a specialist.

At Young Conversions, specialists will complete any parts of the self-build that you don't want to tackle yourself.

A wise self-builder would make an early decision about his or her strengths and weaknesses, secure in the knowledge that many small converters will carry our part-build operations.

■ DIY refurbishment work

If you prefer to carry out refurbishment work yourself on a professionally-built motorcaravan, appliances like cassette toilets, refrigerators, gas water heaters and so on are supplied with comprehensive installation instructions. Many owners complete upgrading projects with pleasing results – but it's important to get a qualified gas fitter to make final gas connections and to conduct safety tests on any gas-operated items.

In addition to upgrading appliances, it's worth adding that Seitz windows and roof lights are also accompanied by clear instructions. Many older motorcaravans can be improved by the addition of a large roof light. If you want to refurbish a VW camper van, Danbury Motorcaravans can supply retro-fit interiors which follow the original style, are pre-assembled for customers and are ready for screwing into position. They also supply 'rock & roll' fold out beds for VW installation.

■ Self-build kits

Several motorcaravan kits have appeared on the market. . . and then disappeared. The author's first project was a Starcraft which is briefly described later. In essence this kit comprised a box chassis, some GRP mouldings with a mediocre finish, seven panes of glass with window rubbers, and a wad of typed notes. You also had to purchase a Cortina car in order to retrieve its cab, engine and running gear which all added up to a challenging operation. In fact it took two years to complete the Starcraft – longer than it had taken to complete a self-build four bedroom house and landscape its half-acre plot. Nevertheless, the subsequent ten or so years of motorcaravanning experiences were enjoyable in spite of being punctuated by more than a fair share of mechanical breakdowns. Lessons were learnt in the process.

It was recognised much later that the Rickman

Rancher was a considerably easier camper van kit to complete and pre-owned examples of these vehicles are still occasionally offered for sale.

In Germany, there is also the self-build Athano from Pleitner PS Wohnmobil GmbH which is sold in various build stages to suit customers' requirements. This is a large A-Class moulding designed for installation on a VW chassis cab.

■ Prototype and bare shells

Every now and again, prototype vehicles appear in classified advertisements. There have also been conversions undertaken using the GRP shells of former British Telecom vans. In reality, complete shells do not appear on the market very often but GRP moulds, together with mouldings, take up considerable space in a factory and will eventually be sold or destroyed.

For example, the Mystique coachbuilt described later started with an incomplete set of mouldings; further examples from this discarded prototype have also been offered for sale more recently. So have GRP coachbuilt mouldings from the Shamrock, an attractive coachbuilt model which was manufactured in Eire a few years ago.

A self-build A-Class kit

The Athano is a self-build German A-Class which is sold in various build stages.

Furniture modules are available for Athano builders who don't want to design their own.

Caravans grafted on flat-bed trucks often lack the finesse of more conventional models.

■ Converting existing vehicles

Other projects involve the conversion of buses, ambulances, prison vans, and a variety of other commercial vehicles. A few painstaking builders create an attractive motorcaravan; others construct a vehicle whose design is not exactly endearing. In particular, trailer caravans bereft of wheels and mounted on the rear of a flat bed lorry lack the finesse associated with the traditional image of a motorcaravan. Irrespective of the quality of the accommodation inside, it should be noted that these vehicles are not accepted by some site owners whose opinion regarding the suitability of a vehicle may differ from that of the owner.

To summarise, there are several approaches to DIY motorcaravan construction and the task is not as straightforward as it might appear at first sight. Some self-built vehicles are certainly as good as those completed by professional builders. On the other hand, alongside the personal triumphs are many half-finished enterprises that have fallen by the wayside. It's easy to run out of steam – or money for that matter – and incomplete projects often appear in the classified advertisements in magazines. For that reason, it's important not to have any misapprehensions about a self-build enterprise. There are both advantages and disadvantages in this approach to ownership and it certainly involves a lot of work.

Administrative requirements

As the construction of a motorcaravan proceeds, it is a legal requirement to inform the Driver and Vehicle Licensing Agency (DVLA) at Swansea of changes to the information recorded in section D of the V5 Vehicle Registration Document. These relate to such things as model/type, VIN/Chassis/Frame number and body colour. Alterations have to be recorded in Section E of the V5 and submitted to the Agency. After 24 March 1997, a new registration document was introduced and Form V100 (available from the Post Office) provides information on vehicle registration.

Customs and Excise used to be involved, too, because VAT payments had to be made on DIY motorcaravan conversions. However, this is no longer the case because VAT is now paid on Light Commercial Vehicles at the time of the original purchase.

It is also important to be aware of the Single Vehicle Approval (SVA) regulations. If you embark on a major motorcaravan project in which a base vehicle is derived from a variety of vehicle components – as in the case of the Starcraft and Rancher – you have to submit the vehicle for an SVA approval test.

The SVA procedure has often been described as a boosted MOT test specifically designed for one-off vehicles built in the United Kingdom. Some people regard it as a UK concession, appropriately introduced in view of the UK's long-standing and unique component car industry. Whereas the Type Approval Regulations are strictly applied across Europe, the SVA test scheme in the United Kingdom has enabled vehicles built on a small scale to gain official authorisation for use on public roads. Articles explaining the SVA test and procedures are often published in kit car magazines.

However, very few self-built motorcaravans need SVA approval because the majority of conversions are based on a standard van or chassis-cab base vehicle whose manufacturers have already had the vehicle Type Approved.

Insuring self-built motorcaravans

Where a vehicle remains a van, it should be insured as such. However, you need to consult insurers about the position during and after a conversion. For example, installed equipment could be worth a large sum of money and it is important that this is covered. You might also be required to obtain an Engineer's Report before an insurance company will extend the terms.

Many insurance specialists who offer policies for professionally-built motorcaravans are not able to insure self-built vehicles. In consequence, many DIY owners take out policies with insurance companies specialising in kit cars. However, one motorcaravan insurer, Shield Direct, also arranges special policies for self-build vehicles as long as they comply with certain criteria. Whilst the criteria change now and again, the requirements are currently as follows:

1) Engine size must not exceed 2992cc
2) Value of motorcaravan must not exceed £40,000
3) There must be at least one fixed bed of a minimum length of 6ft
4) There must be a seating area with a fixed table
5) A permanent installation is required for housing a water container

Insurers may require the self-build vehicle to have at least one 6ft (1.83m) bed in order to qualify as a motorcaravan.

6) There must be either a wardrobe or cupboards
7) There must be a permanently fitted gas or electric hob
8) There must be windows installed on both sides of the habitation area
9) There must be a habitation entrance door – either sliding or opening outwards
10) After the initial acceptance of insurance, the conversion must be completed within 90 days
11) Four photographs have to be submitted, two of which must show the interior; the others must show the exterior, one of which is required to have the number plate visible.

At present, there are certainly insurers who will issue policies for self-built vehicles but this is something to check carefully before embarking on a DIY project.

Weight watching

One of the most important things to check at repeated intervals is the weight of a vehicle and the load on its axles. Far too many self-builders proceed with constructional work, completely oblivious of the base vehicle's capacities in terms of:

• Maximum technically permissible laden mass (MTPLM)
• Mass in running order
• Maximum user payload
• Maximum axle weights.

These terms were explained in Chapter Two and the accompanying technical tip box should be noted. It is obviously most important that furniture and storage systems are as light as possible without compromising their fitness for purpose, a matter discussed in Chapter 9. Ultimately, the lighter the construction, the more personal effects can be carried before reaching the MTPLM limit.

Even owners of professionally-built motorcaravans get an unexpected surprise when putting their fully-laden vehicle on a weighbridge. It can be extraordinarily easy to exceed the overall weight limit as well as exceeding individual axle

loading limits – and that's a criminal offence. There is no doubt that the addition of a lot of accessories and the transport of items like a motor-scooter make significant inroads into the available payload of a vehicle.

Sources of help

For several years the definitive document for the manufacturers of motorcaravans was the NCC/SMMT Code of Practice 201: *Habitation Requirements Relating to Health & Safety for Motorcaravans*. This was published in September 1992 but subsequently replaced on 23 October 1998 by European Norm (EN) 1646.

Since the European Norms are concerned with elements like health and safety, amateur builders should comply with the standards laid down in the relevant documents. Typical habitation matters include the strength, stability and slip-resistance of entrance steps. Bunk beds are important, too, and standards are set regarding minimum headroom, mechanical strength, protection to prevent occupants from falling out, a means of safe access and so on.

Another helpful publication, the *Private Conversions Manual*, is a 60-page guide compiled by The Motor Caravanners' Club and on sale to its members. Similarly useful are the *Home Conversion Notes* by Mike Jago, editor of *Motorcaravan Motorhome Monthly*, available free to readers who send a stamped addressed envelope to the editorial office.

Components

It was mentioned earlier that tracking down components can be one of the DIY builder's biggest problems. Whereas a caravan or motorhome dealer will carry many items in the accessory shop, these are seldom constructional items.

Experience has shown that it's certainly helpful to investigate products used in the building industry, the marine industry and the furniture industry. It is also helpful to find out about components used by classic car restorers, kit car builders, commercial vehicle and bus converters and, of course, motorcaravan builders. Many materials and components used in these industries can be employed in the construction of a motorcaravan.

Prior to building the Mystique, the author visited a trade exhibition for bus, ambulance and truck

Technical tip

When a vehicle is fitted out as a motorcaravan, packed with holiday items and carrying a full complement of occupants, it must not exceed the maximum technically permissible laden mass (MTPLM) of the base vehicle – nor for that matter should either axle have to support more than its specified maximum weight. From the outset, it is important to start by checking the unconverted vehicle on a weighbridge and to establish what scope remains for additions and alterations. Then as the conversion work proceeds, it is crucial to bear in mind the urgency of keeping the weight in check – and to return to a weighbridge at intervals in order to monitor progress.

Commercial quality stainless steel hinges are supplied by Albert Jagger Ltd.

Robust paddle-style door handle assemblies are available from Europa Mail Order.

converters. That tracked down several suppliers of commercial vehicle components and the large catalogue from Albert Jagger was especially helpful. Stainless steel external hinges and a number of body components were subsequently purchased.

Ships' Chandlers are another source of fittings and by attending boat shows you will find products that can be used in motorcaravans as well. For example, rubbing mouldings used along the gunwhales of small boats were used to cover a roof joint on the Starcraft. But as a caveat, there seem to be fewer true chandlers today; many seem to have switched from supplying esoteric boat fittings to selling nautically styled designer clothing. Presumably the profit margins are greater.

Kit car component suppliers also deal in hinges, door catches, bonnet stays, and a host of useful items. The door catch on the Mystique was chosen from the Europa Catalogue of car parts and it is undoubtedly more robust than the catches fitted on many manufactured motorhomes.

For furniture components, drawer units, wire baskets and kitchen products, the Woodfit Catalogue is very useful. Also of note is the huge Hafele catalogue, but it's hard to obtain a copy if you're not a tradesperson. In reality, many of the smaller motorcaravan manufacturers obtain components from Hafele and are willing to supply them to DIY builders.

It was also mentioned in Chapter 7 that domestic waste pipe is an ideal component for use in

motorcaravans and this can be obtained from any building or plumbing merchant. Also from the building trade are adhesive sealants like Gripfill and Sikaflex which enable a motorcaravan builder to bond timber to GRP or metal surfaces – not to mention many other combinations of materials. These kinds of products are important when creating fixing points along the sides and roof panels within the living area.

In the caravan and motorcaravan industries, there are also suppliers with useful catalogues such as ABP (American RV accessories), Autocraft Motor Caravans, AVA Leisure, CAK, Just Kampers (VW parts), Reimo, RoadPro, Towsure, Waeco and others. In most instances there's a mail order service as well.

In some cases a breakers' yard is well worth a visit. Admittedly there are not many caravan breaking yards in this country but a few owners run efficient warehouses where parts are racked and displayed. For example, The Caravan Centre in Pontypool was mentioned earlier in this chapter. Similarly, specialists like Magnum Caravan Surplus and O'Leary Caravan Supplies are further important points of contact. Their stock-in-trade includes many surplus unused items bought from large motorcaravan manufacturers.

Suffice it to say, anyone building a DIY motorcaravan has to be prepared to travel to purchase parts. Many of the items sold in local DIY super stores are too heavy for use in a motorcaravan and you need to look beyond these outlets for a lot of the components required.

Van or coachbuilt?

Not surprisingly, most self-built projects are panel van conversions. It is certainly a lot easier to convert a vehicle which is already roadworthy, water-tight and usable. By contrast, starting with a cab and a bare chassis is much more involved, although a few DIY enthusiasts tackle a coachbuilt model.

There's another reason why a panel van

Converting a van   Most self-build motorcaravans are van conversions. . .

. . . and from the start you can work protected from the weather.

conversion is such an attractive proposition for the DIY builder. You may have noticed that professional van conversions are surprisingly expensive and for a similar outlay you can purchase a considerably larger coachbuilt model. This is because van conversion work doesn't lend itself to speedy production-line building techniques. Moreover, it's difficult to have more than two people working inside a van at once, whereas the appliances and supply systems on many coachbuilts are made with several fitters working simultaneously on an unrestricted bare floor. The walls are added much later.

It also takes longer to construct furniture which fits closely to the contoured sides of a van. That affects the selling price as well. In contrast, fixing furniture units to the flat, sandwich construction walls of a coachbuilt model is considerably quicker and time means money. However, elements like labour costs which help to set the asking price on a professionally-built van conversion, are of little concern to the DIY enthusiast.

Common construction tasks

Irrespective of the type of motorcaravan being built, two elements are important. Firstly, insulation is needed in the walls, roof and floor. Secondly, the walls of the habitation area need windows.

Needless to say, this is not a DIY Build Your Own Motorcaravan book and this chapter is only intended to show the sort of things which are achievable. On the other hand, insulation and window installation are matters of general interest; for example, owners of professionally-built models often wonder if a large roof window could be fitted to their motorcaravan. Hence the following section:

Insulation

Insulation is essential in a motorcaravan and this helps to retain heat in winter and to reduce the effects of direct sunshine in the summer. However, whilst this thermal element is important, don't forget that the acoustic properties of insulants mustn't be overlooked either. On sites situated near a major road or a railway line, any product which reduces noise is to be valued.

It was explained in Chapter 3 that large manufacturers construct composite panels for walls, floor and ceilings using block insulation boards; these are bonded to sheets of plywood in an industrial press. In self-build vehicles, the traditional approach described in that chapter has to be used instead. For example, when insulating the walls of the Mystique, Sikaflex 252 adhesive sealant or ISOPON P40 was used to bond battens to the interior of the GRP bodyshell, 25mm polystyrene was placed between the battens, and 3mm decoratively faced wall and ceiling ply was finally bonded to the frameworks using Evo-Stik Resin W woodworking adhesive

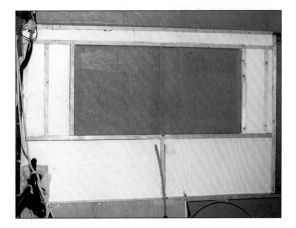

Insulating the walls in a GRP shell

A framework of 25mm (1in) struts was bonded to the wall using Isopon P40 or Sikaflex 252.

At the corners of a window framework, tiny pilot holes were drilled to identify the position outside.

Panels of 25mm (1in) polystyrene were cut and pushed tightly into position.

A 3mm decorative wall ply was fitted to the struts.

Using a 'wool' type insulant

Insulating a panel van is most important to reduce both heat loss and noise – this is an Auto-Sleepers van conversion.

This GRP moulded door had to be insulated with a 'wool'-type insulant because of its contoured shape.

Insulating a floor with Styrafoam

These 36mm boards of Styrafoam are used in both the motorhome and building industries.

This insulated floor was built-up in situ, with a channel incorporated to allow cables to cross the floor.

A quick way to bond a material to a wood or GRP panel is to mix up some Isopon P40.

or Sikaflex 252. **Note:** *In 2004, Sikaflex launched Sikaflex 512 Caravan adhesive sealant which is particularly appropriate for this type of work; moreover the product is more widely available for motorcaravanners than other Sikaflex products.*

When flat surfaces need lining, polystyrene panels are fine but if these start to move and chafe against frame members, the material creates annoying squeaking noises. So in many places, especially contoured surfaces and areas with irregular depth, quilt ('wool') insulation such as Rockwool is to be preferred. This is used by manufacturers, too, as the accompanying photograph shows.

In contrast, Styrafoam is used in the fabrication of composite floor panels as described in Chapter 3. However, self-builders do not have the machinery to construct bonded panels like this. So in the Mystique DIY project, 36mm panels of Styrafoam were laid on 19mm (¾in) floor ply and held tightly in place with a framework of softwood battens. The battens were glued and screwed to the floor and 6mm (¼in) ply was glued on top to produce a strong and well-insulated panel. The final construction is quite heavy, but it will never suffer from the delamination problems described in Chapter 3. In the Starcraft, pre-formed insulated boards were purchased instead from a local branch of the national supplier, Sheffield Insulations.

The construction of a timber sub-frame is no different in a van conversion except that a panel van has metal strengthening struts on the inside. Once again, an adhesive sealant like one of the Sikaflex products will bond timber battens to the metal panels of a van.

In some instances, however, it is easier to use a polyester paste which has been pre-mixed with a mulch of chopped glass strands. Two popular examples, used in car repair work, are Isopon P40 and U-Pol B. Sold in car accessory stores, these products are prepared on a scrap of plywood by mixing in a catalyst often referred to as hardener. Setting times depend on air temperature but as a guide, a blob of polyester paste the size of a golf ball will require three blobs of hardener the size of garden peas.

These two items should be mixed thoroughly on the board (a decorator's knife is useful for this), applied liberally to the strengthening wood which is then positioned on the GRP panel. The work will have to be held in place using temporary struts while the paste is setting, but once it starts to cure, the product hardens rapidly and decisively. Depending on temperature and the amount of catalyst used, this takes just five to ten minutes. In low temperatures, more hardener may be needed to achieve this.

Forming apertures in panel vans

Where it is necessary to form anything from a large aperture (such as for a window) to a small hole (such as for some waste water pipes), it is essential that the structural integrity of a panel van is not compromised. In some instances professional advice should be sought. The same is true in the case of a GRP moulding.

It is also important to treat any bare metal edges that become exposed when holes are formed. Professional manufacturers are especially thorough in this respect and the self-

Installing windows and rooflights

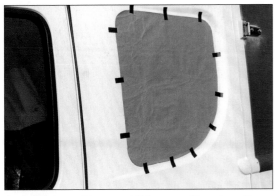

Approved glass cut by a specialist was used to make patterns which were 4mm larger all round.

A jigsaw was used to cut the aperture, running at slow speed and with a blade suitable for GRP.

A wood rasp is often useful for tidying up irregularities, but don't make the aperture too large!

A rubber moulding with grooves to suit the glass and GRP thickness is fitted. Its central web was 4mm.

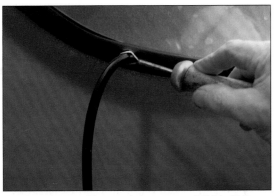

A tool was borrowed from a windscreen specialist to fit the locking rubber key to secure the glass.

To make the travel windows look part of the cab, satin black paint was applied from a spray can.

Fitting a glass window in a GRP moulding

In some instances, a single-glazed window has to be fitted into a van or coachbuilt. This was the case with all the windows in the Starcraft and two travel windows near the cab of the Mystique. The traditional means of attachment employs a rubber surround which expands once the glass is offered-up and a locking insert is added. The accompanying photographs show this being done and you must obviously use the appropriate type of glass for a road-going vehicle.

Fitting Suitz double-glazed framed acrylic windows

In the habitation area, it is better to use double-glazed acrylic framed windows like the type made by Seitz. The prospect of cutting a large aperture in either a van or a GRP bodyshell is rather daunting but this type of framed window can be fitted remarkably easily. The fact that the inner frame is screwed tightly to the outer frame means that the completed assembly grips the reinforcing wooden surround which strengthens the aperture. The result is certainly weatherproof and the accompanying photographs highlight some of the stages in a typical installation.

Using small pilot holes drilled from inside, the cutting line was marked and protective tape added.

Masking tape prevents a jigsaw from marking a painted surface and the material is soon cut.

A barbed wood rasp can trim any irregularities as well as the timber frame around the aperture.

Several times during the trimming process, a Seitz S4 framed unit was offered up to check the fit.

The outer frame and the inner cassette holding the blinds are parted and ribbon sealant is added.

The outer frame is pressed into place and aligned; screws in the inner frame pull the two units together.

builder should be no less scrupulous in his or her approach.

Similarly, rubber grommets and protective collars are needed to shield sharp edges. This protection is especially important when electric cabling passes through openings.

Case histories

In the remaining part of this chapter, five contrasting case histories are presented in order to exemplify different types of project.

These include:

1) A van conversion built on a tight budget
2) A renovated VW T2 Camper
3) The Rancher and Starcraft kit projects
4) A British Telecom van conversion
5) The Mystique coachbuilt project.

The purpose of reporting on real build-ups is to illustrate some of the tasks that have to be tackled. The first project also shows how a lot of money was saved by dismantling an old caravan so that its furniture and appliances could be re-used in a motorcaravan. However, these case histories are selected to typify motorcaravan projects rather than to steer readers through a set of step-by-step instructions. That would fill a book in itself.

Renault Trafic van conversion

Builders: Alison and John Freame

Notes on the base vehicle

When the Trafic was launched by Renault in the early 1980s, its raking front and angular lines were distinctive. Minor facelifts appeared in 1990 and five years later, alternative engines were introduced: a 2.2-litre petrol unit appeared and the 1.7 litre version was withdrawn. Commercial users normally prefer a diesel power unit and early 2.1-litre units were later replaced by a 2.5-litre engine. There has also been a 1.9-litre diesel version.

Though never prominent, the Trafic has been used by several panel van converters and a few coachbuilts appeared, too. The Machzone low-profile Ecu, the Autohomes Ariane, the Elddis Eclipse and the Ranger from Holdsworth were examples. Today, a Renault Trafic is still manufactured, albeit of a much revised design, and Danbury manufactures a conversion with an elevating roof on the short-wheelbase vehicle.

Without doubt, the Trafic's raking front was some years ahead of its time and it deserved a higher profile amongst motorcaravan manufacturers. It certainly appealed to amateur converters and when this project was completed several years ago, the builder-owners were more than happy with the results.

Project overview

This unusual project was a 'conversion' on the part of the owners as well as the vehicle. Alison and John Freame owned an elderly Elddis Shamal touring caravan but felt a motorcaravan would suit them rather better. The problem was that having recently moved house, they had only around £5,000 to spend at current prices.

Second-hand models falling within this price bracket are usually in a pretty poor state, so they decided to tackle a self-build project. An advertisement for a vegetable van appeared in a local Lincolnshire paper and the price was attractive even though the vehicle was somewhat long in the tooth. With five previous owners, the B-registration long-wheelbase, 2.1-litre diesel Renault Trafic Hi-Line had 68,000 miles recorded on a 'clock' that wasn't working. However, diesel engines are noted for longevity and the Renault was structurally sound.

The Trafic ran well, the five-speed box was smooth, fuel consumption was acceptable at around 26mpg and the vehicle was bought with a new MOT certificate for under £2000.

As regards conversion potential, the interior height was particularly good; even with the intended addition of insulated ceiling board, it was clear that a headroom of around 6ft 2in (1.88m) could be achieved.

Conversion details

The first problem arose when the cost of a new fridge, cooker, pumped water system, mains electricity supply, side windows, roof light and so on was calculated. Moreover, no-one was

It started as an old vegetable van, but John and Alison transformed it into a motorcaravan.

The budget was tight so the interior used all the items taken from a dismantled Elddis caravan.

A lot of money was saved by installing the kitchen unit removed from the old Elddis Shamal.

Viewed through the double doors at the rear, the interior has plenty of space for two people.

interested in buying John and Alison's 1975 Elddis Shamal 14ft touring caravan which would have helped to pay for purchases. Undaunted, John took the bold step of deciding to dismantle the caravan and re-install all its fixtures, fittings and furniture in the Renault. The furniture had to be modified, of course, but at least it was light and appropriately constructed.

Building the interior

The dismantled caravan also provided 3mm decorative plywood and polystyrene insulation. Even the windows were prepared for re-use although that was a questionable strategy as caravans were not usually fitted with safety glass when this Shamal was manufactured. The only large item left was the robust chassis and its running gear; that was sold to a local scrap merchant who wanted to build a trailer.

As regards body conversion, the shell of the

Making some modifications here and there, John and Alison fitted the original storage boxes from the caravan.

The bunk bed system re-used the original supports and mattresses taken from the caravan.

Renault Trafic needed little alteration. Metal struts ran across the roof to provide structural integrity and John subsequently fitted two full-length 36mm by 15mm (1½in by ⅝in) timber battens from one end to the other. When fixed firmly with an epoxy adhesive, these provided anchorage points for the ceiling panels which came next. The importance of wooden sub-frames such as this was mentioned earlier in this chapter.

Openings in the roof for a skylight and cut-outs in the sides for windows were prepared using an electric jigsaw (John had undertaken this kind of work in a previous panel van project). It was also decided to fit a new skylight which cost £36 from a caravan dealer.

Two more lengths of aluminium channel were fixed inside along the full length of the van at the top of the wall. This represented the intersection of wall and ceiling panels and the angled slots held the edges of the boards in place. John's experience as an interior decorator was also evident from the smart way he used a wallpaper frieze to add a tasteful finish around the top.

Fitting the furniture was next. John and Alison installed the caravan's wardrobe, the bunk bed with its metal supports and brackets, the kitchen units, hob, fridge and water supply. The original foot pump worked irregularly but the purchase of a Whale submersible unit solved the problem.

Exterior work

Funds were now low and a quotation to respray the exterior was excessive; so paint was purchased from an accident repair specialist and applied using high-quality brushes. Whilst few coachbuilders adopt this traditional approach today, an expert can achieve acceptable results, given warm, wind-free weather. The conversion was finished after nine weeks of dedicated work – helped by long summer evenings.

The Trafic in use

As always with a self-built project, fine tuning was needed. In particular there were problems with the fuel-injection system which took time to cure. But in the living area, the conversion was a pleasing success. Even more impressive was the fact that the true origin of interior fixtures and fittings was scarcely discernible.

Conclusion

Understandably, John and Alison Freame were delighted with the fruits of their labours. Determination and resourcefulness provided an inexpensive entry into the world of motorcaravanning.

Sourcing parts as they did is certainly in keeping with recycling sentiments. As mentioned earlier, there are several caravan breakers around the country, and re-using products and materials in this way will keep the costs down. Some elderly caravans eventually become site huts; others house hens. The reincarnation carried out by Alison and John Freame was a much more noble metamorphosis.

BEFORE: The dilapidated 1973 VW Type 2 with a Westfalia interior was in very poor shape.

VW Westfalia
Owner: Steve Rowe

Notes on the base vehicle

The VW Camper has played an important part in motorcaravan history and the models from Volkswagen are categorised as follows:

• Type 25: This was the third-generation vehicle and it was radically different.

AFTER: When a serious restorer takes on a project, the transformation can be quite remarkable.

Not a lot of the front was left, but replacement panels are obtainable from Just Kampers.

With new steel panels welded into place, and rusty remnants removed, the paint job isn't far away.

• Type 4: The front-wheel-drive Transporter ran from 1991 to 2003.
• Type 5: Motorcaravans built on this new model were shown at European exhibitions in late 2003.
Note: There are several books published on the history of these VW vehicles; Haynes repair manuals are available for the Type 2 1700-2000cc models, the Type 25 1600-2000cc air-cooled models, and the Type 25 1900-2100cc water-cooled models.

Over the years, many conversion specialists have used these base vehicles; some retained a fixed roof, many installed an elevating roof, whereas more recent models tended to have a high-top moulding added.

In recent times, enthusiasts have ascribed cult status to 'Vee Dub' Campers. Young people are especially keen collectors, with surfers prominent amongst the devoted owners.

On account of the sustained interest in the vehicle, Beetles UK imports Brazilian-built Mk2 VWs. The sister Company, Danbury, also fits elevating roofs and supplies retro-fit pre-built furniture and 'rock & roll' beds for DIY converters. Completed conversions are also available and current models include the Danbury Rio and the Surf.

Just Kampers supplies thousands of VW parts for Type 2 and later models from 1968 on; the catalogue lists over 2500 vehicle and ancillary parts.

Project overview

Steve Rowe, former editor of *Motor Caravan Magazine*, drove a VW when he was a student. Ten years later he decided to re-live the experience so paid a visit to BPS Campers, a company which used to carry out VW restoration work.

The company held a stock of dilapidated camper vans awaiting restoration and Steve chose a 1973 Type 2 VW Westfalia Continental with a rising roof – or at least the remnants of a rising

roof. He wanted a complete refurbishment, both inside and outside, and realised that this would take six months to complete. Steve then planned to add some modern comforts himself such as a blown-air gas heater and a mains supply system.

Today, BPS no longer carries out restorations but a former employee, Andy Glazier, has set up The Farnborough VW Centre and continues to offer this service for enthusiastic owners.

Renovation details

In the restoration pictured here, Andy Glazier had to cut away rusty panels so that new steel sections could be welded into place. Where necessary, completely new body panels supplied by Just Kampers were also fitted, many of which are still obtainable from this specialist supplier.

For the renovator, reclaimed parts are sometimes available such as complete door units,

Rust had developed around the wheels and more panel sections had to be removed and replaced.

some of which are imported from California. The kinder weather on America's west coast means that scrapped vehicles are often surprisingly free of rust.

Although Steve's VW Westfalia looked grim both below the floorpan and above, the refurbishment left nothing to chance. Even chassis sections that looked suspect were replaced and the accompanying illustrations show the painstaking efforts in progress. This thoroughness of workmanship is still in evidence at The Farnborough VW Centre and the fact that many parts are still available is something that would-be renovators should bear in mind. In addition, there are lively Owners' Clubs.

Building the interior

Work inside an old VW Camper is the subject of considerable debate among enthusiastic owners. Some stick rigidly to the original design, reinstating elderly appliances and living stoically with a lack of modern conveniences. As far as Steve was concerned, he wanted the Westfalia's characterful interior retained and tidied-up but knew from his earlier VW that these vehicles are not particularly warm in winter.

So Steve decided to have a modern heating system fitted. He also wanted a mains system installed and ordered a Powerpart Kit and battery charger. The author installed this on Steve's behalf and the system was complemented by a leisure battery and a 12V fused distribution unit – both discreetly located. In consequence, the visual appearance of the original 1973 interior was hardly altered.

A Trumatic E2400 heater was fitted by a gas specialist; these compact appliances can be mounted in very small spaces. An electronic panel controls the heater's operation and an external balanced flue has to be fitted so that fresh air for combustion is drawn in from the outside and waste fumes discharged externally, too. In addition, an air intake is required *indoors so* that the Trumatic's fan can draw air from the living space, direct it across a heat exchanger and then return it to the interior duly heated. This is delivered via a warm air duct and in the small living space of a VW there's no need to fit an elaborate system of outlets. An older Trumatic E Series heater had been fitted several years earlier in the Starcraft and the notable output from these units can certainly be confirmed.

Conclusion

The blend of ancient and modern resulted in comfort without a loss of the vehicle's character. Even though a 1973 VW isn't 'vintage' in the motoring sense, motorcaravans have advanced considerably since conversions started using VW Mk2 models. Without doubt, much pleasure can be derived from reviving classic campers and Steve Rowe's VW is a fine example of its type.

It was decided to clean the interior and to retain as much of the original furniture as possible.

The Starcraft, Ranger and Rancher kit projects

Builders: John Wickersham (Starcraft)
John & Justin Wickersham (Ranger)
John White (Rancher)

Notes on the base vehicles

Most Starcrafts were built using a late Cortina fitted with a 2-litre ohv Pinto engine. However, the model built by the author used a Cortina Ghia fitted with a 2.3-litre V6 engine; it provided plenty of power for a coachbuilt camper van.

After two years building the Starcraft, the next kit car project was a Rickman Ranger. The originators of this off-road style vehicle were Derek and Don Rickman. Having achieved renown as very successful motocross motorcyclists and having built exceptionally good motorcycles, their attention turned to the Ranger kit car. It was based on a Mk1 or Mk2 Ford Escort and most builders used a 1600cc cross-flow engine. Whilst the Starcraft had been a difficult project, the Rickman Ranger was much more straightforward.

In fact the Ranger was such a popular car that the Rickman engineers increased the dimensions of the chassis, an employee, John White, designed a compact shell and a motorcaravan version called the Rancher was born. The mechanical elements

A Cortina 2.3 Ghia saloon seems an unlikely base vehicle for a motorcaravan.

were almost identical to those used in the Rickman Ranger, and here was a well thought-out camper van constructed in a similar fashion. However, most Rancher builders preferred to fit the more powerful Ford 2-litre ohv Pinto engine used in the Cortina.

The remains of the cab were mounted on the new chassis, together with the rebuilt engine.

GRP panels were used to cover the doors, and a large shell, new wings and bonnet were added.

Once the engine had been retrieved, the steel sections forward of the cab were scrapped.

Project overviews

So here are two quite different motorcaravans built from kits and both types are supported by member clubs with a number of enthusiastic owners. They exemplify the determination that some people have to own a motorcaravan of their own.

Starcraft

This was an ingenious way to transform a family saloon car into a small coachbuilt motorcaravan. The wheelbase dimension of the Cortina was

With a GRP shell installed, the long job of fitting-out the inside of the vehicle took months to complete.

retained, which meant the propshaft didn't have to be modified. However, to cope with the additional overhang at the rear, two Indespension trailer suspension units were bolted to the new box section chassis in order to provide additional support. The rear-most wheels were unbraked and the Indespension units and their mounting points had to sustain quite severe stress from the tyre friction which occurred when negotiating tight corners.

To many, the appearance of this six-wheel vehicle is stunning; to others it's ghastly. Either way, the rear suspension system, originally designed for a family saloon car, was subsequently required to provide support for a laden motorcaravan. No one ever talked about loading limits and a construction like this using car parts would hardly meet today's rigorous standards. Nor would the idea of having unbraked wheels in contact with the road. However, with some plywood packing to compensate for the pronounced sag of heavily compressed coil springs, the ride quality was surprisingly rather good.

Overall, the project was exciting, sometimes demoralising, and perversely rather enjoyable. In reality, many Starcraft kits were never finished, a number remain in use and there are still two active Owners' Clubs. Bob Black MBE, Chairman of The Caravan Club, was one of the tenacious self-builders who completed a Starcraft. The author of

this book was another, and through the Starcraft, an interest in touring caravans was extended to embrace a complementary interest in motorhomes.

The photographs alongside give an idea of the work involved in building a Starcraft.

Rancher

In contrast, the Ranger and the Rancher were rather less radical. At the same time, cutting up a Ford Escort donor vehicle can be just as involved as cutting up a Cortina. It was just as dirty, too, and cleaning/renovating all the parts was an unavoidable chore. However, both the Ranger and the Rancher chassis were robust and the quality of their GRP bodies was particularly pleasing. For instance, the doors were already hung on the hinges and glass had been pre-fitted at the factory before a kit was delivered. Furthermore, to assist with fitting-out work in a Rancher motorcaravan, GRP modules were designed which included kitchen furniture, a wardrobe, overhead lockers and so on. These were optional, but pre-built assemblies like this can save a lot of time, especially for anyone whose woodworking skills are limited.

In reality, the idea of using GRP furniture isn't unusual and a similar strategy has been followed by Barry Stimson who designed the original Romahome. Barry has continued creating and

When finished, a Starcraft is a distinctive six-wheeled vehicle – but some were never completed.

Most of the parts for a Rickman Rancher came from a Mk1 or Mk2 Ford Escort saloon.

To save time, it's possible to buy refurbished brake assemblies with new discs.

Fitting out the interior could be hastened by purchasing GRP modular furniture units.

Once cleaned and painted, an Escort front suspension unit was ready to be transplanted to the Rancher.

The pre-mounted rear door offers plenty of scope for creating an internal layout which meets your personal requirements.

installing moulded cabinets in his more recent compact motorcaravans like the Provence, the Mediterranee and many other innovative designs.

So whereas Rancher builders had to engage in the hard graft of retrieving an engine and the running gear from Ford donor vehicles, at least the construction of this motorcaravan was much more straightforward than the challenge of fitting out a Starcraft.

The photographs alongside again show what building a Rancher kit motorcaravan entailed and pre-owned models are occasionally advertised for sale. But that's as far as the story goes. In Britain at least, motorcaravan kits of this kind seem to have disappeared – at least for the time being.

Notes on the base vehicle

Several commercial vans as well as public service vehicles are often converted into motorcaravans. In this particular instance, a Ford Transit rear-wheel drive British Telecom van was converted by professional builders. Several amateurs have carried out similar conversions and reports suggest that the work has proceeded without too many problems.

In practice, few professional manufacturers have used Ford light commercial vehicles as the base for a coachbuilt model, the main exception being Auto-Sleepers. For example, the Amethyst, Excelsior, Legend, Pescara, Pollensa, Ravenna and Rienza have all been constructed on Ford vehicles.

Project overview

One of the least endearing features of a standard BT van is the rear end with its industrially constructed double doors. The conspicuous hinges and security fastenings betray its commercial design and would look most out of place on a motorcaravan. Conscious of this, the builders of the one shown here dispensed with the rear doors. Instead, a mould was prepared by laminating GRP over the panels of a side wall so that the contoured shape could be replicated. This was then used to mould an infill panel which

From the outside, the Rancher is an attractive camper van which accommodates two people.

This professional conversion created a large motorcaravan from a commercial vehicle.

The in-fill panel at the rear is a great improvement on the original double doors.

replaced the doors at the back and the result was much more agreeable.

Another task when converting a BT van is to create a link between the cab and the living quarters. This involves cutting away a section from the back of the cab – a job that also had to be undertaken when building the Mystique described next. In truth, any kit car enthusiast knows that a hacksaw, jigsaw, lump hammer and sharpened bricklayer's bolster will soon scythe through the steel panels used for vehicles. Professional builders achieve a neater result using more conventional cutting equipment.

Fitting out

The layout inside featured a toilet cubicle to the rear of the driver's seat, a centrally situated kitchen on the offside, and a large lounge across the rear of the living area. On this particular

A large lounge area is built at the back and this converts into a sizeable bed.

To the rear of the driver's seat, a washroom/toilet has been fitted; next to this is the kitchen.

Far right: the converter has created a linking entrance between the cab and the living area.

A wardrobe has been placed adjacent to the entrance door, and this also houses the electrical controls.

conversion the interior achieved a feeling of spaciousness and the cabinets were well-built. Externally a BT van tends to look a little top heavy but the smart living quarters on this conversion were hard to fault.

Conclusion

The converted van had a strong, one-piece bodyshell with none of the obvious junctions which often lead to leaks when a vehicle gets older. There's no doubt that a DIY enthusiast starting with a robust shell like this would have plenty of scope to design and build a well-appointed motorcaravan. It would certainly be easier than starting with a completely bare chassis; that presents an even greater challenge, as the commentary on the Mystique reveals next.

Technical tip

Glass reinforced plastic (GRP) moulding

It is beyond the scope of this book to describe how glass fibre moulds and mouldings are made. Nevertheless it is worth recording that V & G Caravans near Peterborough can create 'one-off' GRP projects for customers. For instance, if you own an older motorcaravan and a rear body skirt gets damaged beyond repair, V & G can make a replica. Even if the original moulded component had been manufactured in ABS plastic, the company is able to create a replacement using GRP. This service is not only unusual; it is a life-line for owners of vehicles which receive damage when the motorcaravan manufacturer is no longer in business. Locker lids, lamp housings, wheel spats and all sorts of body sections can be made to special order.

The Mystique coachbuilt project.

Builder: John Wickersham.

Aims and objectives

One of the privileges of working as a contributor to motorcaravan magazines is having an opportunity to drive and conduct live-in tests using a wide variety of vehicles. On the face of it, the work sounds rather glamorous: in practice it involves a lot of travelling, extensive photography, detailed recording of factual information and a painstaking analysis of all the information gathered. Nevertheless, it does reveal the finer qualities of a product as well as its points of weakness.

Over a number of years it becomes apparent what features you find personally attractive. Everyone buying a motorcaravan has to consider what they want to use it for and we all have

The Mystique coachbuilt used a Fiat Ducato 2.8 turbo diesel Maxi base vehicle.

different purposes in mind. So when planning to build a motorhome yourself, many of the pleasing features seen previously can be incorporated into the new project. In addition you have an opportunity to try out new ideas of your own.

At the beginning of this chapter, several explanations were given for the fact that a surprising number of people decide to build their own motorcaravan. There's no simple reason, of course, and in the author's case, there were some professional considerations as well for embarking on this enterprise.

To begin with, when a magazine reader sees an article explaining how to carry out a repair or fit a particular appliance, he or she would reasonably assume that the writer has done the job themselves. That can be far from the truth. In two decades spent contributing to DIY magazines, house-building magazines, car-building magazines and caravanning magazines, the author has found on countless occasions that some accounts are contrived. Articles on how to build a garden wall written by journalists who've never even mixed mortar are rather more common than readers might realise. So are photographs of DIY decorators clad in clean clothes and with clean hands who are pretending to paper a lounge.

For practical accounts to have any worth, it is the author's view that a writer needs to be closely involved with his or her subject matter. In the examples reported here, experiences gained through building motorcaravans have proved invaluable when passing advice to others in magazines, writing books, and compiling product installation manuals.

Building things yourself also makes you more appreciative of the problems facing professionals. It's easy to criticise others: trying to get things right yourself is quite another matter. Nevertheless, there have been inexcusable faults in some of the motorcaravans that the author has tested. And it's surprising how reluctant many manufacturers are to try out new ideas, new products and new designs. In Britain, for example, you expect to see exciting concept vehicles at motor car shows, but you seldom see concept motorcaravans at exhibitions (except in Germany) and that is rather a pity. With these points in mind, the Mystique was destined to be different.

Some clear aims and objectives were noted down when the project was first considered. These included the following intentions:

- The base vehicle had to be fitted with a powerful engine that would easily achieve the maximum speeds permitted by law.
- From the outset, it had to be able to tow.
- The vehicle had to have as much payload as reasonably possible.
- A Fun Tech 338cc micro-car support vehicle would provide supplementary transport and there should be a facility for transporting this, or two motor-scooters, inside. A hatchback rear door would therefore be a key design feature.
- Since the loads would often vary, a computer controlled, reactive air suspension system would be needed so that the motorcaravan would ride level irrespective of the load being carried.
- Recognising that a number of motorcaravans exceed the rear axle loading limit, the vehicle

To use the Mystique's full carrying potential, it was necessary to construct a large hatchback door.

Full headroom was achieved in the lounge (which also serves as a garage for the micro-car) by fitting a lift-up bed.

For extra convenience the bed is left made-up, and it can be lowered for use in less than ten seconds.

had to have as small a rear overhang as reasonably possible.
- For comfort, a permanently made-up bed was wanted, albeit with an elevating system to prevent an unnecessary loss of daytime living space.

These were the broad aims and there were also some personal dislikes to come to terms with. For example, there was a resistance to constructing a large over-cab 'lump' – a feature which must surely have an adverse effect on fuel consumption. The preferred thinking was to facilitate better streamlining by fitting a high level bed at the back, with a garage/lounge underneath. This idea of creating a rise at the rear rather than over the cab fitted in well with the decision to incorporate a large hatchback door.

Without doubt, the body configuration was unusual, and the package of chassis and suspension alterations had not been tried before. There were also a number of habitation features that would break from usual practices. This sort of thinking is all very well, but how could the body be constructed?

Quite by accident the design sketches being prepared bore close resemblance to a project which had been developed a few years earlier by Barry Stimson. His remarkable designs have included extraordinary concept cars featured in the national press, exciting sports boats, designs for high speed cross-continental buses and plenty of unusual motorcaravans, including the first Romahome. It is doubtful if anyone in Britain has his wealth of experience and willingness to break away from tried and tested traditions. So a phone call was made and it transpired that Barry was short of space and was about to scrap some large prototype mouldings which had once contributed to the creation of an award winning project.

A number of key items were missing but the broad character of the remaining GRP mouldings was in keeping with the features appearing in

the sketches mentioned earlier. Instead of these mouldings being scrapped, they were collected together and loaded on to a large trailer so that another unusual vehicle could be created.

The base vehicle

The pieces of Barry Stimson's prototype shell that were remaining had been designed to fit on a Fiat or Peugeot chassis cab. Without doubt, the Fiat 2.8 turbodiesel met all the expectations listed above and many converters also know its fine credentials. This has a lively engine and its cab is comfortable, too.

Long deliberations led to a decision that only a long-wheelbase Fiat Maxi chassis would be suitable. Barry's original bodies had been paired with medium-wheelbase Peugeots and there was a considerable overhang at the back. That was contrary to the author's intentions, as listed earlier. What's more, even a long wheelbase version did not completely support the ideas for transporting motorbikes, a Fun Tech micro-car, or DIY materials like bags of cement. This had to be a motorcaravan which would earn its keep as a

Parts of this damaged prototype shell were found but the mouldings were about to be scrapped.

When suspension air is released, tyre height increases inside and this factor influenced the wheel box design.

load carrier but without exceeding rear axle limits. A long rear overhang was *not* appropriate.

Fitting a replacement AL-KO Kober chassis was considered, but at the time the company didn't appear to have progressed far into the world of air suspension. Drinkwater Engineering in Leyland was much further ahead and had already installed computer-controlled reactive air suspension systems on many regional ambulance fleets. This product includes an air release control which lowers a vehicle, thereby making it easier when loading-up. It's also a useful facility when a motorhome is parked on a sloping pitch.

In addition, many of the trucks on Britain's roads have been built with major chassis modifications undertaken at Drinkwater's Leyland works. The alterations receive the full approval of the respective vehicle manufacturers. Equally any work contributing to improved payload and the issue of a revised data plate is carried out with the full approval of the Vehicle Certification Agency. Drinkwater Engineering was largely unknown in the motorcaravan industry, but the company certainly had the credentials to carry out the modifications envisaged.

So a new Fiat Maxi chassis cab was ordered, and many of the optional elements like a high output alternator and auxiliary driving lights were added to the purchasing form. It took ten months to arrive and was delivered direct to Leyland. At Drinkwater Engineering, the rear axle was removed, extended in length by 225mm (9in), and strengthened as part of an MTPLM upgrade. The leaf spring suspension was scrapped and replaced by a computer-controlled air suspension system. The chassis was lengthened amidships as shown in Chapter 4, which meant that the body moulding for the living quarters would be accommodated without having to add extension sections rear-wards of the back axle. In other words, there would be no large overhang at the back. The base vehicle was also checked on the British Leyland weighbridge, the new weight date noted and upgrade plates were then supplied to show a maximum technically permitted laden mass (MTPLM) of 3850kg.

Today, Drinkwater Engineering is now part of the TVAC group in Leyland and hundreds of owners have since followed in the author's trail to have upgrading work carried out to improve their permitted payloads.

The body

The bare chassis was driven 200 miles home and the work which followed was carried out in the garden. Sturdy outriggers for the chassis were designed and built by a local factory so that the

The Fiat 2.8 tdi Maxi LWB was delivered to Drinkwater Engineering for chassis/suspension alterations.

floor of the bodyshell would be totally supported width-ways. Some manufacturers overlook this important element.

Recognising that brains are often better than brawn, and with only a trolley jack available, an idea was worked out for placing the bodyshell on the chassis. Judicious trimming of the side skirts and the construction of support trestles enabled the base vehicle to be reversed under the raised shell. The overcab moulding posed a bigger problem and this was lowered from a handy oak tree using old climbing rope, pulley blocks and a neighbour. Soon afterwards Sikaflex sealant was crucially important for bonding the forward section to the cab. Many manufacturers similarly use this extraordinary product.

However, it was decided to avoid an over-zealous application of sealant at junctions where adjacent panels meet. Even though Sikaflex sealant doesn't discolour as readily as it used to, irregularities in the joining points were disguised using sections of wing piping which is sold mail order by classic car restorers like Woollies.

All in all, Barry Stimson's skill had created a bodyshell which looked as if it had always been part of the cab – instead of an after-thought stuck on the back. For instance there aren't the ugly vertical protrusions that you usually find to the rear of cab doors at the point where the narrower cab meets the wider living area. Most body designers fail to create a gentle transition where the cab meets the habitation moulding. Poor design here not only compromises the streamlining of the vehicle, it can cause wind noise and provides an inappropriate place of rest for moribund moths and flies.

Lastly, the colour. It seems curiously disappointing that nearly all coachbuilt motorcaravans are white, whether you like it or not. The Swift group produced a startling break with tradition by exhibiting a one-off metallic blue Kon Tiki motorhome in 2003 – and then expressed surprise that a number of visitors to the exhibition wanted to purchase it! Colour adds character and the motorcaravan here has large panels which were finished using Moondust Silver cellulose paint from Halfords. Cans of satin black spray paint helped the cab windows blend with travel windows in the living area. Finally the graphics were created as a one-off project by Graphicraft, the specialist which supplies Auto-Sleepers, Avondale, Bailey, Explorer, Swift and many other caravan/motorhome manufacturers with their finishing decor.

Fitting out

As stated already, the interior reflected personal requirements and a lot of motorcaravanners would consider many of the ideas intolerable. For instance, Seitz blind and screen systems are so effective when it's dark that there had never been any intention to fit curtains. Ironically, the absence of curtains is seldom noticed by visitors who look

Rather than lift the heavy moulding on to the chassis, the vehicle was reversed underneath it instead.

inside – although for many owners a lack of velvet drapes would cause sleepless nights.

So would the absence of a full-size domestic cooker. But not everyone wants an oven and a four-burner hob. A good grill and a compact microwave oven take up much less space – and save on weight as well. That is down to personal needs, and other breaks with tradition can be seen in the following specification list:

- It was decided to have a diesel-fuel water and space heating system installed. In spite of the product's successful use in boats and lorry cabs, Eberspacher hydronic units had not been fitted in a British coachbuilt motorhome before. However, development work had previously been successfully carried out in Murvi van conversions and the benefits of this system were clear. Eberspacher heating is described in Chapter 6.
- A retractable mains coupling cable would be designed and fitted, and this was another innovation. Frankia motorcaravans have since

The only way to fit the overcab moulding was to lower it from an oak tree using old climbing ropes.

The Mystique was the first British coachbuilt to be fitted with an Eberspacher Hydronic heating system.

started fitting a similar system in which the cable is dispensed and wound back on to a permanently installed drum.

- A 12V supply system was needed to offer lighting in zoned areas, thereby providing maximum illumination levels wherever and whenever required. This led to the installation of 27 12V lights, most of which are halogen, along with four master panels so that lighting can be controlled:
  i) inside the entrance
  ii) from the kitchen
  iii) from the lounge
  iv) from the high-level double bed.
  A remote key fob switch also activates glow lights at floor level to illuminate a route to the toilet which is sufficiently discreet not to awaken other sleepers. This elaborate 12V system was developed with specialists at BCA Leisure, and used BCA high-quality wiring looms. The company's products are well-known by major manufacturers and are used in caravans/ motorhomes from the Explorer Group, Bailey Caravans and others.

- As a reaction prompted by the usual parsimonious provision of mains sockets, this motorcaravan is fitted with eight 13 Amp sockets with additional hidden cables just in case further sockets are needed in the future.
- The cab seats have turntables in order to contribute to the seating provision in the living space. In addition, a facility was devised to permit the speedy installation of two further automotive seats for occasions when four people will be using the vehicle. These feature integral safety belts and were described in Chapter 9.
- The kitchen was designed with a large lift-out storage box to speed up food packing back in the house. And since many British manufacturers completely overlook the importance of a waste bin, a compact one was fitted within a sliding drawer unit from Woodfit. The fresh water supply system with water purifier and the domestic waste water system incorporating deep water traps was described in Chapter 7.
- Internal decoration had to be contemporary, simple in style and built with easy-clean surfaces. For wet weekends or when engaging in muddy sports, a vinyl floor covering was important. At the same time, two large, edge-bound carpet sections were made for the living areas and a third was specially made for the cab.
- A shower room was constructed using parts of a Stimson-designed GRP moulded cubicle, thereby ensuring there would be no risk of water damage to adjacent structures.
- Essential for this motorcaravan, a good security system was needed and the sophisticated system from Van Bitz was described in Chapter 10.

Overall, the specification was very different from most motorcaravans but that was the whole point of the exercise.

The swivelling cab seats become part of the living area; two additional vehicle seats can be bolted in as well.

Batteries and the 230V consumer unit were housed in a special locker with a retractable cable reel.

Conclusion

Ideas for this project motorhome reflected personal requirements and many people would assert quite strongly that its layout wouldn't meet their approval. Neither might it be a sales success for a manufacturer. But herein lies the fun of self-build. This one was built by me, and for me, to suit trips to muddy campsites, sandy beaches, ski resorts and rocky mountains during any season of the year.

Of course there were problems along the way. For instance, a lack of proper tools made it quite difficult to find a way of neatly cutting out the back of the cab. It even took four months to design and build a hatchback door complete with gas springs. However, that turned out to be one of the most useful things, especially when the seats in the lounge are folded back. The hatchback makes it easy to stow motor-scooters, white water canoes, snow skis, wood from the timber yard and even a worn-out washing machine on its last-ever journey to the local council tip. Another unexpected bonus of the hatchback has been its value as a sun porch; all it needs now are some slide-on canvas sides.

Not surprisingly, it took twice as long to build the Mystique as it took to build the Starcraft. Equally, there are some more bits and pieces to add in the future. On account of the fact that it was built outdoors, bad weather often held things up. So did the need to go to work and earn a living. There were also many delays when sequential photographs had to be taken, although some of these have proved useful for illustrating this book. So it was scarcely surprising that the job stretched out over a period of four years!

In that time, the vehicle also became a test bed and was the first motorcaravan to be fitted with a Status 530 directional TV aerial – as described in Chapter 10. Following trials, modifications were made by the manufacturer and the improved aerial now on sale has become an important accessory product. The Mystique was also used to test the first Remis concertina cab blinds brought into Britain – also described in Chapter 10.

Throughout the building period, the vehicle was regularly used, and had been since the shell was first secured to the chassis. It's surprising how ideas take shape when it's a dark December night and you're lying on a hard plywood floor in a sleeping bag. Computer-aided design is all very well, but when you take up residence in a bare shell with no door, no windows, and no access to the cab, you soon find out where you need to fit 'this' or 'that'. Accordingly, this motorcaravan was developed over a period of time, rather than built to a rigid plan.

In hindsight, a few things would be done differently were it possible to go back to the beginning again. For instance the lift-up bed is probably the most comfortable motorhome bed in the world, but it's rather heavy and is situated

When the rear floor had been insulated and lined, the rear of the cab was removed in stages.

high above the floor. When the construction was completed, it was hardly surprising to note an increase in the vehicle's body roll when negotiating tight bends and mini-roundabouts. Thanks to air suspension, it's no worse than the roll experienced with many coachbuilts, but were there to be a next time, a lower bed and one of the clever cantilevering systems seen in professional models would probably be installed instead.

That aside, most elements have been pleasingly successful. But why is it called 'Mystique'?

Firstly it had to bear a name that hadn't been used for a motorcaravan before. Secondly there are many owners who think they know every motorhome, then spot this one and get decidedly puzzled. But the Mystique remains a mystery model, even though this book has revealed its secrets. . .

Kit car builders often resort to unconventional methods when cutting away parts of a vehicle.

Standards and regulations

Supplied by Martin Spencer, Technical Manager for The Caravan Club.

Definition of a motorcaravan

For the purpose of definition, the European Directive for Whole Vehicle Type Approval contains the following statement:

'...a motorcaravan is a Special Purpose M1 Category Vehicle constructed to include at least the following equipment: seats and table, sleeping accommodation which may be converted from the seats, cooking facilities, storage facilities. The equipment shall be rigidly fixed to the living compartment; however, the table may be designed to be easily removable.'

A motorcaravan's design is influenced by a range of standards and regulations. As a general rule, regulations are legally binding, whereas most standards are 'advisory', meaning compliance with them is voluntary, although it may be a requirement of schemes such as the SMMT/NCC badge of approval (see below). Most aspects of base vehicle design tend to be controlled by regulations, while much of the habitation area is guided by standards. In both cases, national requirements are steadily being replaced by European ones, meaning that UK and imported models are being built to increasingly similar rules and guidelines.

Requirements have become more stringent over time, but it is very rare that new demands are made retrospective. The outline requirements mentioned below relate mainly to new vehicles, but indications of when important changes were introduced are also given. This section is intended to provide only an overview of what is a very complex topic.

Base vehicle

For many years, the main document controlling the design of all motor vehicles used on the UK's roads has been the Road Vehicles (Construction and Use) Regulations. This covers allowable dimensions and weights, brakes, wheels and tyres, rear view mirrors, speedometers and a wide range of other topics. One key area not covered by 'C&U' is the lighting on the exterior of the vehicle which is detailed in the Road Vehicle Lighting Regulations (RVLR). Both are constantly being amended, as new or revised national and international requirements (usually European Directives) are incorporated. When you buy a motorcaravan, you should be able to assume that the manufacturer or importer has checked that it is compliant with these requirements, in the same way you do for a car. However, the system for checking compliance is much more stringent for cars, due to the process of Type Approval, of which more below. If you are buying a custom-built vehicle or a low-volume import, and especially if it originates from outside the European Union, it may be wise to look for the common signs of non-compliance, such as a kph-only speedometer or unusual lighting configurations. If in any doubt, ask questions of the retailer, or even consider if an independent pre-purchase inspection of the vehicle might be necessary.

Despite the origin of most base vehicles in the commercial vehicle sector, motorcaravans are classed as a 'Special Purpose' variant of the passenger car category ('M1') for legislative purposes.

From 1998, passenger cars have had to comply with a process known as European Whole Vehicle Type Approval (EWVTA). This certifies that the car complies with a wide range of legal requirements, similar in scope (and compatible with) C&U and RVLR. If you have bought a new car since that time, it will have come with a Type Approval Certificate stating this. The aim of EWVTA is to ensure that the vehicle is safe and roadworthy when first sold, and also to enable it to be sold in any European Community country without requiring further testing. EWVTA will extend to other vehicle categories in due course. At the time of writing, it is likely that new designs of motorcaravan will have to comply from July 2008, while designs already in production will have to comply from July 2010. While helpful in ensuring safe and legal vehicles, and useful in promoting vehicle sales across Europe, the administrative burden of EWVTA will have some impact on manufacturers, especially smaller ones. Very low-volume manufacturers will not be expected to comply with the full process, but instead are likely to have to submit sample vehicles for a kind of enhanced MOT test, known as Single Vehicle Approval (SVA). This would also become a requirement for self-builders. While clearly a concern for the motorcaravan industry, the introduction of EWVTA in the car sector has not seen the large-scale disappearance of models and makes, nor substantially increased prices. Even the kit car industry, which has many parallels to the motorcaravan sector in terms of scale and diversity, has survived.

Habitation area

Historically, there have been relatively few legal controls on this area of a motorcaravan. For instance, the legal requirements which apply to gas installations in houses and other buildings do not apply to privately-used caravans, and because they are motor vehicles, the furniture in motorcaravans does *not* need to comply with the legislation relating to the fire safety of domestic furnishings. Some areas *are* legally controlled, however – for instance, the installation of mains electrics must comply with BS 7671 'Regulations for Electrical Installations (IEE Wiring Regulations 16th Edition)'. From 1989, though, the Society of Motor Manufacturers and Traders (SMMT) introduced 'The Motor Caravan Code of Practice', which was then updated from September 1992 in a joint SMMT/National Caravan Council (NCC) 'Code of Practice 201'. This specifies various requirements relating to the health and safety of the habitation area, but is not a legal requirement. As a UK initiative, it applies only to UK-produced vehicles (and official imports), and not all manufacturers and importers adopt it.

If a motorcaravan displays the SMMT/NCC 'CoP 201' badge, its design will have been inspected and approved by NCC Certification Engineers. Designs without this approval may still be safe and extremely well-produced – it's just harder to be certain that this is the case.

Things changed again from September 1998, when many new European Standards were adopted as British Standards in the UK:

BS EN 1646-1 'Habitation Requirements Relating to Health and Safety'. Covers amongst other issues entrance step design, door dimensions, bunk strength and safety, drinking and waste water system designs, heating requirements, fire precautions and handbook requirements.

BS EN 1646-2 'User Payload'. Definitions of vehicle weight and payload terminology, and minimum user payload requirement.

BS EN 1648-2 '12V Direct Current Extra Low Voltage Electrical Installations'. Installation, performance and safety requirements.

BS EN 721 'Safety Ventilation Requirements'. Requirements and evaluation methods.

In 2002, an additional European Standard was added, covering the gas system:

BS EN 1949 'Specification for the Installation of LPG Systems for Habitation Purposes in Leisure Accommodation Vehicles and in Other Road Vehicles'. Safety, performance and installation requirements for cylinder storage, pipework, appliances and flues etc.

These replace and enhance the requirements previously covered in CoP 201. Again they are not legally binding, but their European relevance means that more manufacturers are adopting them.

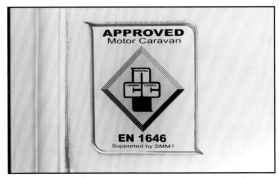

Vehicles checked for compliance by the NCC carry a revised badge of approval, which states 'EN 1646' on it, indicating the main habitation standard, although the certification checks carried out by the NCC cover a wider range of topics as well as those detailed in the standards. As European Standards, these have been, or are being, adopted by countries throughout Europe (although not at the same time in each country), meaning that imported motorcaravans are more likely to comply with them as well. The NCC is willing to inspect and certify imported motorcaravans, but overseas manufacturers may simply claim compliance with the standards, without going through the certification process.

Towing brackets

Many motorcaravan owners fit their vehicle with a towing bracket, perhaps to tow a boat or car trailer, or maybe a luggage trailer. Most motorcaravans are rated for towing by their manufacturer (and hence have a defined towing limit, which must not be exceeded). When fitting a towing bracket to a car sold since August 1998, the bracket must itself be Type Approved in accordance with European Directive 94/20EC. This requirement does not currently apply to motorcaravans, although this will undoubtedly change once EWVTA is extended to include this sector. Type Approved towing brackets are already available for some base vehicles, though, and these are a good choice due to the stringent test requirements for them. Alternatively, look for a towing bracket which has passed the requirements of the British Standard BS AU 114b, or the similar International Standard ISO 3853.

Rear-mounted accessories

Many motorcaravans have accessories such as cycle carriers, ladders and storage boxes fixed to the rear of the body. When permanently fixed, these are considered to be part of the vehicle structure, and hence part of its overall length. This can sometimes cause problems with the legally permissible rear overhang, for which there are two alternative definitions. The first option is simple – the overhang must be not more than 60 per cent of the wheelbase of the vehicle. The alternative is more involved – the maximum distance which the rear of the vehicle swings out when pulling away from a stationary position on a 12.5m radius turn must not be more than 0.8m.

Number plates

Like other motor vehicles, all motorcaravans must display legal number plates front and rear which comply with BS AU 145. The latest version of this standard (BS AU 145d – which will be marked in the bottom right hand corner of the plate) applies to plates produced from September 2001. Note that number plates made after this date for use on cycle carriers or trailers attached to motorcaravans also have to conform to the new standard.

Seat belts

Motorcaravans first used since October 1988 must have seat belts for the driver and for the row of seats next to the driver. Belts are not legally required for the seats in the habitation area, but are clearly desirable, and should be used if available. Few motorcaravans have rear seat belt installations which have been subjected to testing as stringent as that for the front seats.

Tachographs

Current and likely forthcoming legislation on tachographs will not mean that even the largest motorcaravans need such devices unless the vehicle is being used for commercial purposes, and generally only then if it is being used to transport goods. However, the extension of tachograph regulations may mean that more and more base vehicles used for conversions have tachographs fitted. Self-builders may come across these and wish to have them removed.

Speed limiters

Currently, large trucks are fitted with 56mph speed limiters, and the legislation requiring this is likely to be broadened to cover smaller classes of goods vehicle as well. Due to their classification as Special Purpose M1 category vehicles, this will not be a requirement for motorcaravans, but limiters may be fitted to base vehicles as standard, and will need to be de-specified when the base vehicle is ordered by the converter, or removed as part of the conversion process.

Contact addresses

Please note: This address list was correct at the time of going to press. It includes specialist suppliers and manufacturers whose products and services have been mentioned in this book. Several of the firms have web sites and these are easy to locate using search engines.

The motorcaravan manufacturers listed here are specialists offering bespoke building services and individual fitting operations such as the installation of high top roofs. To contact the many other manufacturers and importers, readers are advised to consult the monthly Buyers' Guides in magazines such as

1. *MOTORCARAVAN MAGAZINE*,

2. *MOTORCARAVAN, MOTORHOME MONTHLY*,
and
3. *WHICH MOTORCARAVAN*.

A.B. Butt Ltd,
Frog Island,
Leicester,
LE3 5AZ
Tel: 0116 251 3344
(Supply and installation of solar panels)

ABP Accessories,
27 Nether End,
Great Dalby,
Leicestershire,
LE14 2EY
Tel: 08700 115111
(American RV Accessories including Camco products)

A.C. Holdings,
4, Breckland Business Park,
Watton,
Norfolk, IP25 6UP
Tel: 01953 884999
(Mail Order for A Glaze Total Surface Protection)

Adrian Flux Insurance,
126 London Road,
Kings Lynn,
Norfolk,
PE30 5ES
Tel: 08700 777888
(Insurance of kit cars and conversions)

Adroit Services,
18 Monks Road,
Swineshead,
Boston,
Lincolnshire, PE20 3EL
Tel: 01205 820004
(Cruise Control, Reversing Aids)

Airflow (UK) Ltd,
Crown House,
Faraday Road,
Newbury,
Berkshire RG14 2AB
Tel: 01635 569569
(Trickle battery chargers)

Albert Jagger Ltd,
Centaur Works,
Green Lane,
Walsall,
West Midlands, WS2 8HG
Tel: 01922 471000
(Manufacturers/suppliers commercial vehicle fittings)

Alde International (UK) Ltd,
14 Regent Park,
Booth Drive,
Park Farm South,
Wellingborough,
Northamptonshire,
NN8 6GR
Tel: 01933 677765
(Central heating systems, Gas leak detector)

Amber Plastics Ltd,
Broombank Road,
Chesterfield Industrial Estate,
Sheepbridge,
Chesterfield, S41 9QJ
Tel: 01246 453544
(Inboard fixed tanks)

Al-Ko Kober Ltd,
South Warwickshire Business Park,
Kineton Road,
Southam,
Warwickshire,
CV47 0AL
Tel: 01926 818500
(AMC conversions)

Apollo Chemicals Ltd,
Sandy Way,
Amington Industrial Estate,
Tamworth,
Staffordshire
B77 4DS
Tel: 01827 54281
(Manufacturers of adhesives for repairing delaminated composite panels)

Autocraft Motor Caravans,
Fan Road Industrial Estate,
Fan Road,
Staveley,
Chesterfield,
Derbyshire
S43 3PT
Tel: 01246 471199
(High top fitting service, accessory sales)

Autogas 2000 Ltd,
Carlton Miniott, Thirsk,
North Yorkshire YO7 4NJ
Tel: 01845 523213
(Caratank LPG bulk storage tanks)

Auto Glym,
Works Road, Letchworth,
Herts SG6 1LU
Tel: 01462-677766
(Vehicle cleaning products)

Autovan Services Ltd,
32 Canford Bottom,
Wimborne,
Dorset BH21 2HD
Tel: 01202 848414
(Major body repair and rebuilding work)

AVA Leisure,
Unit 3,
Skitts Manor Farm,
Moor Lane, Marsh Green,
Edenbridge,
Kent, TN8 5QX
Tel: 0870 757 2277
(Roof fitting service, accessory supplier, van converter)

A. Baldassarre,
Upholsterer and Coachtrimmer,
103, Coventry Road,
Queens Park,
Bedford MK40 4ES
Tel: 01234 359277
(Upholstery work, foam supply and soft furnishings)

BCA Leisure Ltd,
Unit H9,
Premier Way,
Lowfields Business Park,
Elland,
West Yorkshire HX5 9HF
Tel: 01422-376977
(Manufacturers of Powerpart mains kits)

Beetles UK Ltd, -
Danbury Motorcaravans

Belling Appliances,
Talbot Road,
Swinton,
Mexborough,
South Yorkshire S64 8PR
Tel: 01709 579900
(Belling cookers, hobs and water heaters)

Bradleys,
Old Station Yard,
Marlesford,
Suffolk, IP13 0AG
Tel: 01728 747900
(Mail Order supplier of ABS repair kits and paint products for plastic)

Brian Hughes Generators,
Glen Cottage,
Hampton Malpas,
Cheshire, SY14 8JQ
Tel: 01948 820580
(Honda leisure generators and rain covers)

British Car Auctions Ltd,
Sales & Marketing Department,
Expedier House,
Portsmouth Road,
Hindhead,
Surrey GU26 6TJ
Tel: 01428 607440
(Motorcaravan auctions)

British Rubber Manufacturers' Association Ltd,
6 Bath Place,
Rivington Street,
London, EC2A 3JE
Tel: 020 7457 5040
(Trade Association advising on tyres)

Bulldog Security Products Ltd,
Units 2, 3, & 4, Stretton Road,
Much Wenlock,
Shropshire TF13 6DH
Tel: 01952-728171/3
(Bulldog security devices and posts)

C.A.K. - See Caravan Accessories

Calira Apparatebau,
Trautmann KG,
Lerchenfeldstr. 9,
87600 Kaufbeuren,
Germany,
Tel: 08341/9764 0
(LED water level gauges)

Calor Gas Ltd,
Athena Drive, Tachbrook Park,
Warwick CV34 6RL
Tel: 0800 626626
(Supplier of butane, propane and LPG products)

The Camping & Caravanning Club,
Greenfields House,
Westwood Way,
Coventry CV4 8JH
Tel: 01203 694995

The Caravan Club
East Grinstead House,
East Grinstead,
West Sussex RH19 1UA
Tel: 01342 326944

E.E. Calver Ltd,
Woodlands Park,
Bedford Road,
Clapham,
Bedford MK41 6EJ
Tel: 01234 359584
(Indoor motorcaravan storage)

Calypso Sleeping Systems,
E-Con Consulting Gmbh & Co.KG,
Bergstrasse 20,
D-59329
Deutschland
Tel: 00 49 2523 953341
(Calypso Aqua stop and coir mattress underlay products, mattress support systems)

Campingaz
Coleman UK Inc.,
Gordano Gate,
Portishead,
Bristol BS20 7GG
Tel: 01275 845024
(Supplier of Campingaz butane and LPG appliances)

Carafax Ltd,
Rotterdam Road,
Sutton Fields Industrial Estate,
Hull HU7 0XD
Tel: 01482 825941
(Caraseal ribbon and cartridge sealants)

Car-A-Tow - See Pro-Tow

Caravan Accessories (C.A.K. Tanks) Ltd,
10 Princes Drive Industrial Estate,
Kenilworth,
Warwickshire CV8 2FD
Tel: 0870 757 2324
(Water tanks and components, electrical products, appliances, ventilators, cabinet hardware)

The Caravan Centre,
Steadmans Yard,
Tal y Wain,
Pontypool, MP4 7RL
Tel: 01495 774999
(Specialist breakers supplying caravan/motorhome products)

The Caravan Seat Cover Centre Ltd,
Cater Business Park,
Bishopsworth,
Bristol, BS13 7TW
Tel: 0117 941 0222
(Seat covers, new foam, new upholstery, made-to-measure curtains)

Carcoon Storage Systems Int. Ltd,
Orchard Mill,
2 Orchard Street,
Salford,
Manchester, M6 6FL
Tel: 0161 737 9690
(Trickle chargers)

CarPlan Products,
Tetrosyl Ltd,
Bury,
Lancashire,
BL9 6RE
Tel: 0161 762 6609
(Vehicle cleaning products)

Carver products - See Truma

CEC Plug-In-Systems,
Grange Park Lane,
Willerby,
Hull HU10 6EQ
Tel: 01482 659309
(12V control components, water level sensors, gauges, electronic alarm)

Concept Multi-Car,
Unit 4A/B,
Pennypot Industrial Estate,
Hythe,
Kent, CT21 6PE
Tel: 01303 261062
(High top roof installation, Reimo products, van conversions)

Country Campers,
The Grove,
Three Gates Road, Fawkham,
Kent, DA3 7NZ
Tel: 01474 707929
(High top roof installation, van conversions to order)

Crossleys,
Unit 33A, Comet Road,
Moss Side Industrial Estate,
Leyland,
Lancashire PR26 7QN
Tel: 01772 623423
(Major body repair and rebuilding work; partner branch in Darlington, Co. Durham)

Customer Enquiries (Vehicles),
DVLA,
Swansea SA99 1BL
Tel: 0870 2400010
(Guidance on vehicle registration)

Danbury Motorcaravans/Beetles (UK),
Unit 1,
Bristol Mineral Works,
Limekiln Road,
Rangeworthy,
South Gloucestershire, BS37 7QB
Tel: 0870 1202356
(VW Type 2 Campervans with modern conversions, Type 2 VW Brazilian imports, supply of retrofit interiors)

Design Developments,
24 Carbis Close,
Port Solent,
Portsmouth,
Hampshire PO6 4TW
Tel: 023 9237 9777
(Barry Stimson design consultant and motorcaravan manufacturer)

Dometic Ltd,
99 Oakley Road,
Luton,
Bedfordshire, LU4 9GE
Tel: 01582 494111
(Refrigerators, air conditioners, toilets.)

Driftgate 2000 Ltd,
Little End Road,
Eaton Socon,
St Neots,
Cambridgeshire PE19 8JH
Tel: 01480-470400
(Manufacturers of XCell Mains inverters)

Drinkwater Engineering - see TVAC

Dynamic Systems International Ltd,
The Oakes, Bracken Rise,
Brandon,
Suffolk, IP27 0SX
Tel: 01842 810338.
(Ventair 15 mattress anti-condensation underlay)

Eberspächer (UK) Ltd,
10 Headlands Business Park,
Salisbury Road,
Ringwood,
Hampshire, BH24 3PB
Tel: 01425 480151
(Petrol and diesel-fuelled water & space heaters)

Elecsol Europe Ltd,
47 First Avenue,
Deeside Industrial Park,
Deeside,
Flintshire CH5 2LG
Tel: 0800 163298
(Elecsol carbon fibre leisure batteries)

Electrolux Leisure Appliances - See Dometic

Essanjay Motohomes,
Unit 2,
Sovereign Business Park,
48 Willis Way,
Poole,
Dorset, BH15 3TB
Tel: 01202 683608
(Motorhome servicing, components, removable steering wheels)

Europa Specialist Spares,
Fauld Industrial Estate,
Tutbury,
Burton upon Trent,
Staffordshire
DE13 9HR
Tel: 01283 815609
(Vehicle trims, light clusters, and all specialist vehicle parts)

Exhaust Ejector Co Ltd,
Wade House Road,
Shelf,
Nr. Halifax,
West Yorkshire,
HX3 7PE
Tel: 01274 679524
(Replacement acrylic windows made to order)

Exide Leisure Batteries Ltd,
Customer Services,
6-7 Parkway Estate,
Longbridge Road,
Trafford Park,
Manchester,
M17 1SN
Tel: 0161 7863333
(Exide Leisure Batteries)

Farécla Products Ltd,
Broadmeads,
Ware,
Hertfordshire,
SG12 9HS
Tel: 01920 465041
(Caravan Pride G3 acrylic window scratch remover, GRP surface renovator)

The Farnborough VW Centre,
10 Farnborough Road,
Farnborough,
Hampshire,
GU14 6AY
Tel: 01252 521152
(High quality VW Campervan restorations)

Fiamma accessories
Contact your motorcaravan dealer

Foam for Comfort Ltd,
Unit 2,
Wyther Lane Trading Estate,
Wyther Lane,
Kirkstall,
Leeds
LS5 3BT
Tel: 0113-274 8100
(New synthetic foam, latex, composite bonded foam)

Franks Caravan Spares,
16/27 Wigmore Street,
Stopsley,
Luton,
Bedfordshire LU2 8AA.
Tel: 01582 732168
(Caravan breakers and sales)

Froli Kunststoffwerkwerke Fromme GmbH,
Liemker Strasse 27,
D-33758 Schloss Holte,
Germany.
Tel: 49 (0) 52 07 / 95 00 0
(Froli bed support systems)

Gaslow International,
The Manor House,
Normanton-on-Soar,
Leicestershire,
LE12 5HB
Tel: 01509 843331
(Gas leak gauges, refillable cylinders, LPG components)

General Ecology Europe Ltd,
St. Andrews House,
26 Brighton Road,
Crawley,
RH10 6AA
Tel: 01293 400644
(Nature Pure Ultrafine water purifier)

Grade UK Ltd,
3 Central Court,
Finch Close,
Lenton Lane Industrial Estate,
Nottingham
NG7 2NN
Tel: 0115 986 7151
(Status TV aerials and accessories)

Gramos ABS Repair Kits - See Kingdom Industrial Supplies

Häfele UK Ltd,
Swift Valley Industrial Estate,
Rugby,
Warwickshire,
CV21 1RD
Tel: 01788 542020
(Furniture components and hardware)

HBC Systems UK,
12 Stuart Road,
Halesowen, B62 0ED
Tel: 0121 421 4373
(Professional system for repairing aluminium body panels)

Hella Ltd,
Wildmere Industrial Estate,
Banbury,
Oxfordshire OX16 3JU
Tel: 01295 272233
(Hella Towing electrical Equipment)

Hornchurch Motor Caravan Centre,
5–7 Broadway Parade,
Elm Avenue,
Hornchurch,
Essex RM12 4RS
Tel: 01708 444791/443782
(Custom-made roof racks, cycle
racks, motorcycle racks and ladders)

Independence 2000,
Unit 5,
Tanfield Lea Industrial Estate South,
Stanley,
Co. Durham, DH9 9QX
Tel: 01207 282 200
(GRP vehicle over-bumper in
matching white)

Just Kampers,
Unit 1,
Stapeley Manor,
Long Lane,
Odiham,
Hampshire, RG29 1JE
Tel: 01256 862288
(Mail Order VW Camper and
Transporter parts 1968–2004;
accessories)

Kenlowe Ltd,
Burchetts Green,
Maidenhead,
Berkshire
SL6 6QU
Tel: 01628 823303
(Radiator cooling fans and automatic
transmission oil coolers)

Kingdom Industrial Supplies Ltd,
6/10 Bancrofts Road,
Eastern Industrial Estate,
South Woodham Ferrers,
Essex,
CM3 5UQ
Tel: 01245 322177
(Mail Order, Gramos repair kits for
ABS plastic)

Lab-Craft Ltd,
Church Road,
Harold Wood,
Romford,
Essex, RM3 0HT
Tel: 01708 349320
(Electrical appliances, lighting units)

Lattoflex Bed Systems,
Thomas GmbH + Co. Sitz- und
Liegemöbel KG
Walkmühlenstrasse 93
27432 Bremervörde, Germany
Tel: 0049-4761 979138
(CaraWinx mattress support systems)

Leisuredrive DIY,
Unit 10,
Corporation Street,
Manchester,M4 4DG
Tel: 0161 832 2891
(Installer of high tops, van converters,
supplier of unit furniture)

Leisure Plus,
Unit 5,
New Road Industrial Estate,
New Road,
Hixon,
Staffordshire, ST18 0PJ
Tel: 01889 271692
(Wholesaler of adhesives,
delamination repair products,
sealants)

Marlec Engineering Ltd,
Rutland House,
Trevithick Road,
Corby,
Northamptonshire NN17 5XY
Tel: 01536 201588
(Wind and Solar systems)

**Magnum Mobiles and Caravan
Surplus,**
Unit 9A,
Cosalt Industrial Estate,
Convamore Road,
Grimsby DN32 9JL
Tel: 01472 353520
(Caravan/Motorcaravan Surplus
Stock)

Marquis Motorhome Centre,
Winchester Road,
Lower Upham,
Southampton
SO32 1HA
Tel 01489 860666
(Hire and buy scheme)

Maxview,
Common Lane,
Setchey,
King's Lynn,
Norfolk
PE33 0AT
Tel: 01553 813300
(TV aerials, satellite TV products, free
guidebooks)

Mer Products Ltd,
Whitehead House,
120 Beddington Lane,
Croydon,
Surrey
CRO 4TD
Tel: 020 8401 0002
(Mer Car Care products)

Morco Products Ltd,
59 Beverley Road,
Hull HU3 1XW
Tel: 01482 325456
(Water Heaters, accessories)

The Motor Caravanners' Club,
22 Evelyn Close,
Twickenham,
Middlesex TW2 7BN
Tel: 020 8893 3883

Motorhome Information Service,
Maxwelton House,
Boltro Road,
Haywards Heath,
West Sussex
RH16 1BJ
Tel: 01444 453399

Munster Simms Engineering Ltd,
Old Belfast Road,
Bangor,
Co. Down,
Northern Ireland
BT19 1LT
Tel: 02891 270531
(Whale semi-rigid pipework, pumps,
taps and plumbing accessories)

The National Caravan Council,
Catherine House,
Victoria Road,
Aldershot,
Hampshire
GU11 1SS
Tel: 01252 318251

**National Inspection Council for
Electrical Installation Contracting,**
(NICEIC)
Vintage House,
37 Albert Embankment,
London SE1 7UJ
Tel: 020 7564 2323
(Certification to confirm a
motorcaravan is correctly wired for
mains electricity)

The Natural Mat Company,
99 Talbot Road,
London, W11 2AT
Tel: 0207 9850474
(Airflow slatted sprung
beech bed systems, mattress anti-
condensation coir underlay)

**Noise Killer Acoustics
(UK) Ltd,**
103 Denbydale Way,
Royton,
Oldham, OL2 5UH
Tel: 0161 643 8070
(Noise reduction systems for
motorcaravans)

Nu Venture Campers,
Unit 7,
Actons Walk,
Wood Street,
Wigan,
Lancashire,
Tel: 01942 238560
(Motorcaravans built to customer
specification)

Nu Venture Motor Homes,
Unit 2,
Seven Stars Road,
Wallgate,
Wigan,
Lancashire, WN3 5AT
Tel: 01942 494090
(Motorcaravans built to customer
specification)

O'Leary Spares and Accessories,
314 Plaxton Bridge Road,
Woodmansey,
Nr Beverley,
East Yorkshire, HU17 ORS
Tel: 01482 868632
(Retailer of surplus stocks purchased
from caravan manufacturers)

PGR Products Ltd,
16 Crofton Road,
Lincoln,
Lincolnshire LN3 4NL
Tel: 01522 534538
(Wheel clamps)

Pleitner's PS Wohnmobil GmbH,
Laerstrasse 16,
33775 Versmold,
Deutschland.
Tel: 0049 054 23 20 40 0
Web:www.pleitner.de
(Dealer linked with VW based Athano
self build A Class)

Pro-Tow
Unit 1,
565 Blandford Road,
Hamworthy,
Poole,
Dorset BH16 5BW
Tel: 01202 632488
(Car-a-Tow towing frames; Solar
Solutions solar panels)

PWS,
Unit 5,
Chalwyn Industrial Estate,
Old Wareham Road,
Parkstone,
Dorset, BH12 4PE
Tel: 01202 746851
(Racks, protector bars, custom-made
tow bars)

Pyramid Products Ltd,
Unit 1,
Victoria Street,
Mansfield,
Nottinghamshire NG18 5RR
Tel: 01623-421277
(Levelling ramps and accessories)

Premier Glass Fibre Ltd,
Upper Floor,
52 Spencer Street,
Oadby,
Leicestershire, LE2 4DP
Tel: 0116 2718391
(Bak-Paka rear mounted storage
boxes)

Rainbow Conversions,
10, Century Way,
March,
Cambridgeshire, PE15 8QW
Tel: 01354 659072
(Van conversions built to order;
Vohringer ply & accessories)

Reimo Motorcaravan Conversions,
Collingham Street,
Off North Street,
Cheetham,
Manchester, M8 8RQ
Tel: 0161 8391855
(High top roof installation, component
supply and van converter)

Remis UK, - Through accessory
dealers
(Remis blinds, flyscreens, roof
windows)

RoadPro Ltd,
Stephenson Close,
Drayton Fields,
Daventry,
Northamptonshire, NN11 5RF
Tel: 01327 312233
(Accessories, chargers, reversing
aids, TVs)

Ryder Towing Equipment Ltd,
Mancunian Way,
Ardwick,
Manchester M12 6HW
Tel: 0161 273 5619
(Electrical towing equipment &
'The Practical Guide to Towbar
Electrics')

Safe and Secure Products Ltd,
Chestnut House,
Chesley Hill,
Wick,
Bristol BS30 5NE
Tel: 08700 727234
(SAS security devices and posts)

Sargent Electrical Services, Ltd,
Unit 39,
Tokenspire Business Park,
Woodmansey,
Beverley, HU17 0TB
Tel: 01452 678987
(12V controls and panels)

SF Detection Ltd,
Hatch Pond House,
4 Stinsford Road,
Nuffield Industrial Estate,
Poole,
Dorset BH17 0RZ
Tel: 01202 645577
(SF350 Carbon monoxide detector)

Shurflo Ltd,
Unit 5,
Sterling Park,
Gatwick Road,
Crawley, RH10 9QT
Tel: 01293 424000
(Water pumps)

Sika Ltd,
Watchmead,
Welwyn Garden City,
Hertfordshire AL7 1BQ
Tel: 01707 394444
(Sikaflex cartridge sealants and
adhesive sealants)

Silver Screens,
P.O. Box 9,
Cleckheaton,
West Yorkshire, BD19 5YR
Tel: 01274-872151
(Insulated window covers)

**The Society of Motor
Manufacturers and Traders,**
Forbes House,
Halkin Street,
London SW1X 7DS
Tel: 0171 235 7000

Solar Solutions - See Pro-Tow

Sold Secure Trust,
5C Great Central Way,
Woodford Halse,
Daventry,
Northamptonshire, NN11 3PZ
Tel: 01327 264687
(Sold Secure Test House)

Somar Transtec,
Unit 33,
Northwick Business Centre,
Blockley,
Gloucestershire, GL56 9RF
(Power assisted steering specialists,
automatic gear systems)

Spinflo, Ltd,
4 -10 Welland Close,
Parkwood Industrial Estate,
Rutland Road,
Sheffield, S3 9QW
Tel: 0114 - 2 738157
(Grills, Hobs, Ovens)

Stoves plc, Company name
changed to:
Glen Dimplex Cooking Ltd,
Stoney Lane,
Prescot,
Merseyside L35 2XW
Tel: 0151 426 6551
(Grills, Hobs, Ovens)

SVO,
Redman Road,
Porte Marsh Industrial Estate,
Calne,
Wiltshire SN11 9PR
Tel: 01249 815141
(Power assisted steering, disabled
adaptations)

Symonspeed Ltd,
Cleveland Garage,
1 Cleveland Road,
Torquay,
Devon TQ2 5BD
Tel: 01803 214620
(Air assistance units and SOG toilet
system)

TB Turbo Ltd,
Turbo House,
Port Royal Avenue
Off Willow Lane,
Lancaster
LA1 5QP
Tel: 01524 67157
(Autoclutch, Turbo charging
conversion, intercoolers, LP Gas
tanks, engine performance chips)

TEK Seating Ltd,
Unit 32,
Pate Road,
Leicester Road Industrial Estate,
Melton Mowbray,
Leicestershire
LE13 0RG
Tel: 01664 480689
(Cab seating and
upholstery)

Thetford Ltd,
Centrovell Estate,
Caldwell Road,
Nuneaton,
Warwickshire, CV11 4UD
Tel: 024 76 322700
(Norcold refrigerators, toilets and
treatments)

TOWtal,
332 King Street,
Fenton,
Stoke-on-Trent, ST4 3DA
Tel: 01782 333422
('A' Frames, electric brake actuators,
trailers, scooter racks)

Truma UK,
Truma House,
Beeches Park,
Eastern Avenue,
Burton-upon-Trent,
Staffordshire DE13 0BB
Tel: 01283 511092
(Space heating and water heating
systems, gas components, Carver
spares)

Trylon Ltd,
Thrift Street,
Wollaston,
Northamptonshire NN29 7QJ
Tel: 01933 664275
(Resins, glass and guidance on glass
reinforced plastics)

TVAC,
Centurion Way,
Leyland,
Lancashire, PR26 6TZ
Tel: 01772 457116
(Air suspension systems and
motorhome weight upgrades)

Ultimate Design,
37 Pytchley Road,
Kettering,
Northamptonshire NN15 6ND
Tel: 01536 514400
(Cruise control kits, navigation
systems)

van Aaken Developments Ltd,
Telford Avenue,
Crowthorne,
Berkshire, RG45 6XA
Tel: 01344 777 553
(Tuning chips for vehicles including
motorhomes)

Van Bitz,
Cornish Farm, Shoreditch,
Taunton,
Somerset TA3 7BS
Tel: 01823-321992
(Strikeback T Thatcham-Approved
security, gas alarm, Battery Master)

Van Window Specialists,
Unit 4,
Riverside Works,
Methley Road,
Castleford,
West Yorkshire, WF10 1PW
Tel: 01977 552929
(Made-to-measure windows, supply
and fit, VW van conversions)

Varta Automotive Batteries Ltd,
PO Box 402,
Broadwater Park,
North Orbital Road,
Denham,
Uxbridge,
Middlesex,
UB9 5AG
Tel: 01895 838993
(Gel leisure batteries)

Vehicle & Marine Window Co.,
Victoria Street,
Birmingham
B9 5AA
Tel: 0121 772 6307
(Window manufacturers, fitters and
suppliers)

V & G Caravans,
107 Benwick Road,
Whittlesey,
Peterborough,
Cambridgeshire,
PE7 2HD
Tel: 01733 350580
(Replacement replica panels in GRP)

Vöhringer Importers,
1 Butterwick Drive,
Herongate,
Shrewsbury,
Shropshire,
SY1 3XE
Tel: 01743 3
50580
(Stockist information for lightweight
decorative plywoods)

Waeco UK Ltd,
Unit G1,
Roman Hill Business Park,
Broadmayne,
Dorset,
DT2 8LY
Tel: 01305 854000
(Compressor refrigerators, reversing
aids, navigational aids)

Watling Engineers Ltd,
88 Park Street Village,
nr. St. Albans,
Hertfordshire
AL2 2LR
Tel: 01727 873661
(Specially designed towing brackets)

Webasto Product UK Ltd,
Webasto House,
White Rose Way,
Doncaster Carr,
South Yorkshire, DN4 5JH
Tel: 01302 322232
(Diesel-fuelled heaters, water
evaporative air conditioners)

Whale – see Munster Simms

Witter Towbars,
Drome Road,
Deeside Industrial Park,
Deeside,
Chester CH5 2NY
Tel: 01244 284500
(Towbars and cycle carriers)

Woodfit Ltd,
Kem Mill,
Whittle-le-Woods,
Chorley,
Lancashire PR6 7EA
Tel: 01257 266421
(Hinges, fittings, hardware, wire
storage baskets and catches)

Woolies,
off Blenheim Way,
Northfields Industrial Estate,
Market Deeping,
Peterborough PE6 8LD
Tel: 01778 347347
(Trim, accessories and window
rubbers)

W4 Ltd,
Unit B, Ford Lane Industrial Estate,
Arundel,
West Sussex
BN18 0DF
Tel: 01243 553355
(Supplier of 230v kits, double-pole
switched sockets, socket testers,
ribbon sealants)

Young Conversions,
Unit 47, Barton Road,
Water Eaton,
Bletchley, Milton Keynes,
Buckinghamshire
MK2 3BD
Tel: 01908 639 936
(Full or part conversions on any base
vehicle, stage payment conversion,
one-off designs)

ZIG Electronics, Ltd,
Saxon Business Park,
Hanbury Road,
Stoke Prior,
Bromsgrove,
Worcestershire
B60 4AD
Tel: 01527 577800
(12V controls, chargers, water level
sensors and gauges)

Zwaardvis, BV,
PO Box 115,
5480 AC Schijndel,
The Netherlands,
Tel: 31 (0)73 549 2074
(Aluminium high stability table pillars
and sliding
mechanisms)

Index

Author Acknowledgements

This manual embraces many technical topics and I am indebted to the countless experts whose advice, encouragement and help has enabled me to write this book. Others have loaned important photographs which add to its visual impact. I would particularly like to thank:

Simon Collis, Editor, Motorcaravan Magazine, who gave permission to use some library photographs of the Mystique motorcaravan from IPC Media Ltd.

Martin Howlett, Sales & Marketing Manager of Avondale Coachcraft who made special arrangements to provide the inspirational cover photograph.

Gordon King, Commercial Director, BCA Leisure who has passed on so much technical advice relating to motorcaravan electrical systems.

Hugh Lamberton, Technical Manager of Dometic for proof reading large sections of the manual, particularly the chapter on Refrigerators.

Louise McIntyre, Project Manager, Haynes Publishing for helping to produce such a well-presented manual.

Steve Rowe, Editor, Caravan Magazine, who gave permission to use photographs of his VW Campervan, loaned by IPC Media Ltd.

Martin Spencer, Technical Manager of The Caravan Club whose advice, proof reading and contribution in Appendix A has bestowed an important authoritative edge to the technical content.

Other titles of interest from Haynes Publishing

Driving Abroad (2nd Edition)
By Robert Davies
ISBN: 1 84425 048 2

Glovebox Car Book
By Steve Rendle
ISBN: 1 85960 792 6

The Caravan Handbook
By John Wickersham
ISBN: 1 85960 801 9

The Caravan Manual (3rd Edition)
By John Wickersham
ISBN: 1 85960 333 5

The Bike Book
By Fred Milson
ISBN: 1 84425 000 8

The Motorcycle Book
By Alan Seeley
ISBN: 1 85960 868 X

The Digital Photography Manual
By Winn L. Rosch
ISBN: 1 85960 995 3

For more information please contact
Customer Services Department, Haynes Publishing, Sparkford, Yeovil, Somerset BA22 7JJ, UK

Tel. 01963 442030 Fax 01963 440001
Int. tel: +44 1963 442030 Fax: +44 1963 440001

Email: sales@haynes-manuals.co.uk
Web site: www.haynes.co.uk